Identity Crisis

Identity Crisis

Standing Between Two Identities of Women Believers from Muslim Backgrounds in Jordan

Sarah Yoon

Foreword by Terry Muck

WIPF & STOCK · Eugene, Oregon

IDENTITY CRISIS
Standing Between Two Identities of Women Believers from Muslim Backgrounds In Jordan

Copyright © 2015 Sarah Yoon. All rights reserved. Except for brief quotations in critical publications or reviews, no part of this book may be reproduced in any manner without prior written permission from the publisher. Write: Permissions, Wipf and Stock Publishers, 199 W. 8th Ave., Suite 3, Eugene, OR 97401.

Wipf & Stock
An Imprint of Wipf and Stock Publishers
199 W. 8th Ave., Suite 3
Eugene, OR 97401

www.wipfandstock.com

ISBN 13: 978-1-62564-857-0

Manufactured in the U.S.A.

This book is dedicated to my late mother, Sungkuk Yun.

Contents

Foreword by Terry Muck | ix
Preface | xiii
Acknowledgments | xv

1 Introduction | 1

2 Women's Identities in Christianity and Islam | 26

3 Women in Jordan | 61

4 Narratives of Banaat al-urdun (Daughters of Jordan) | 96

5 Analysis | 133

6 Conclusion | 166

Appendix | 179
Bibliography | 181
Subject Index | 193

List of Tables

Table 1: Interview with Muslim Women | *101*

Table 2: Interview with BMB Women | *118*

Table 3: Jordanian BMB Women's Theories and Challenges to Form a New Identity | *146*

Table 4: Jordanian BMB Women's Challenges to Create a New Identity | *147*

List of Figures

Figure 1: The Process of BMB Women's Identity Formation | *157*

Foreword

AFTER YEARS OF TELLING Jordanian Muslim women the story of Jesus, Sarah Yoon identified a problem. Among those Jordanian Muslim women who embraced the implications of what Jesus did and decided to follow the Jesus Way, many very quickly reached an impasse. To paraphrase the Apostle Paul, "what they wanted to do (follow Jesus) they found themselves unable to do" (Rom 7:18). Sarah Yoon wondered why this happened. Although she acknowledged the traditional missiological wisdom that this impasse was the result of cultural factors—family, friends, nation—that were Muslim, not Christian, making it very difficult for these women to become Christian, Sarah thought there was more to it than that. She suspected that in addition to cultural difficulties, there were equally inhibiting personal issues at play. An identity crisis was taking place. Raised and socialized to see themselves as Muslim women, they simply could not take the leap to see themselves as Christian women. What they want to do, they do not do.

Conversion to Christianity has many facets. Scholars who study it, missiologists who encourage it, and theologians who explain it never run out of new angles to explore. Conversion—the religious change that takes place in a previously non-Christian person to a person who embraces some form of Christianity—is considered by many to be the foundational act of a human being. Conversion is a return, a reversion if you will, to what God originally intended us to be in the garden of Eden. It is the end of one way of living and the beginning of another. People who were once "lost" are now found. It involves both a radical change of heart and mind, and a gradual growth process toward becoming more like Jesus. Over time, usually by joining with other similarly transforming people, new Christians acquire a new set of beliefs and behaviors that mark them as Christian. Given this obvious importance it is little wonder that many theories of conversion have emerged over the years.

Lewis Rambo has related the extensive psychological findings of decision making to religious conversion. Jim Engel has helpfully delineated a process of "becoming Christian" that begins with a general awareness of God and ends with a life of service in building God's kingdom. Andrew Walls uses the stay of a Christian missionary to China, Timothy Richards, to show that at least part of the converting process involves finding a specific role of service, ordained by God, carried out by us. Many have written about the aspects of cultural conversions or christianization that include the transformation of entire cultures from non-Christian to Christian, whatever that may mean in different contexts. Lesslie Newbigen emphasized the cumulative nature of the transforming process, observing that in India, at least, "becoming Christian" is the result of many contacts with Christians and Christian acts of charity.

Sarah Yoon's work among Jordanian believers of Muslim backgrounds adds to this impressive array of work by focusing on identity, hybridity, and complex cultures. By focusing on individual issues of complex religious identity, Dr. Yoon does not eschew the work that has been done on conversion as seem purely through the theological lens of God's gracious authority toward us all, nor the crucial insights of cultural anthropologists who note the crucial and unavoidable impact of culture on religious choices, nor the practical wisdom of mission workers who have devoted their lives to telling the good news to these who have not heard. But Dr. Yoon's focus on identity has resonances with several global realities that mission workers ignore at their peril: The global reality (1) that it is extremely unlikely that significant Muslim cultures will become Christianized; (2) that competing missions from Muslims, Buddhists, Hindus, and others will simply melt away; (3) that historical missions to Muslim women and men have been largely ineffective if measured by the number of converts; and (4) that women are rarely seen as significant players in the mission equations and scenarios.

Thus, the challenge is to learn how to encourage the conversion to Christianity of people who choose to remain cultural Muslims, cultural Hindus, cultural Buddhists; to "convert" other religious missions to become partners in our common human religious quests for human flourishing, not competitors—without giving up on the uniqueness of Christianity; to acknowledge the uniqueness—and importance—of women's religious quests, seen not *over against* male quests, but as complementary to them;

and to have enough humility to participate in the *missio Dei* without so dramatically turning it into the *missio humana*, thereby giving up our tendencies toward an over-reliance on human measures of effectiveness and instead trying to see "effectiveness" through God's eyes. All this, Sarah Yoon's argument does.

Terry Muck
Executive Director, Louisville Institute

Preface

THIS BOOK IS DESIGNED to help people understand BMB (believer from Muslim background) women's situation in Jordan. Islam is not only a religion, but the foundational root of all Muslims' lives in all areas of life. A Muslim finds the meaning of life and her/his primary identities from Islam. When a Muslim converts to Christianity or any other religion, she/he faces a great deal of confusion regarding oneself and dilemmas about one's circumstances. Hence, although some Muslims have an interest in and respond to the good news of the gospel, many of them leave this newfound faith in a short time without specific reasons. In contrast to the general assumption that many new converts or seekers leave their new faith because of persecution or pressure from family members or communities, I seek to show that the major reason they leave is that they face identity confusion primarily inside of themselves.

Jordan is a traditional Islamic country. Jordanian women also format their identities upon Islamic values under gender-oriented social and religious influences. This research is about the identity crises new women believers face when they come from an Islamic background in the Jordanian context. It studies how Jordanian Muslim women have built on their women's identity and what kind of identity crises they go through. It consists of a total of six chapters. The first chapter deals with my autobiographical background for research, observations regarding believers from Muslim backgrounds (BMB) in Jordan and theoretical research about conversion, Islamic religious traditions, and identity. The second chapter studies the identity of women in Christianity and Islam, as defined by the Bible and Qur'an, respectively. The third chapter deals with the life and identity of Jordanian women. It searches a general context of Islamic backgrounds of Jordan, Jordanian understanding and relationship with Christians in their history and society and women's identity under these sociocultural influences. The fourth chapter includes interviews with Muslim women, BMB women and Christian women workers who are involved in ministries to BMB women. The fifth chapter is findings and analysis on the research. It figures out the challenges of women and reasons of identity crisis of BMB women in the conversion process. The final chapter gives integrative summaries and suggestions for further study.

When a Muslim woman converts to Christianity, she experiences that her existing Muslim identity interferes in the formation of the new identity of being a Christian, so she faces an identity crisis between her old Muslim identity and her new Christian identity. Hence she is challenged by the discontinuity of the past in the process of creating her new identity. It includes not only the religious dimension, but also sociocultural dimensions.

Acknowledgments

Praise the Lord. Praise the Lord, O my soul. I will praise the Lord all my life; I will sing praise to the Lord all my life

(PSALM 146:1–2, NIV).

Special thanks go to Jordanian Muslim women and BMB women who are the motive and reason for my research and ministry along with Dr. Terry Muck, who is a mentor and has helped me to finish my research.

I am also deeply grateful to my family. Jaehyung Yoon, my husband, and Taehuyn and Dohyun, my two sons have always been patient with me and have supported me in diverse ways.

1

Introduction

Autobiographical Background to the Study

I WAS BORN AND raised in a sincere Buddhist family. Following my family, I went to a Buddhist temple and practiced Buddhist rituals since I was young. When I was eleven years old, I had heard about Christianity from my elementary school Christian teacher. I hated to hear about Christianity, but at the same time I was very curious to hear what it was like. I was wondering: if every religious adherent claimed that they believed in the true God—such as Buddha for Buddhists, Jesus Christ for Christians—then who is the true God? Is Buddha the true God or Jesus Christ or anyone else? I decided to learn more about Christianity. I went to church alone without telling my family, but it was hard for me to secretly continue going to church. I could not keep telling lies whenever I went out to go to church on Sunday. Hence, my family eventually found out, and it took a long time to obtain permission to attend church.

During that time, I had very mixed feelings and various thoughts of myself. For me, choosing another religion from my family meant betraying them and admitting that they would go to hell because of their unbelief of Jesus Christ. However, my heart was already moving more toward God than Buddha while I had known God and Jesus. God protected me and helped me keep my faith through all difficulties and eventually brought salvation to my family. I dedicated my life to sharing the truth with those who don't know Jesus Christ, and have become a worker overseas serving the Arabs in Jordan for over ten years.

In Jordan, I have found that the dynamics of people's life and perspectives are influenced by various factors from Arab traditionalism

Identity Crisis

to postmodern tendencies. I have seen that many Muslims want to know more about Jesus Christ and to become Christians. At the same time, I have watched Jordanian converts face huge tensions in the process of changing their religion, and how difficult it is for them to become established in their new faith. In particular, women seem to have more hardships in becoming Christian than men.

Here are my experiences with two women (a BMB and a seeker) in Jordan.

- Case 1

    Kaldiye[1] worked as a nurse at the Christian hospital and attended the meetings for patients in which Christian staff share the gospel with Muslim patients. One day she came to me and said that she understood what I had shared at the meeting and wanted to know more about Jesus. I explained the gospel and the cost for her of becoming a Christian. In spite of that, she wanted to accept Jesus as her Savior, so we prayed together and Jesus Christ became her Savior in September 2008. She and I started having a Bible study, and I found out that it was not easy for her to follow the general style of Bible study that answers questions about the Bible at a beginner level. However when I asked about her faith in Jesus Christ, she clearly understood the redemption of Jesus Christ and the content of the gospel. She only made it to two Bible studies with me, and because of her mother's illness, she had to leave the hospital. In spite of her circumstances, she made many appointments with me for Bible studies over the phone, but she didn't keep most of them. Later, she didn't even answer my phone calls. This all happened within three months.

- Case 2

    Fatima was a graduate student in one of the universities in Jordan. She was hospitalized at the Christian hospital for a month in July 2009. Through Christians who worked at the hospital, she heard the gospel for the first time in her life. Although she did not accept Jesus Christ as her Savior, she could not deny her interest in knowing more about Jesus and Christianity. After leaving the hospital, she searched the internet and looked for more information about the subject. One day in November I met her at the university in which she studied and I gave her a Bible and several other Christian books. Fatima was very happy with the books. In fact, she was

1. All names in the book are pseudonyms, excluding where I have quoted an author.

actually looking for some of the same books that I had given her. I invited her to have a Bible study with me and she gladly accepted. However, she made an excuse and didn't come to the first Bible study. I made another appointment with her, but she didn't appear again. After that, she never even answered my phone calls.

Along with these cases, I've watched many other Jordanian women and men seekers and believers stagnate in their faith or give up seeking about their new interest/faith in Christianity. The spirit of Islam is embedded in all customs and traditions, and extends "throughout all activity, thought, and feeling" of Muslims.[2] Islam is the crucial basis of identity for Muslims. The term "Muslim" refers to their total identity, not just their religious identity. Therefore making the choice to leave Islam and to follow Jesus Christ has serious costs for converts in all the diverse dimensions of their lives.

Statement of the Problem

Nur Armangan, a Turkish BMB and missiologist, states that many converts from Islamic backgrounds "give up their new faith within the first two years of their initial decision."[3] Traditionally, it is known that believers from a Muslim background (BMB) have threats/realities of persecution from family, community, society, or the secret police. However, I have also observed the important phenomenon that even before persecution or having their new faith exposed, many seekers or initial believers give up seeking the new truth and return to their previous phase. My experience shows that this phenomenon is found to occur more among female BMBs in particular, because of the unique circumstances in religious and sociocultural aspects in Jordan. Therefore, the social and religious issue my research addresses is that many female BMBs in Jordan experience difficulties to keep their faith, particularly in a context like Jordan where becoming a Christian is illegal for Muslims. Some of them stop seeking their new faith and/or return to their old beliefs.

There are many factors contributing to their difficulties and one of them is the critical factor of identity crisis. Specifically then, I set out to do research on the problem: It is extremely difficult for female BMBs in

---

2. Patai, *The Arab Mind*, 146.
3. Armangan, "Conversion," 59.

Jordan to become and stay Christians, because of all the identity issues such a conversion raises.

Assumptions and Questions for Research

Why do BMB women have difficulties keeping their new found faith and does this phenomenon happen with a higher occurrence among female Muslim BMBs or seekers? First of all, the nature of conversion "involves not just adopting a set of ideas but also converting to and from an embodied worldview and identity."[4] When people decide to convert or to seek a new faith, there are not only different theological ideas to be changed, but many other aspects of their life are also in need of conversion—mind, culture, identity, and even worldview. I observed that these fundamental issues often occur at the beginning of their conversion. When a Muslim becomes a Christian, the construction of a new identity as a Christian is an absolute necessity that needs to be addressed. However, one's existing Muslim identity can interfere in the formation of the new identity of being a Christian, so the person faces an identity crisis between their old Muslim and new Christian identities.

Secondly, with reference to identity, Muslim women exist in unique milieus in which to construct their identities. These identities must fall in line with Islamic religious traditions and customs. Historically, it is known that "Muslim women have not been free to define their own identities, or to be agents of social change."[5] Women's identity in an Islamic society such as Jordan is limited by gender-oriented social influences and customs.

Hence, the assumption of this research is that the unavoidable "identity crisis" is one of the reasons that make Jordanian BMB women experience difficulties making the decision to follow Christ or to keep their new faith after conversion, particularly in the early phases of their seeking. Based on this assumption, I addressed the significant research question: *When Jordanian Muslim women convert to Christianity, what kind of difficulties and identity crises do they go through?*

---

4. Norris, "Converting to What?," 171.
5. Sharify-Funk, *Encountering*, 134.

Delimitations of the Research

By and large there are two streams of thoughts on gender in modern Islamic societies. Conservatives in Islam consider that the preservation of traditional gender relationships is important to the social structure of Islam.[6] In contrast, feminists apply a feminist critique to the patriarchal aspect of Islam, asserting that "an extensive rereading of history and reinterpretation of the texts" is necessary to find the original meanings of them.[7] In contemporary Muslim women's identity studies Fatima Mernissi (1987), Amina Wadud (2006), Nimat Hafez Barazangi (2006), and others focus on proving equality between Muslim men and women and debunk how women's status is degraded according to *sharia* law (Islamic law) and Islamic traditions. My focus in this research has been on how ordinary Jordanian Muslim women have constructed their identities under commonly accepted conservative Sunni understandings of the Qur'anic descriptions about women and sociocultural standards. Hence, I did not deal with the debate on women's rights and the equality of Muslim women's social status in comparison to men or the interpretation of the Qur'an and Islamic religious traditions. Furthermore, in quoting and referencing voices about Muslim women's circumstances, I tried to describe the most common Middle Eastern view of women. Sometimes words can convey different meanings according to different cultural contexts. For instance, Yvonne Yazbeck Haddad refuses to apply the concept of women's liberation used in the West when referring to the East. She differentiates the meaning of the liberation in the Middle East from the West. According to her, women's liberation in the West seeks for women's politically won rights, but in the Middle East it "continues to seek her liberation within the confines of the role assigned to her by Islam, that of a wife and a mother."[8]

Secondly, the target group of my research did not include new women believers and seekers evangelized by insider movements or C5 and C6, which is actively carried out in South Asia and other Islamic regions.[9] In-

---

6. Clarke, "Women in Islam," 188.
7. Barazangi, *Woman's Identity*, 34.
8. Haddad, "Traditional Affirmations," 80.
9. The level of Contextualization for Muslim mission by John Travis: C1 Traditional church using outsider languages; C2 Traditional church using insider language; C3 Contextualized Christ-centered communities using insider language and religiously neutral insider cultural forms; C4 Contextualized Christ-centered communities using insider language and biblically permissible cultural and Islamic forms; C5 Christ-centered

sider movements, or C5 and C6 believers, are not yet found in significant numbers in Jordan. Therefore I did not deal with identity issues of converts from these movements in Jordan. Rather, all women whom I interviewed had been evangelized through traditional evangelistic ways that use verbal proclamation and approaching locals through mission institutions such as hospitals and NGOs (non-governmental organizations).

Lastly, I conducted interviews with three different groups: Muslim women, BMB women, and female Christian workers serving Jordanian women. Interviews with Muslim women about their identities were conducted randomly. These women came from various educational backgrounds, ages, and social statuses in Bedouin village and urban settings. Eleven Jordanian female BMBs were interviewed. Due to the fact that in Jordan it is illegal to change one's religion according to *sharia* law, it is very difficult to publicly or privately meet converts. Therefore, I approached the small number of interviews in depth to discover what kind of processes they went through when they changed their religion. For interviewees who have served in Jordan, I chose those who has been in Jordan over twenty years and have been committed to ministry for Muslim women throughout.

Although the stories of women who left their newfound faith are useful to inform this research about what kind of difficulties they went through, I had deliberately excluded interviewing these women because of the following reasons:

1. My interviews with BMB women already cover identity issues which are common—whether these women have left or kept their new found faith;

2. I have added into my understanding of this phenomenon and my own personal experiences with women who once converted but left their faith, which is embedded in the entire analysis process of this paper;

3. Engaging these women again is extremely difficult in the context of Jordan where conversion is illegal. The consideration for security for these interviewees and myself does not allow me to freely engage them.

---

communities "Messianic Muslims" who have accepted Jesus as Lord and Savior; C6 Small Christ-centered communities of secret/underground believers ("insider" pertains to the local Muslim population, "outsider" pertains to the local non-Muslim population) (Travis, "The C1 to C6 Spectrum," 304–10).

Introduction

Definition of Key Terms

BMB: This is a term which is used frequently in the mission field and academia to point out a Christian believer who was a Muslim and grew up with an Islamic background. Traditionally the term MBB (Muslim Background Believer) was often used, but in the last decade the preferred term has become BMB (Believers from a Muslim background) because it is Christ-centered, not background-centered.[10] The other name used to delineate new converts from the Islamic world is "a follower of *Isa* (Jesus)". In this paper, I used the term BMBs exclusively. Because I understand that the conversion of BMBs is gradual or a process rather than a sudden event, BMBs in my paper include those who decide to believe in Jesus as their Savior once even though some of them have had long periods to adapt new faith through many things.[11] I defined seekers as those who are simply inquiring about the gospel, but have not yet become BMBs.

Conversion: Today, the concept of conversion has become more complicated to define in our pluralistic religious as well as multicultural environments. In his book *Understanding Religious Conversion* Lewis Rambo defines "conversion as a process of religious change that takes place in a dynamic force field of people, events, ideologies, institutions, expectations and orientations."[12] Rambo adds that "there is no one cause of conversion, no one process, and no one simple consequence of that process."[13] In the sociological perspective, conversion means "a transformation of one's self concurrent with a transformation of one's basic meaning system and it changes the sense of who one is and how one belongs in the social situation."[14] In my study, I defined conversion in this multifaceted, complex way that has religious, cultural, and psychological dimensions.

Identity: Identity related to one's self-definition is simply answering the question "Who am I?" People can answer it from a biological, physical and religious perspective. Meredith B. McGuire, in *Religion: The Social Context*, explains that this question of "Who am I?" is answered in terms of "This is

---

10. Evans, "Discipling," 159.

11. Generally there are two types of conversion experiences accepted: gradual (or process) and sudden (or event). Many scholars discuss this issue such as Gaventa, *From Darkness to Light*; Peace, *Conversion in the New Testament*; Saliba, *Understanding New Religious Movements*, etc.

12. Rambo, *Understanding*, 5.

13. Ibid., 5.

14. McGuire, *Religion*, 73.

where I belong," and connects self-identity to a social aspect, "because it is constructed through ongoing interactions with others."[15] Gé M. Speelman emphasizes that "an individual's personal identity" is constructed from the internalized representations of one's own culture and social environment.[16]

Identity Crisis: In the eight stages of social-emotional development, Erik Erikson introduces the concept and emphasizes "identity crisis" which happens when moving to the next vital stage of personality in one's life cycle.[17] As a fundamental unconscious process, identity in Erikson's understanding integrates personality as well as connects a person to the outside society. During an identity crisis, a person questions and struggles with one's self and loses one's peace of mind and even sense of purpose.[18] Ruthellen Josselson defines an identity crisis as "the experience of questioning what we have taken as a given: 'I have always been like this, but perhaps I could still be otherwise. I could make and live out different choices.'"[19] This identity crisis can be elevated "by inner change or social dislocation."[20]

Collectivism: The core elements of collectivism are that "groups bind and mutually obligate individuals."[21] Collectivism describes the process whereby one comes to understand one's self in the context of the relationship between self and others, and is complementary to the concept of individualism. D. Oyserman understands collectivist societies as communal societies, which are characterized "by diffuse and mutual obligations and expectations based on ascribed statuses."[22] He adds that "in these societies, social units with common fate, common goals, and common values are centralized; the personal is simply a component of the social, making the in-group the key unit of analysis."[23] In this vein, a group membership is a central aspect of one's identity and becomes a source of one's judgment in life matters.

15. Ibid., 52.
16. Speelman, *Keeping Faith*, 32–37.
17. Erikson's Eight Stages of Development are 1. Trust vs. Basic Mistrust, 2. Autonomy vs. Shame and Doubt, 3. Initiative vs. Guilt, 4. Industry vs. Inferiority, 5. Identity vs. Role Confusion, 6. Intimacy vs. Isolation, 7. Generativity vs. Stagnation, and 8. Integrity vs. Despair (Erickson, *Identity*).
18. Josselson, *Finding Herself*, 13.
19. Josselson, *Revising Herself*, 27.
20. Ibid., 28.
21. Oyserman, Coon, and Kemmelmeier, "Rethinking Individualism," 5.
22. Ibid., 9.
23. Ibid.

Introduction

Theological and Analytical Frameworks

Frameworks of Theories

I MADE USE OF three theoretical frameworks in my research: *Conversion Studies, Islamic Religious Formation,* and *Identity.*

Conversion Studies

In this research, I discussed religious conversion theories related to identity crisis formation in the conversion process rather than motifs of conversion. John Lofland and Norman Skonovd (1981), Lewis R. Rambo (1993, 1999), C. E. Farhadian (1999), Gé M. Speelman (2001), and Massimo Leone (2004) studied the process of conversion and they posited diverse phenomena when conversion occurs. All of them commonly mentioned an interim stage or crisis of establishing oneself in one's new faith and its influences in the process of conversion. This interim stage of conversion is the basis of understanding identity issues of BMB women in Jordan. I compared these scholars' understandings of conversion with what I discovered about conversion among Muslim women in Jordan.

Islamic Religious Formation

I researched the ways in which Islamic doctrines and worldviews were lived out in Jordan in relation to identity construction. Religion is both individual and social.[24] Jonas Adelin Jørgensen states that religious identity denotes the self-identification of individuals or groups in terms of religious faith.[25] Therefore religion facilitates a foundational resource for believers to determine their own identity. Wilfred Cantwell Smith defines Islam as a "total framework of being imbedded in which each component part of the lives of the Muslims, each thing that they see, each object that they touch, each sentence that they utter or receive, takes on meaning."[26] This investigation of an Islamic definition of religious identity in various perspectives showed how BMB women's previous identities were established.

---

24. McGuire, *Religion*, 6.
25. Jørgensen, *Jesus Imandars*, 28.
26. Smith, *Belief*, 25.

Identity Crisis

The Qur'an is the primary resource from which to define and construct one's self-identity as Muslims. The Hadith (Muhammad's sayings) and the Sunnah (Muhammad's deeds and sayings) are also critical Islamic traditions that contribute to their identity. In relation to the Sunni tradition in Jordan, these Islamic sacred books are fundamental assets. Wherever possible I tried to isolate what these texts said about women's identity construction, even though the texts were largely patriarchal.

Identity

Today's world is increasingly defined by the two forces of globalization and postmodernism. Therefore, people's understanding of "self" has changed. Modernistic beliefs and traditional identities have been threatened by these influences and individuals' choices of religion are more flexible than before. These phenomena also have influenced Muslim women's self-presentation, education, career life, and so on. In order to do thorough research on identity, I dealt with the issue of women's identity with three perspectives: postmodern and transitional, sociopsychological, and women's cultural perspectives.

Zigmunt Bauman (2007) and Manuel Castells (2004) articulated characteristics of identity in postmodern and transitional societies, and developed ideas on how globalization, urbanization, advanced technologies, and contemporary ideas affect self-identity. From the sociopsychological perspective, identity is understood to have a close connection to culture. Culture influences people's emotion, worldview, and self-understanding. The works of Harry C. Triandis (1995) show clear features of how one's concept of self-understanding and social behavior are influenced by one's society's cultural meanings and complexities, such as an individualistic or collectivistic tendency. Çiğdem Katiğçibaşi (2007) and Gary S. Gregg (2007) have proven how this cultural model in Arab societies deeply affects Arab people's understanding of self and their behaviors. Regarding the unique picture of women's identity, Josselson (1987, 1996) discusses this in relation to diverse milieus of society, family tradition, education, and ages. Her four categories of women's identity—Guardians, Pathmakers, Searchers, and Drifters—describe the general features of women's identity in the development of life from youth to middle age.

The milieu of Jordanian BMB women is different from Jordanian male BMBs. Jordanian BMB women have distinctive identities in contrast to their male counterparts. For the analysis of the identity crisis of Jordanian BMB women, I integrated all the aforementioned theoretical frameworks to research identity construction of Jordanian women and analyze identity crises in their conversion process. I predicted that Bauman and Castell's understanding of identity informed basic characteristics of identity in relation to current transitional Jordanian sociocultural situations. Triandis, Katiğçibaşi, and Gregg's crosscultural sociopsychological model also explained how Jordanian women's behaviors are influenced by Jordanian religious and sociocultural factors. Furthermore Josselson's categorization helped to explore the process of women's identity construction and to analyze the difficulties that Jordanian women face in the next step of their life's decisions. Rambo and Speelman's concept of discontinuity from one's previous religion gave foundations to explain what confuses BMB women when they begin forming their new beliefs. All these theories were useful not only to understand the construction of Jordanian women's identity, but also to anticipate the diverse hindrances which exist inside and outside of their circumstances in the process of settling in to their new faith at the initial phase. I expected that my research in the specific Jordanian context would add nuances to all these theories of identity construction, revealing the unique pattern of Jordanian women's lives. In my research I was also aware that for an appropriate investigation on Jordanian women's identity issues, categorization or analysis of Western concepts of women had to be applied very carefully to Jordanian women.[27] Historical differences and sociocultural relativity had to be acknowledged to analyze theories properly.

Literature Review

My literature review was based on three segments: identity in the interim stage related to conversion theories; the formation of identity in a transitional society under the influence of postmodernism and cultural influences; Muslim women's identity both globally and locally in Jordan. Furthermore, I also examined Muslim women's understanding of "self"

---

27. In Frances S. Adeney's research about motivation of Indonesian Christian women to be leaders in religious institutions where there is usually resistance and barriers to such, she points out the dangers of using a single set of standards, even if accepted in a Euro-American context, to analyze Indonesian women's life (Adeney, *Christian Women*, 168).

Identity Crisis

and the interpretation of it in the Islamic Scripture and traditions, such as the Qur'an, Hadith, and other Arabic literature.

Conversion

Conversion studies over the years have developed and included religious, social, anthropological, and psychological disciplines.

Religious and Sociopsychological Understanding of Conversion

In Christian understanding the word conversion has been widely used as an "external act of religious change" or a "critical internal religious change in persons."[28] Conversion means returning to God and being transformed by God in the Bible. The Hebrew root *subh* is the main word used in the Old Testament to express to "turn, return, bring back, restore," and *niham* is also related and means to "be sorry or to regret."[29] The Greek word for conversion *epistrepho*, *metanoeo*, and *metamelomai* are used. *Metanoeo* means to repent and the associated noun *metanoia* is repentance.[30] *Epistrepho* means actual turning and repenting.[31] In the Old Testament, God continually called Israelites to turn away from their sins and idol worship and return to him.[32] Therefore, conversion in the Old Testament denotes "both 'repent' and 'repentance.'"[33] In the New Testament usage, repentance means turning away from "sin, selfishness, darkness, idols, habits, bondages and demons, both private and public."[34] In this sense, Christopher J. H. Wright notices that the calling of Israel to return to God in the Old Testament had continuity with the New Testament context and defines the nature of conversion as the radical rejection and displacement of all other gods, inclusion and allegiance to Christ and a radical ethical transformation.[35]

---

28. Walls, "Converts or Proselytes?," 2.
29. Brown, "Conversion," 353.
30. Ibid.
31. Ibid.
32. Ibid.
33. Wright, "Implications," 14.
34. Wallis, *The Call*, 5.
35. Wright, "Implications," 15.

Introduction

From the theological perspective, there are various emphases to interpret the concept of conversion within Christian hermeneutics and practical implications. General theological issues regarding conversion in Protestant circles are categorized according to who brings it (God or man), how long it takes, and whether it is individual or corporate focused in its representation of conversion.[36] According to their different theological understandings, people emphasize "the activity of God, people, or a co-mixture of God and people in bringing in about conversion" respectively.[37] In traditional Christian theology, conversion is understood as an integral work of God related to the issues of sanctification and soteriology.[38] The Reformed tradition understands conversion "as a part of the broader plan of God in vocation, or the 'calling' of the elect to receive salvation" with their election and predestination.[39] Calvin understood grace to be irresistible. Therefore, "the work of the Holy Spirit's regeneration precedes faith and repentance is the fruit of faith."[40] In the Lutheran view, it is "the recognition of humanity's utter sinfulness by the law of God that causes one's repentance and conversion and in faith this is completed."[41] By contrast, churches in the Armenian and Wesleyan tradition and others in the Holiness movement understand "the freedom of human response to the gospel and the view that conversion precedes regeneration."[42] Therefore, conversion is "what humans have to do; regeneration is what God alone can do."[43]

In a sociological perspective, conversion means "a transformation of one's self concurrent with a transformation of one's basic meaning system and it changes the sense of who one is and how one belongs in the social situation."[44] There are great varieties in characteristics of conversions. McGuire highlights the individuation in the conversion process. He asserts that "religions in modern contexts must actively work at generating members' individual choices and commitments," but in traditional societies "young people's belonging to the group's religion in the future is taken so

---

36. Gibbs, "Conversion," 276–82.
37. Chacko, *The Phenomenon*, 5.
38. Mckim, "The Mainline," 123.
39. Ibid., 125.
40. Ibid.
41. Ibid., 130.
42. Ibid.
43. Ibid.
44. McGuire, *Religion*, 73.

Identity Crisis

for granted that youth need only to learn how to perform their own roles in that group."[45] Conversion also effects an individual's meaning system, its diverse social relationship and the very identity of convert.[46] McGuire explains social, psychological, and ideational perspectives of conversion.

> The social component consists of the interaction between the recruit and other circles of associates (e.g., parents, friends, co-workers). The psychological component refers to emotional and affective aspects of conversion as well as to changes in values and attitudes. The ideational component includes the actual ideas the convert embraces or rejects during the process. These ideas are rarely very philosophical or theological; they are simply a set of beliefs that both justify the new meaning system and negate the former one.[47]

Furthermore, McGuire states the cases of disenchantment in the conversion process. He asserts that "like the commitment process, the disengagement process involves the pushes and pulls of various social influences."[48] He categorizes four stages that are characteristic of role exit: first doubts, seeking and weighing role alternatives, a turning point, and establishing an ex-role.[49]

In psychological explanations, William James suggests that religious conversion is "a profound step in the creation of a self."[50] In the same vein, Rambo describes that the conversion process has various stages and diverse phenomena in each stage. In *Understanding Religious Conversion*, Rambo defines "religious conversion is one of humanity's ways of approaching its self-conscious predicament, of solving or resolving the mysterious of human origins, meaning, and destiny."[51] He adds that "Conversion takes place within a dynamic context [which] is the integration of both the superstructure and the infrastructure of conversion and it includes social, cultural, religious and personal dimensions."[52]

---

45. Ibid, 75.
46. Ibid., 77
47. Ibid.
48. Ibid., 91.
49. Ibid.
50. Douglas, "Conversion," 260.
51. Rambo, *Understanding*, 2.
52. Ibid., 20.

Introduction

According to Rambo, the context of conversion includes Encounter, Crisis, Quest, Interaction, Consequences, and Commitment in the process of conversion. This systemic model shows that complicated conversion context encompasses a vast panorama of conflicting, confluent, and dialectical factors that both facilitate and repress conversion.[53] In particular, the Commitment stage includes pivotal decision-making and new identity-forming. Anselm L. Strauss in *Mirrors and Masks: The Search for Identity* also explains that this Commitment stage in the conversion process involves "conviction as to what is right and proper as well as its converse: what is worth striving for, fighting for, what is to be avoided, abhorred, considered cheap or sinful, and so on."[54]

Lofland and Skonovd's 1981 research on the conversion stories of young people in the U.S. debunks the reasons about the transformation of religious identity in the conversion process and deals with the interim stage, which is understood as identity crisis. Although the research was done in the U.S. for converts to Christianity, they prove that, according to various conversion motif types, the process of conversion is complex. They also suggest that in each motif there are also five variations: degree of social pressure, irregular duration, level of affective arousal, affective content, and belief-participation sequence after conversion. With these variations, people experience an interim stage between their old and new faiths that causes crises within converts.[55]

Speelman distinguishes the conversion process as three phases: the old faith (the context), the interim period (crisis and quest), and the new faith (encounter, commitment and consequences).[56] She also points out the tension between the old self and the new self in the conversion process. Through the investigations of "continuity and discontinuity of identity issues among ex-Muslims and ex-Christians," Spleeman assures the reader

---

53. Ibid.

54. Strauss, *Mirrors*, 39–40.

55. Conversion Motifs: 1. Intellectual conversion: the person seeks knowledge about religious or spiritual issues from books or media 2. Mystical conversion: prototypical model: Saul of Tarsus 3. Experimental conversion: a major avenue of conversion in the 20C because of great religious freedom. Potential convert experience without faith 4. Affectional conversion: interpersonal bonds, personal experience of being loved, nurtured and affirmed by group and its leaders 5. Revivalist motif: in nineteen century than twenty century centuries, individuals are influenced by the meetings and social influences 6. Coercive motif: specific conditions need to be present: brainwashing (Lofland and Skonovd, "Conversion Motifs," 373–85).

56. Speelman, *Keeping Faith*, 306.

that "conversion is often experienced as a total upheaval of one's identity, a complete break with the past."[57] She states that because of building the "new self" with the building blocks of the "old self," in the first stage of peoples' conversion, converts often are confused.[58]

Identity Crisis in Conversion Process

Generally, "crisis" in conversion studies is mentioned as a kind of starting point when one faces certain situations in her/his life where they doubt their old beliefs. However, during the process of conversion, a person who is seeking a new faith meets another crisis of identity, called an interim stage. Outside the crisis, a person takes a step to look to another faith, but inside the crisis, the person is put into tension between their old and new faiths.

Regarding a convert's identity crisis, Rambo points out in another work (1999) with Farhadian that conversion is the passage between the time of disbelief and the time of belief.[59] There is an "interim period between the discarding of the old faith and the adoption of the new, a period of quest and it can be a stage of doubt and searching."[60] They suggest that there will often be a psychological struggle that a person might experience while converting from one religion to another.[61]

Rambo also argues in *Understanding Religious Conversion* that "resistance is the normal or typical reaction of both individuals and societies to conversion attempts."[62] According to him, conversion sometimes brings emotional grief. Rambo points out that after conversion, many converts experience grief over lost relationships and connections with outsiders and prior beliefs. Hence conversion experience is painful for many converts because it uproots converts' whole lives and sometimes causes confusion inside of converts about their decision.

Conversion also brings confusion of integration between personal and social (or communal) identity to converts. Leone in *Religious Conversion and Identity: The Semiotic Analysis of Texts* affirms that the 'destabilization

57. Ibid., 304.
58. Ibid.
59. Rambo and Farhadian, "Converting," 10.
60. Speelman, *Keeping Faith*, 306.
61. Rambo and Farhadian, "Converting," 10.
62. Rambo, *Understanding*, 35.

of the self' is part of the first stage of conversion.⁶³ Leone asserts that identity is the critical issue in all the various and different types of religious changes a person may have.⁶⁴ He explains identity crisis as:

> Encountering with a new system of religion provokes a destabilization of the self . . . On the one hand, the destabilization of the self implies the loss of personal identity. This means that converted people do not know how to coherently organize the different (and often opposite) religious ideas which they have received from the encounter with the Christian message or which they have developed as a consequence of this encounter. On the other hand, the destabilization of the self implies the loss of social identity. This means that the group or community to which converted people belonged (or still continue to belong) does not know how to coherently integrate them.⁶⁵

Other works also find that even the most devoted converts can often feel as though they are caught between two worlds.⁶⁶ Therefore, conversion experience for converts is a new construction of their identities and gives various challenges to fixed perspectives of themselves and of relationships with the societies.

Identity

Identity is based upon one's self-understanding. It makes a bridge "between who we feel ourselves to be internally and who we are recognized as being by our social world."⁶⁷

IDENTITY IN TRANSITIONAL SOCIETY UNDER THE INFLUENCE OF POSTMODERNISM

McGuire asserts that the edifice of self-identity in modern societies is "qualitatively different from that in traditional societies."⁶⁸ In contempo-

---

63. Leone, *Religious Conversion*, 13.
64. Ibid., 175.
65. Ibid., 79.
66. Carrothers, *Identity*, 13.
67. Josselson, *Revising Herself*, 27.
68. McGuire, *Religion*, 53.

rary societies, the individual's social situation cannot be fixed. If traditional societies have power in family, community, and society to nurture individuals' religious senses, nowadays these processes have "seriously weakened to offer the individual a stable source of belonging and identity."[69]

Bauman also demonstrates new challenges of identity in our temporary societies in *Liquid Times: Living in an Age of Uncertainty*. Bauman describes that our societies have passed "from the 'solid' to a 'liquid' phase of modernity" in which any social forms of identity can "no longer keep their shape for long."[70] In addition, he debunks the idea that politics loses its power in uncontrolled global (and in many ways extraterritorial) space and the community can no longer guarantee certain safe-zones against individual failure.[71] Therefore long-term thinking, planning, and acting are not efficacious for living in these societies and changing individual lifestyles.[72]

Castells is another researcher who contributes to foundational identity issues related to contemporary society. He proposes three aspects of identity in contemporary societies: Legitimizing Identity, which is introduced by the dominant institutions of society to extend, "rationalizes their domination *vis à vis* social actors," and forms statuses deeply rooted among people or made by civic associations;[73] Resistance Identity, which is "generated by those actors who are in positions/conditions devalued and/or stigmatized by the logic of domination";[74] and Projective Identity, which is when social actors, on the basis of whatever cultural materials are available to them, build a new identity that redefines their position in society and seeks the transformation of the overall social structure.[75]

Castells considers Resistance Identity as a vital form of identity building of our network society to alienate people: "It constructs forms of collective resistance against otherwise unbearable oppression, usually on the basis of identities that were apparently, clearly defined by history, geography, or biology, making it easier to essentialize the boundaries of resistance."[76] Islamic fundamentalists have this strong resistance identity

69. Ibid., 58.
70. Bauman, *Liquid Times*, 1.
71. Ibid., 1–2.
72. Ibid., 3.
73. Ibid., 9.
74. Castells, *The Power*, 8.
75. Ibid., 8–9.
76. Ibid., 9.

against Western Christianity or culture. They reflect on themselves as what they name "the exclusion of the excluders by the excluded."[77] Speelman also affirms that "identity always rests on the dynamics of mirroring oneself in others with whom one is in relationship."[78] Therefore, the others evoke the reply: "I am like her/him" or "I am not like her/him."

Castells also points out the weakness of the traditional partiarchalism in transitional societies challenged by the rise of an informational, global economy and technological changes.[79]

> New generations are being socialized out of the traditional pattern of the patriarchal family, and are being exposed from an early age of the need to cope with different settings, and different adult roles. In sociological terms, the new process of socialization downplays to some extent the institutional norms of the patriarchal family and diversifies the roles within the family.[80]

Identity in Cultural Influences

Michael Rynkiewich defines culture as "a more or less integrated system of knowledge, values and feelings."[81] He, therefore, suggests that the sociocultural perspectives of the researcher "ask how these people perceive the world around them, how they feel about the things they see . . . how these people actually behave and in particular, how people acquire an identity, negotiate social relations and form groups."[82] Robert J. Schreiter in *Constructing Local Theologies* expresses that cultural tradition provides resources for identity and culture gives specific boundaries for one to recognize the world to which one belongs. This boundary "appears in roles, in status markers, and in the line between publicly discernible behavior and privately held truth."[83] Speelman states that culturally determined frames are regarded as "normal" for a particular culture and the basis of people's

---

77. Ibid.
78. Speelman, *Keeping Faith*, 35.
79. Castells, *The Power*, 193.
80. Ibid., 243.
81. Rynkiewich, *Soul*, 64.
82. Ibid.
83. Schrieter, *Constructing Local Theologies*, 105.

Identity Crisis

behavior and thinking.[84] Therefore, when one's identity, central values, and norms are produced within a certain framework of their culture, it works as a block from the outside world. Culture is the principal agent from which to construct one's identity. Hence, Arabic society's unique cultural elements, in particular related to Islam, have a strong connection with Muslim's identity formation. For instance, June Price Tangney and Gabriele Taylor's research proves how shame and other emotions affect one's self-conceptualization.[85] According to Tangney, "shame, guilt, embarrassment, and pride are members of a family of 'self-conscious emotions' that are evoked by self-reflection and self-evaluation."[86]

In cross-cultural psychology, Herry C. Triandis shows the connection between one's individualistic or collectivistic identity tendency to one's egocentric or sociocentric behavior.[87] He understands that culture shapes one's purpose of life and one's ideal images of who one wants to be.[88] Çiğdem Katiğçibaşi and Gary S. Gregg work in Turkey and Morocco, respectively, on specific applications of cross-cultural psychology to Muslim societies. Katiğçibaşi, a Turkish woman psychologist, studies the linkage of one's self-understanding related to development of life in Muslim culture in her book, *Family, Self, and Human Development Across Cultures*.[89] Gregg, in *Culture and Identity in a Muslim Society*, researches the transitional status of a Muslim's identity between tradition and Western-style modernity through "young Moroccans' self-presentations to be pervasively shaped by the volatile cultural struggle."[90] In the same vein with Triandis and Katiğçibaşi, Gregg draws attention to how the collectivist orientation of Muslims' influences format Muslims' identity as sociocentric selves. According to them, Muslims, particularly the younger generations, are struggling between the two cultures of sociocentrism and egocentrism.

---

84. Speelman, *Keeping Faith*, 49.
85. Tangney and Dearing, *Shame and Guilt*; and Taylor, *Pride*.
86. Tangney and Tracy, "Self-Conscious Emotions," 446.
87. Triandis, *Individualism*.
88. Ibid., 10.
89. Katiğçibaşi, *Family*.
90. Gregg, *Culture*, 3.

Introduction

IDENTITY OF WOMEN

When considering identity expressions, women's identity is described more in relational context with others. Josselson understands that identity has built on a process of integration and interpretation one's life, and asserts that

> Identity is what integrates our own diversity, gives meaning to the disparate parts of ourselves, and relates them to one another. Identity is how we interpret our own existence and understand who we are in our world. I am a woman, but my identity as a woman is my unique way of being a woman in the culture in which I live. And so on with other aspects of my (or your) identity.[91]

She draws four categories of the general types of women's understanding of "Self": Guardians, Pathmakers, Searchers, and Drifters in her development of women's identity.

Guardians construct their identity to follow their parents or other authoritative influences when they are children: "They are likely to feel— This is how I am because it's how I was raised or how I've always been."[92] Guardians know where they are going without having considered any alternatives.[93] It is possible for them because when they were little girls they "absorbed the values and attitudes of their families and still held fast to them, or as adolescents, found someone else to cling to who would define what was right for them."[94] Therefore these Guardian-type of women usually do not question religion while continuing in the beliefs and practices of their childhood "because they blindly adopt their parents' standards."[95] Pathmakers make their identities according to their own achievements or commitments.[96]

Searchers are those who are still in the stage where they are trying to find their identity. The search for one's identity leads to an "*identity crisis*, which refers to an acute form of confusion and disorientation that affects

---

91. Josselson, *Revising Herself*, 30.

92. Ibid. Josselson developed it on J. E. Marcia's four types (statutes) of identity formation based on the presence or absence of crisis and commitment in occupational and ideological (religious and political) realms: "Foreclosure, Achievement, Moratorium and Diffusion" in *Finding Herself*, 29.

93. Ibid., 37.

94. Ibid.

95. Ibid., 42.

96. Ibid.

individuals, peoples, nations, and institutions."⁹⁷ In their case, "they are in an 'identity crisis' filled with conflict, torn between the demands and expectations of their parents that were firmly inside of them and the wish to extricate themselves and make their own choice."⁹⁸ Searchers have a difficult time integrating their identities and choosing a way to live, because they are "on the road to choice, in the midst of the struggle, and stumbling through the period of exploration."⁹⁹ However, they are deeply engaged in questioning and have a sense of self-awareness.¹⁰⁰ According to Josselson, becoming a Searcher is dependent upon how much one will allow new experiences to be profoundly meaningful.¹⁰¹ They want to keep their old self as a safety precaution in order to "come back to claim it" at any time.¹⁰² In this period, "the presence of supportive others appears to be necessary in consolidating an independent identity."¹⁰³ Lastly, Drifters live without any struggling or having a clear commitment in their identity. In some aspects, they do not mind or care about their identities.

Research Methodology

The focus of this research is on the identity issues of female Jordanian BMBs throughout the conversion process with religious, anthropological, and psychological perspectives. I applied qualitative research methodology in my research. Due to the religious circumstances of Jordan, it was extremely difficult to publicly meet a lot of female Believers from Muslim Background. In this sense, the qualitative research was useful to find identity, because it has special functions in order to investigate "complex and sensitive issues."¹⁰⁴ Qualitative research is defined as "a set of interpretive, material practices that make the world visible."¹⁰⁵ In addition, the nature of qualitative research "begins with assumptions, a worldview, the possible

---

97. Theron, "Devastating Grace," 33.
98. Josselson, *Revising Herself*, 105.
99. Ibid., 106.
100. Ibid.
101. Ibid., 138.
102. Ibid.
103. Ibid.
104. "Qualitative Measures."
105. Denzin and Lincoln, "Qualitative Research," 3.

use of a theoretical lens and the study of research problems inquiring into the meaning individuals or groups ascribe to a social or human problem."[106]

In particular, case studies through interviews were an important method to produce my qualitative research. In-depth interviews helped to bring understanding of how people think and what they experienced during the conversion process. Therefore, I conducted three kinds of interviews: one type with Jordanian Muslim women and another with BMB women. Interviews with Jordanian Muslim women investigated how they built their women's identity. Other interviews with Jordanian BMB women investigated what kinds of identity crises they went through in the process of conversion. The third set of interviews observed identity crises from the perspective of overseas workers who had worked with both Muslim and BMB women. All interviews were semi-structured with both focused and open-ended questions. The semi-structured interview allowed "for planned questions around specific issues and general items but also employ(ed) the freedom of an unstructured approach."[107] I audiotaped the interviews and then provided transcriptions and notes. My interviews were personal and one-on-one.

In carrying out this research and through the process of analysis, I acknowledged that I brought three perspectives to the work: Language, Outsider Perspective, and Religion. I have studied spoken and classic Arabic at language schools for several years, but my Arabic has limits to understanding the Qur'an and Jordanian Arabic. Hence, for the interviews, I received help from a Christian female translator to interpret and translate the interviews in the transcriptions. Regarding the analysis of Jordanian Muslim and female BMB's identity issues, my research findings were from a Christian outsider perspective. I have lived in Jordan, but I am not a Jordanian. Therefore, when I investigated the identities of Jordanian women's sociocultural milieu, I had an etic (outsider) not an emic (insider) perspective. Finally, although I am a BBB (Believer from a Buddhist Background) and share some similar experiences to BMB women in Jordan, I have approached the religious perspectives of Jordanian Muslim women's life from a Christian viewpoint.

---

106. Creswell, *Qualitative Inquiry*, 37.
107. Ammerman et al., *Studying Congregations*, 206.

Significance of the Research

Some research has been carried out on the conversion of Muslims to Christianity and Muslim women's conversion. The majority of that research, however, is about the reasons for conversion and how to bring about the conversion of Muslims. There are few studies about how these converts construct their new identities while they are settling into their new faith. Some articles and research have been done which raise issues on the return of BMBs to Islam and identity issues by Seppo Syrjänen, Kathryn Kraft, and Edward Evans. Syrjänen and Evans dealt with BMBs in Pakistan, and Kraft conducted her research about BMBs in Lebanon and Egypt respectively, but none of these focused on women and identity issues at the beginning stage of conversion. Rather they discuss general problems of BMBs in those countries.[108] Therefore, this study will be helpful to understand the conversion process in relation with women's identity.

Secondly, existing research about the evangelism of Muslims is heavily, in fact almost exclusively, targeted to Muslim men. In Arab countries and Islamic cultures, women have a unique culture and milieu, and are treated separately from men, in general. Hence, reaching out to Muslim women and discipling them cannot be done simply using the methods which target men. This study specifies the Jordanian Muslim women's milieu as well as new believers' unique circumstances in the process of conversion.

Thirdly, this research offers a foundation in order to develop an appropriate way of discipleship for BMB women and protect them from leaving at the initial stage of their new faith. This research's focus on identity crisis contributes in producing a new model of discipleship for BMBs which considers a convert's identity formation.

Lastly, but most importantly, this study shows an appropriate missiological theory to complement and combine existing theories, which are reflected in the study that refers to identity in the conversion process. Bauman's theory explains the uncertainty of contemporary society to decide an individual's life. Castell's three categorical identities also illustrate the important characteristics of identity referring to our network societies. However, both Bauman and Castell give general characteristics of the fluidity of people's identities in modern life, and any associated issues, by focusing more on the social and political realm, and do not deal with the crisis or problems people face during the formation of their identities in

---

108. Syrjänen, *Searching for Meaning*; Kraft, *Searching for Heaven*.

contemporary society. Although Triandis, Katiğçibaşi, and Gregg describe relationships between identity formation and culture, it is not enough to apply to specific Jordanian Middle Eastern circumstances, and to account for the transition process from collectivism to individualism. In the case of Josselson, she gives an outstanding explanation about characteristics of adult American women's identities, which have been formed throughout their lives. She categorizes four types of women's identities and they are helpful to understand how women format their identities related to decision-making, in particular. Although her work grants a general frame of women's identity, it is not enough to explain Middle Eastern women's identity formation under Islamic influences.

2

Woman's Identities in Christianity and Islam

As an academic principle, comparative theology is considered a sharing between scholars who have different worldviews about "the investigation of the concept of ultimate reality, the final human goal and the way to achieve it."[1] In this chapter, for the purpose of comparison of women's identity in Christianity and Islam, I will focus on the nature of women's identity in the accounts of creation of human beings, and explore how the Bible, the Qur'an, and other Islamic traditions explain the status of women in both religions. This comparison of women's identity between Christianity and Islam makes clear how Muslim women form their identity and what kind of new religious identities BMB women form in the process of conversion.

McGuire states that religion makes the adherent perceive and know the world in which they belong and its experiences and rituals "continually reproduce and transmit to the next generation the collective sense of 'who we are' and 'what it means to be one of us.'"[2] Islam is a religion of strict religious practices. The function of rituals "reminds the individual of its belonging, [and] creates an intense sense of togetherness" according to McGuire, and in this way Muslims are built together as one religious body.[3] Hence, one's religion ties with not only divinity but also to the society and community he/she belongs. Jørgensen also supports the idea of religion as a resource of creating one's own identity and attributing meaning to the

1. Ward, *Religion*, 339.
2. McGuire, *Religion*, 20.
3. Ibid., 21.

world he/she belongs to.⁴ By religious commitment the solid communal identity is created among adherents.⁵ Islamic doctrine is very closely knitted both with people's sense of their own identity and with community life structured in Arab Muslim communities.⁶

Identity of Women in Islam

Regardless of the ethnicity or race, for a Muslim Islam has to be "the first source of identity, not an 'additional' ideological superstructure."⁷ In the Qur'an, the revelation of Allah is the standard of all Muslims' lives, and defines who human beings are and how they live. In particular, identities of Muslim women are closely bound by the Islamic traditions. Melani McNeal affirms that "interpretations of these sources lay a burden upon them that excludes and diminishes them, leaving them weak and vulnerable, dependent on others to mediate their status and role before God and define their place in the community."⁸ In addition, Muslims' absolutism concerning the Prophet Muhammad, through whom "Allah would reign," allows Muhammad's message (via the Sunnah and the Hadith) and life to be a model of Muslims' practices.⁹ The Qur'an and Islamic traditions prescribe the self-identity of women as multifaceted.

The Qur'anic View of Women's Identity

Self (Nafs) and Creation

In Arabic "self" is translated as *nafs*, and has multiple meanings including soul, spirit, mind, life, animate being, living creature, person, individual, self, personal identity or nature.¹⁰ The Arabic holistic view of human beings is shown in the word *nafs*. Barazangi describes it as the realization of "the existence of God through its relation with itself and nature."¹¹ Sometimes

---

4. Jørgensen, *Jesus Imandars*, 20.
5. Kim, "Differing Concepts," 107.
6. Kraft, *Searching for Heaven*, 35.
7. Al-Faruqi, "Women's Self-Identity," 74.
8. McNeal, "Do Muslim Women Really Need Saving?," 82.
9. Zwemer, *Moslem Women*, 38.
10. S.v. "nafs," in Wehr and Cowan, *Arabic-English Dictionary*, 985.
11. Barazangi, *Woman's Identity*, 43–44.

Identity Crisis

nafs has been used for species in the Qur'an: "And Allah has made for you mates (and Companions), of your own nature" (16:72).[12] Adam and his wife were created the same "*nafs.*"[13] Furthermore, it is clear that the principle of life, soul or self, comes from Allah.[14] In that sense, Al-Faruqi affirms that "the Qur'anic worldview is one in which creation is created with a single purpose—to worship (serve) God... The self-worth of the individual is the same for all."[15]

Allah is the creator of human beings, male and female (49:13), and rewards equally, regardless of gender, those who do good work for the sake of Allah (3:195; 4:32; 16:97).[16] Narratives of the creation of humans are distributed in different parts of the Qur'an (4:1; 6:2; 7:12,189; 15:26; 17:61; 23:12–14; 30:21; 32:7; 37:11; 39:6; 49:13; 55:14, etc.). According to the Qur'an, a woman is created with a man as one entity, and their origin is from a single soul (4:1; 33:35; 49:13).[17] "O mankind! Reverence Your Guardian-Lord, Who created you From a single Persons, created, of like nature, His mate, and from them twain Scattered (like seeds) Countless men and women..." (4:1).

The creation of all animals are from water (24:45), as well as all living things (21:30). Furthermore, a mere "drop of sperm" is also repeated as a factor of the origin of humans (16:4; 36:77; 40:67; 53:45–46; 76:2; 80:19). Human beings are made from clay, and have spirit by the breathing of Allah (32:7–9). In another account, humans are also made from water (25:54). A more detailed description of the biological process of reproduction can also be found:

> Man We did create From a quintessence (of clay); Then We placed him In a place of rest, Firmly fixed; Then We made the sperm Into a leech-like a clot; Then of that clot We made A (foetus) lump; then We made out of the lump Bones, and clothed the bones With flesh; then We developed Out of it another creature. So blessed be Allah, The Best to create! (23:12–14)

---

12. I use 'Abdullah Yusuf Ali's translation of the Qur'an with several noted exceptions (Ali, *The Meaning*).
13. Khan, *Woman*, 30.
14. Anwar, *Gender*, 3.
15. Al-Faruqi, "Women's Self-Identity," 78.
16. Ibid.
17. Ibid., 79.

In some interpretations of creation, Muslims follow the Judeo-Christian understanding, which is shown clearly in the Hadith, Muhammad's message and life. For instance, in contrast to the Bible, there is no mention that human beings are created in the image of Allah in the Qur'an, but in the Hadith it is written that "The Prophet said, 'Allah created Adam in His picture (image).'"[18] Another example is the name of woman. Although the first man is called Adam, the woman does not have a name. She is called his wife in the Qur'an (7:19), but in the Hadith as Eve, in the Islamic tradition "*Hawwā*," and she is believed to be taken out from rib of Adam.[19] Human beings are very special within creation (95:4). They have freedom to choose "either to fulfill their potential as the most honored among God[Allah]'s creation or sin to a level furthest away from God by disobeying or denying Him."[20]

Although "human beings carry an inherent dignity and honor conveyed in the very manner of their creation" (7:10, 31:20), the highest transcendent and untouched status of Allah is distanced from humanity.[21] Therefore as a fundamental conception in Islam in terms of their relationship with Allah, human beings are servants or slaves to their master, but never anything closer.[22]

Women's Image and Status

In general, women are important subjects in the Qur'an and Muhammad's message. There are general disciplines of women in the Qur'an 2:221–41 (marriage, menstruation, divorce, widows, and a dowry), 65:1–7(divorce), 4:3–35, 124–30 (marriage, inheritance, adultery, protection, and dowry), 5:5–6 (marriage and prayer), 24:2–19, 23–27 (adultery), 30–33, 58–61 (veiling, chastity, clothing), 33:4–6, 28–37, 49–59, 73 (modesty, dowry, divorce and reward of faith), and 60:10–12 (marriage). In the Qur'an, the Arabic word '*al-dhakar*' (male) and '*al-unsa*' (female) are used to designate

---

18. The phrase used in this *Hadith* is *a la Surato* in Arabic. This "according to His image" is identical with the term in the Van Dyke Arabic translation of the Bible *Surato 'ala insaan allah fakhalaq* (Gen 1:27) (Kahn, "Translation of Sahih Al Bukhari," 8:246).

19. Ibid., Surah 4:547.

20. Bush et al., *The Religious World*, 321.

21. Siddqi, "Being Human in Islam," 17.

22. Ibid., 18.

Identity Crisis

a biological distinction respectively (3:36).[23] This sexual difference between male and female is continuously repeated in the Qur'an and Hadith.

In the Islamic traditions, women are honored by their pious life and dutiful behaviors. At the same time, however, women are portrayed as negative images and have a limited role. Therefore, in the Hadith, views of women are multiple and contradictory. For instance, Muhammad mentioned that "I have left behind no temptation more harmful to my community than that which women represent for men"[24] but also said that "the whole world is delightful, but the most delightful thing in it is a virtuous woman."[25] The Prophet considered a woman good if she was a delight to her husband's gaze, obeyed his wishes and placed her person and her wealth entirely at his disposal.[26]

EQUALITY

"The natural order of relationships in Islam" is considered a hierarchy.[27] Thus the concept of equality exists in relationship to just rewards, good or bad, in the hereafter, for deeds accomplished during one's life following the will of Allah. This equality between a man and a woman is shown in several verses of the Qur'an such as 4:1; 33:35; 6:164 and so on. Both male and female have originated from one living being, thus have the same dignity and rights.[28] A woman is an independent human being and "*Khalifa*" (representative) of Allah. She has received "the great potentialities for the acquisition of knowledge and fulfillment of her role as the *Khalifa* of Allah on earth."[29] Men and women have religious equality (3:195; 9:71; 33:35), and the reward of faith is promised to both men and women (3:19; 16:97).

> For Muslim men and women,—For believing men and women, For devout men and women, For true men and women, For men and women who are Patient and constant, for men And women who humble themselves, For men and women who give In charity, for men and women who fast (and deny themselves), For men

23. Anwar, *Gender*, 25.
24. Cited in Anwar, *Gender*, 48.
25. Ibid.
26. Khan, *Woman*, 17.
27. Schleifer, *Motherhood*, 85.
28. Jawad, *The Rights*, 42.
29. Badamasiuy, *Status*, 20.

and women who Guard their chastity, and For men and women who Engage much in Allah's praise—For them has Allah prepared Forgiveness and great reward. (33:35)

The Qur'an considers woman *"muhsana*—a fortress against Satan— because a good woman, by marrying a man, helps him keep to the path of rectitude in his life."[30] The Qur'an also honors female figures such as Mary the mother of Jesus Christ and women saints in the Muslim calendar.[31] Women in general are considered to have honored social positions as mother (31:14), wife (30:21; 2:228; 4:19) and daughter (81:8–90).[32] Having children is critical for women and rearing children is the way to enter paradise for women.[33]

> [It is] the realization of God's desire; the fulfillment of the Prophet's call to marry and increase his followers' number; gaining the fruit of a child's prayer. Muslims believe that when parents die and leave a child (son or daughter), his prayer would benefit the dead parents. However, if the child dies before his parents, he would make intercession on his parent's behalf.[34]

Women fulfill the desire of Allah by obeying their husband and having and rearing children. It is even asserted by Aliah Schleifer, in *Motherhood in Islam*, that when a woman dies during the time of procreation, she is considered a martyr because she is the same as a person who is fighting for Allah in Jihad.[35]

Inequality or Differentiation

The image of women in many parts of the Qur'an and traditions are depicted as powerful and dangerous beings.[36] Women by their nature are conduits of evil and allure Muslim men (3:14; 24:31). Therefore women's sexual power needs to be controlled by "polygamy, repudiation, sexual segregation, etc.

---

30. Doi, *Women*, 6.
31. Zwemer, *Moslem Women*, 39.
32. Badamasiuy, *Status*, 24–28.
33. Dagher, *The Position*, 11.
34. Jawad, *The Rights*, 31.
35. Schleifer, *Motherhood*, 54.
36. Mernissi, *Beyond the Veil*, 19.

as a strategy for containing their power."[37] It is believed that "all the trials, misfortunes and woes which befall men come from women."[38] Mernissi adds that a woman in a public space of men upsets Allah "by inciting men to commit *zina* [adultery or sexual impurity]," and the man has everything to lose in this encounter: peace of mind, self-determination, allegiance to Allah, and social prestige."[39] In order to keep a man's purity, women should veil their bodies (24:31; 33:59).[40] Therefore, modesty is the most important virtue asked of women in particular: "O Prophet! Tell Thy wives and daughters, And the believing women, That they should cast Their outer garments over Their persons (when abroad): That is most convenient, That they should be known (As such) and not molested. And Allah is Oft-Forgiving, Most Merciful" (33:59).

> And say to the believing women That they should lower Their gaze and guard Their modesty; that they Should not display their Beauty and ornaments except What (must ordinarily) appear Thereof; that they should Draw their veils over Their bosoms and not display Their beauty except To their husbands, their fathers, Their husband's fathers, their sons, Their husbands' sons, Their brothers or their brothers' sons, Or their sisters' sons, Or their women, or the slaves Whom their right hands Possess, or male servants Free of physical needs, Or small children who Have no sense of the shame Of sex; and that they Should not strike their feet In order to draw attention To their hidden ornaments. And O ye Believers! Turn ye all together Towards Allah, that ye May attain Bliss (24:31).

In Islamic understanding, "women and men are created equal but not identical."[41] In the realms of socioeconomic order, family, and property, the differences between the rights and obligations of the two sexes are much clearer.[42] The *ummah* for Muslims is the "embodiment of the model behavior expected of society and individuals" (3:110).[43] In order to achieve Islamic values and goals for the community (*ummah*, tribes, clans, or

37. Ibid.
38. Al-Ghazali, *Ghazali's Book* cited in Walther, *Women*, 40.
39. Mernissi, *Beyond the Veil*, 144.
40. al-Buti, Ela kul, 98.
41. Braswell, *Islam*, 106.
42. Al-Faruqi, "Women's Self-Identity," 79.
43. Bush, *The Religious World*, 322.

extended family), individuals are considered as part of a community. As a basic essential social unit of this *ummah*, a family becomes a starting point to constitute the ideal Islamic socioeconomic order.[44] At the same time, family and marriage life for women is also essential foundation to grant their identities from the Qur'an and Islamic tradition. Even in the issue of Islamic education, the importance of family stability is emphasized for the future of Muslims and for the sound structuring of Islamic society.[45]

A great deal of the role of women in the Qur'an and other traditions are ascribed to them as wife and mother. Haddad declares that "wife and mother" is not only a role for Muslim women but it is their sole identity.[46] Samuel Zwemer also asserts that one of the important Qur'anic teachings regarding women is "in relation to marriage, divorce, and domestic slavery."[47] Sometimes women are described as men's possessions; "Everything in this world is a piece of property, or a possession. The best possession in the world is a pious woman."[48] In Islam a women's whole life is "placed under the care and authority of males" for their protection.[49] As the protectors and maintainers of women, men are responsible not only for providing, "but, also as a policeman of the Muslim order, and for the discipline and the guarding of his female relatives."[50] It is also the duty of men to keep the family's dignity by protecting the purity of the female members.[51] In this sense, the notion of honor killing shows "that the family's reputation for chastity depends heavily on women's behavior and contour."[52] Therefore, in the Qur'an 4:34–38, it is encouraged that a husband can discipline his disobedient wife as protector and maintainer and "his right to discipline has been recognized and sanctioned by the Qur'an and the Prophet and upheld by centuries of Islamic law."[53] At the same time, a wife should obey

---

44. Al-Faruqi, "Women's Self-Identity," 79.
45. Roald, *Women*, 213.
46. Haddad, "Traditional Affirmations," 63–64.
47. Zwemer, *Moslem Women*, 40.
48. Khan, *Woman*, 17.
49. Beck, "The Religious Lives," 34.
50. Mernissi, *Beyond the Veil*, 82.
51. Al-Faruqi, "Women's Self-Identity," 128.
52. Ibid., 128-29.
53. Haddad, "Traditional Affirmations," 71.

her husband as long as the instructions given are lawful.[54] Obedience to authoritative male family members is a duty for women.

> (Husbands) are the protectors And maintainers of their (wives) Because Allah has given The one more (strength) Than the other, and because They support them From their means. Therefore the righteous women Are devoutly obedient, and guard In (the husband's) absence What Allah would have them guard. As to those women On whose part ye fear Disloyalty and ill-conduct, Admonish them (first), (Next), refuse to share their beds, (And last) beat them (lightly);But if they return to obedience, Seek not against them Means (of annoyance): For Allah is Most High, great (above you all) (4:34).

There are several statements related to divorce (2:227–32, 236; 33:49; 65:1; 66:5). In the process of divorce, according to the Qur'an 2:228, men and women have the same rights, but men are over women. For child custody in a case of divorce, there is no specific mention of which parent is suitable. "According to the view of Islamists, however, it is the father who is responsible for the child's and the mother's economic sustenance for as long as the child is with the mother" (2:233).[55] Traditionally, boys can stay with their mother until two years of age, while little girls can stay with their mother until seven years old, but some countries allow seven years of age for boys and nine for girls.[56]

Not only in divorce, but there are many other aspects of differentiation between men and women in the Qur'an as well in the Islamic traditions. Polygamy is considered "the only reasonable alternative to meet the needs of women for protection and care" from the past history of war and natural disasters.[57] For instance, a man is allowed to have four wives, but he should treat them all equally (4:3). A daughter receives an inheritance half of what male siblings receive (4:11), and two female witnesses have the same weight as one male witness (2:282). Even in the case of the crime of murder, "blood money paid for a woman is half of that paid for a man."[58] Muslim women cannot marry non-Muslims (60:10). This ban is because unbelievers can never treat women in marriage according to the will of

54. Badamasiuy, *Status*, 42.
55. Roald, *Women*, 230.
56. Minces, *The House*, 68.
57. Ibid., 50.
58. Lindholm, *The Islamic Middle East*, 230.

Woman's Identities in Christianity and Islam

Allah.⁵⁹ But Muslim men can marry women from other religious backgrounds after they become Muslim.

Debatable Interpretation about Qur'anic Verses

The Islamic understanding about women and their status in society is becoming polarized according to positions of interpretation about Islamic traditions and literatures. Before the advent of Islam in the Jahiliyya period, female infanticide, female abduction, easy access for men to marry, divorce, and concubinage were practiced.⁶⁰ Muhammad in the early seventh century AD elevated the status of female and gender relations in pre-Islamic Arabia.⁶¹ It was a new religion but also included a social reform movement for the status of women in those days.

The tendency of interpretation of Islamic texts during the medieval time became conservative, and male superiority over the female was supported by prominent exegetes, such as Abu Ja'far Muhammad ibn jarir al-Tabari (d. 923), Abdallah ibn Umar al-Baydawi (d. 1286?), and others in those days. Therefore the traditional interpretation about women in the Qur'an and other Islamic traditions present an anti-woman bias and show social and cultural segregation of women.⁶² According to Haifaa A. Jawad, certain pre-Islamic practices for women reappeared during the Abbasid period, because various social attitudes from invasions of Turks and Mongols were embedded into Islamic cultures and customs.⁶³ Therefore the status of Muslim women was neglected and they were deprived of their rights again.⁶⁴ Barbara Stowasser states that the tendency of a "medieval interpretation of woman's origin and nature denies female rationality and female moral responsibility."⁶⁵ Anwar adds that traditionalists see women "as lacking in reason, apt to go wrong or defective in various ways so that

---

59. Doi, *Women*, 47.

60. Ibid.

61. "After his death religious scholars and administrators elaborated on and exaggerated this position of protection by the male of the female, a process reflected in the patriarchal customs and attitudes of the time" (Beck, "The Religious Lives," 33).

62. Afkhami, "Introduction," 6.

63. Jawad, *The Rights*, 24.

64. Ibid., 24–25.

65. Stowasser, *Women*, 28.

they tend to act on the basis of irrational judgment."[66] Hence women are considered as "incomplete" or have "something missing."[67]

Although conservatives and traditionalists still follow the medieval interpretation and continuously bind women under men's authority, Muslim modern reformists and feminists assert new ways of interpretation. They are against the traditional understanding of denigration of women and claim a different approach to the Qur'an.[68] Davary criticizes the androcentric interpretation of "the identity of women throughout the history of Islam."[69] Anwar also asserts that the established hierarchical gender system shapes the constitution of the self-conceptions among Muslims. She understands that this influence shapes women in the formation of their identities "through dependency on fathers, brothers, husbands, masters, and even tribes," and still affects people until the present.[70] Therefore, according to Anwar, Muslim women have not been able to make their own interpretation, but they just have "become the object of male power, authority, and knowledge whose effects are imprinted on their bodies."[71] In the same vein, Barazangi in *Woman's Identity and the Qur'an: A New Reading* declares that Islamic society stripped off the identity of women in the Qur'an. She states that it is "by assuming that a woman's religion-moral rationality (*Din*) is the responsibility of her male household, Muslim communities have not only denied women the Qur'anic meaning of *din* but also violated the very first principle of Islam, the Oneness of the Deity, as the source of value and knowledge."[72]

By and large, most *tafsir* (interpretations or exegesis of the Qur'an) in medieval times point to strong favoritism of Allah for men and a lot of traditional materials including the Hadith accept women's inferior nature "by the consensus (*'ijima'*) of the learned doctors of law and theology until the eighteenth-century pre-modern reformists began to question their authoritative status."[73] Throughout this period, women were described as weak, but at the same time the threat to the male and society by women's sexual

66. Anwar, *Gender*, 26–28.
67. Ibid.
68. Lindholm, *The Islamic Middle East*, 232.
69. Davary, *Women*, 7.
70. Anwar, *Gender*, 16–17.
71. Ibid., 19.
72. Barazangi, *Woman's Identity*, 34.
73. Stowasser, *Women*, 28.

power was paradoxical. These views dominated the Islamic Scripture-based paradigm on gender.[74] In the Hadith, women are depicted as deficient people "in intellect and religion and most of the inhabitants of Hell are women."[75] The Hadith also says if women are disobedient or ungrateful to their husbands, they will go to hell "while 'obedience' (*ta'ah*) becomes for the wife a legal duty to the extent that she may, if she leaves the marital home without sufficient cause, lose her right to maintenance and dower."[76]

In particular interpretations about sensitive Qur'anic verses, such as 2:228; 4:34 and 176, shows shrewd differences according to the positions respectively. Stowasser in "Gender Issues and Contemporary Qur'an Interpretation," supports this conservative tendency of medieval interpretation about 2:228 and 4:34 to quote two exegetes al-Tabari in *Jami' al-baydan 'an ta'wilay al- Qur'an*, (or *fi tafsir al-Qur'an*), and al-Baydawi in *Anwar al-tanzil*. According to her, Tabari and Baydawi assert that men in general excel or have superiority over women and "entail the man's right to discipline his woman in order to ensure female obedience both toward God [Allah] and himself."[77] In particular, Tabari proves the inferiority of women from the story of the first woman in the Qur'an. Tabari understands that Satan tempted both the man and the woman to disobey the commands of Allah but only approached *Hawwa* to make Adam eat the fruit of the tree which is the promise of eternal life. According to him, "God only cursed the woman not the man and God also made the woman foolish and stupid, while He had created her wise and intelligent."[78] Baydawi also says that:

> Men have been confined prophecy, religious leadership, saintship, pilgrimage rites, the giving of evidence in law-courts, the duties of the holy war, worship in the mosque on the day of assembly (Friday), etc. They also have the privilege of electing chiefs; have a larger share of inheritance and discretion in the matter of divorce.[79]

In modern days *tafsir* still inclines to traditional understandings, in particular of gender issues which have been kept in *sharia* law.[80] However

74. Ibid., 23.
75. Clarke, "Women in Islam," 199.
76. Ibid., 205.
77. Stowasser, "Gender," 33.
78. Ibid., 29.
79. Braswell, *Islam*, 149.
80. Stowasser, "Gender," 33.

Identity Crisis

since the nineteenth century, Islamic modern reformists began to "challenge the authenticity of these traditional and conservative interpretations about gender issues."[81] For instance, the Egyptian modernist Muhammad Abduh (d. 1905) proceeds in understanding of Surah 4:34 "in the God-willed natural order of family, the man is charged with leadership (*qiwama*) to protect domestic life and well-being."[82]

> He is to the wife as the head is to the body. Men merit this "superiority" because of qualities they alone possess, some innate and some acquired . . . Women, in turn, should be gratified that their dependency, even though it is a matter of natural constitution, is actually rewarded with "remuneration" or "wages" (dower and maintenance). The husband's *qiwama [leadership]* over his wife consists not of acts of tyranny but of guidance toward righteous behavior, education, domestic efficiency, house-boundness, and fiscal responsibility to his budgetary guidelines. Then the woman can keep her house in safety and order and bear and raise the children."[83]

Al-Faruqi understands 2:228 and 4:34 based on the socioeconomic distribution of communal responsibility, rather than the female gender's inferiority. She explains that in these verses there is a just differentiation between some rights and responsibilities of men and women, not any "biological difference making men and women anything other than partners."[84] Another feminist who claims reinterpretation of the Qur'an is Barazangi. She affirms that traditional interpretations make women lose their self-identity and need male proxy religio-morality (complementarity), even for the next generation of women.[85] Therefore, she claims that the *qiwama* (leadership) in Surah 4:34 should be understood only as "the domestic and financial obligation vis-à-vis the woman's biologically essential role of procreation and 2:228 shows "an added responsibility for the male when he initiates the divorce process."[86] Davary points out that Muslim women are "the symbolic embodiment of traditions" in Islamic society.[87] Accord-

---

81. Stowasser, *Women*, 28.
82. Stowasser, "Gender," 34–35.
83. Ibid., 35.
84. Al-Faruqi, "Women's Self-Identity," 97.
85. Barazangi, *Woman's Identity*, 52.
86. Ibid.
87. Ibid., 142.

ing to her, "woman's traditional role as wife and mother is associated with domesticity, with chastity, and with equating housework with jihad."[88] This was intentionally emphasized in later commentaries which were not the intention of the Prophet Muhammad and his companions' in their times.[89]

Women in Islamic Traditional Narratives

According to Stowasser, the sin of women in the Qur'an indicates "rebellion against God, unbelief, and also disobedience toward the husband if he be righteous, and virtue is faith to the point of martyrdom, obedience to God, purity, and obedience to the husband if he be righteous: it also is modesty, bashfulness, and motherly love."[90] Women in Islamic traditional narratives show these examples.

Women of the Bible in the Qur'an

In the Qur'an there are important female figures of the Bible, who are symbolic representatives of the ideal woman and shape the present and future reality of Muslim women.[91] They teach values and virtues for Muslim women. For example, in the Qur'an 66:10–12, the wives of Noah and Lot are given as examples to the unbelievers and Pharaoh's wife and Mary the mother of Jesus to the believers.[92] In particular, Mary is considered righteous because her isolation from the people is a good model of "gender segregation at the onset of puberty, and the qualities of chastity and obedience associated with her are said to point to the necessity of virginity at the time of marriage" (19:16–17).[93]

The first woman the Qur'an mentions is the wife of the prophet Adam. As aforementioned, the Qur'an doesn't mention her name or how she was created.[94] However, she is mentioned in several parts of the Hadith and

---

88. Ibid.
89. Ibid.
90. Stowasser, *Women*, 21.
91. Ibid.
92. Ibid.
93. McNeal, "Do Muslim Women Really Need Saving?," 80.
94. Ibid., 25.

Islamic traditions.[95] Stories of some of the women around Moses such as the "bashful gait" of Moses' wife (28:25–26) and the women with other early prophets are used to encourage Muslim women to stay home and be secluded.[96]

Wives of the Prophet

The wives of the Prophets are special figures for Muslim women. It is known that Muhammad was polygamous and had nine or twelve wives in his life.[97] In the Qur'an 33:6, 28, 30 the wives of Muhammad are highly regarded as respected ones as "Mothers of the Believers." According to L. Clarke, because of their closeness to the Prophet Muhammad as well as their own personal virtue, Muslims respect them and take them as pragmatic models for Muslim women.[98] They showed examples of how to be obedient to both Allah and their husband (Muhammad).

> O consorts of the Prophet, Ye are not like any Of the other women: If ye do fear (Allah), Be too complaisant Of speech, lest one In whose heart is A disease should be moved With desire: but speak ye A speech (that is) just. And stay quietly in Your houses, and make not A dazzling display, like That of the former times Of ignorance: and establish Regular prayer, and give Regular Charity; and obey Allah and His Messenger. And Allah only wishes To remove all abomination From you, ye Members. Of the Family, and to make You pure and spotless (33:32–33).

Hence, the behavior and teaching of Muhammad for his wives, and relationship with them have been vital resources for marriage and family life of Muslims.[99] As the Prophet Muhammad became a pioneer of new sacred Islamic history, his consorts came to signify a new beginning of the female example in Islam.[100] Their behavior was recorded and recognized as "*Sunna* (standards of what was lawful and forbidden for Muslims, espe-

---

95. "Adam—Creation of Eve."

96. McNeal, "Do Muslim Women Really Need Saving?," 80.

97. While the Hadith is not unanimous on the number of women whom the Prophet married, the majority of traditions put their number at fourteen, of which nine were alive when the Prophet died (Clarke, "Women in Islam," 190).

98. Ibid.

99. Ibid., 191.

100. Stowasser, *Women*, 85.

cially Muslim women) and then codified (*qua* examples) in the works of early Islamic jurisprudence (*fiqh*)."[101] The Hadith talks a great deal about the Mothers of Believers "as exemplars who strive to keep Islamic norms and values including women's personal comportment, dress, performance of ritual and worship."[102]

Khadijah (the first wife of the Prophet Muhammad), A'isha (a daughter of Abu Bakr), Zainab (a daughter of Quzaima), Saffiyah, and Um Salamah are great sources in the Hadith of Muslim women's lives.[103] The faithful marriage of twenty-five years of the Prophet Muhammad with Khadijah is an ideal model of marriage. Khadijah had faith and belief in her husband and shared her wealth with the prophet.[104] Zainab is also a good example who worked for the poor and is considered a mother of the community.[105] Saffiyah is famous for her intellect and how she taught people about family relations, etc.[106] Um Salamah was also a great scholar and gifted with guidance for the first community of Muslims.[107]

In particular, A'isha is the best known as an unparalleled respected figure among his wives. Although being praised for her sincere religious acts and characteristics, she is most famous for being loved by the prophet.[108] She was present with the Prophet when he received revelations from Allah, so she was asked to give advice even when the Prophet was alive.[109] It is acknowledged that thousands of traditions were given to her directly from the Prophet.[110] Wiebke Walther in *Women in Islam From Medieval to Modern Times* states that "she [A'isha] was much in demand: women asked her for advice on questions of clothing and cosmetics in relation to religious law, and even respected men consulted her on questions of religion and the way life was to be led . . . She is also reported to have laid down the fundamental rules of Arab-Islamic ethics."[111]

---

101. Ibid., 106.
102. Ibid., 115.
103. Clarke, "Women in Islam," 191.
104. Schleifer, *Motherhood*, 86–87.
105. Clarke, "Women in Islam," 191.
106. Doi, *Women*, 141.
107. Ibid., 142.
108. Clarke, "Women in Islam," 190–91.
109. Spectorsky, "'A'ishah," 34.
110. Jawad, *The Rights*, 21.
111. Walther, *Women*, 106.

Identity Crisis

After the death of the Prophet Muhammad, she became an even more powerful person in the Muslim community. She lived long after Muhammad's death and provided great guidance to Muslims.[112] Her father, Abu Bakr, became the first caliph from AD 632 to 634 and this helped to cement A'isha's position among the community.[113] Following the murder of Uthman in 656, she once more emerged as "the center of public attention."[114] She even performed an important role in the "Battle of the Camel."[115] She is mentioned in 2,210 narrations in the Hadith.[116] She also had as her pupil 'Abdullah ibn al-'Abbas, who was one of the Qur'an's best commentators.[117] Although conservatives sometimes understood A'isha's public activities negatively,[118] she is a good example for Muslim women because of her courage, wisdom and noble characteristics.

Identity of Women in Christianity

In Christianity, men and women are created in God's image and likeness (Gen 1:27; 5:1; 9:6; Jas 3:9). The image of God is considered at the core of who we are and defines us as human.[119] The image of God has been granted human "capacity for reason, morality, and spirituality."[120] Thus, the divine image makes humans able to have fellowship with God. This true nature of humanity however was lost because of the fall of humans.

In spite of the defilement of human beings, God saves humans through the redemption of Jesus Christ, and makes them new creations by participating by faith in Christ's death and resurrection. Thus humans are capable of finding their true identity and recovering their nature as being

---

112. Doi, *Women*, 140.

113. Spectorsky, "A'ishah," 34.

114. Walther, *Women*, 107.

115. Spectorsky, "A'ishah," 34; cf. The battle of Camel—Along with Talha and Zubayr, A'isha tried to commit vengeance for the death of Uthman against Ail ibn Abi Talib in Basra. Ali won the battle. Talha and Zubayr were killed and A'isha was sent to Medina. Because she was at the chamber on the Camel during the war, the war was called the battle of Camel (s.v. "The Battle of Carmel," in Kim, *Encyclopedia of Islam*, 226).

116. Doi, *Women*, 140.

117. Khan, *Woman*, 27.

118. Barazangi, *Woman's Identity*, 37.

119. Wright, "Implications," 40.

120. Ibid.

partakers of the divine nature (2 Pet 1:4) and coworkers with God (1 Cor 3:9; 2 Cor 6:1).

The Biblical View of Women's Identity

Image of God and Creation

God created humans from the dust of the ground and gave the breath of life: "Then the LORD God formed a man from the dust of the ground and breathed into his nostrils the breath of life, and the man became a living being" (Gen 2:7).[121] God also created all human beings equally as creatures made according to his image: "Then God said, 'Let us make man in our image, in our likeness, and let them rule . . .' So God created man in his own image in the image of God he created him; male and female he created them" (Gen 1:26–27).[122] He made them as male and female—"as sexually differentiated and hence relational creatures."[123]

The meaning of "image" in this context is the "reflection" of God in his creation.[124] Image is *selem* in Hebrew, and "appears seventeen times in the Old Testament, including the five occurrences in the Genesis texts."[125] By and large, *selem* refers to diverse types of physical representations (Num 33:52; 1 Sam 6:5, 11; 2 Kgs 11:18; 2 Chr 23:17; Ezek 7:20; 16:17; 23:14; Amos 5:26).[126] In particular, two verses use *selem* to describe the momentary "nature of human existence, likening it to a shadow (Ps 39:6) or to the residue of a dream that remains after one awakes (Ps 73:20)."[127] Likeness (*demut*) "derives from the verb *damah* ('be like,' 'resemble') or may be an Aramaic loanword."[128] It means "likeness" or "resemblance" and is used synonymously with *selem*.[129]

---

121. In this paper I use the New International Version (1999) of the Bible, with exceptions.

122. Cf. Gen 5:1–3; 9:5–6; Ps 8; 1 Cor 11:7; 2 Cor 3:18; 4:4; Eph 4:24; Col 1:15; Jas 3:9.

123. Grenz, *The Social*, 269.

124. Cortez, *Theological Anthropology*, 16.

125. Grenz, *The Social*, 186.

126. Ibid.

127. Ibid.

128. Ibid., 187.

129. Ibid..

Identity Crisis

God granted both man and woman the authority of representatives of God (Gen 1:28) without discrimination between male and female. Grenz connects the image of God to kingship ideology of Near Eastern myths and cultures, and relates it to the royal image as "God's vice-regent on earth."[130] The image of God grants similarity between humankind and God (Gen 5:1–3; 9:6).[131] It involves "the capacity for relationship with God as his counterpart,"[132] and allows humans to have "dominion or rulership over creation."[133] Thus the biblical theme of creation of human beings as the image of God shows not just cosmological understanding, but how it is possible for there to be a relationship between God and His creatures.[134] God's creation of human beings is depicted as an expression of his love.[135] God created humankind "by forming a covenant bond with the divine image bearer" and gave them autonomy and free responsibility.[136] God communicates to his creation in dialogical form.[137] The human beings are "free in relation to Godself as God's dialogue-partners."[138]

In God's grace, he respects humankind's "freedom and independence and there is an absence of over-determination" in dialogues with human beings.[139] Furthermore, human beings have the ability to choose "what to do, what habits to cultivate, which cultural influences and role models to follow and what we will become in the future."[140] Mark Cortez, a professor of theology at Western Seminary in Oregon, expounds the meaning of the image of God in humanity with four perspectives: the structural image that applies to human's capacity for "rational thought"; the functional image that applies to human's capacity to "do"; the relational image that applies to human's capacity to relate to God, other humans and creation and is also shown "clearly in the male-female differentiation of humanity"; and finally,

---

130. Ibid., 190–91,198.
131. Ibid., 193–94.
132. Ibid., 195.
133. Ibid., 196–97.
134. McFadyen, *The Call*, 18.
135. Harrison, *God*, 33.
136. Grenz, *The Social*, 281.
137. McFadyen, *The Call*, 20.
138. Ibid.
139. Ibid., 19.
140. Harrison, *God*, 186.

the multifaceted image that applies to "all the various aspects of the human person."[141]

Robert Coleman defines that being made in the image of God makes man a "self-conscious person" and a "spiritual being" who has "immortality," "intelligence," "holiness," and "freedom to decide."[142] Man has understanding about himself, where he belongs, and who he is when in a right relationship with God as His creation. "In self-consciousness, like God, he knows how he is."[143]

The image of God for the human being is like mirroring the divine in right relationship with God.[144] Regarding the image of trinitarian ensemble of Father, Son, and Spirit, the divine image in humanity can be referent to "the relation of humans in community or traceable within the human individual (Gen. 1:26)."[145] McFadyen expounds that the Trinity exists as "a unique community in interdependent moments in a process of mutuality," and the Trinity exists for others.[146] So the Three Persons' mutuality for each other is mirrored in the creation narratives of human beings in Genesis. This displays mutuality, not hierarchical domination.[147]

After the fall (Gen 3:1–8), however, the man lost his intimate relationship and hid himself from God. In Genesis 3, Satan tempted the woman, and she was deceived (2 Cor 11:3; 1 Tim 2:14).[148] She took the forbidden fruit, ate of it, and gave it to the man. The woman and the man disobeyed the command of God which did not allow them to eat fruit from the tree of the knowledge of good and evil. This disobedience of God's command caused sin to enter the world. The defilement of human nature caused the depravation of man's fellowship with God.[149] It causes human beings to be "over against God and individuals over against one another."[150] Grenz states that "the person's 'likeness-to-God', however, has remained part of

---

141. Cortez, *Theological Anthropology*, 18–29.
142. Coleman, *The Heart*, 58–61.
143. Ibid.
144. Grenz, *The Social*, 170.
145. Ipgrave, "Affinity," 27.
146. McFadyen, *The Call*, 27.
147. Ibid., 35.
148. Evans, *Woman*, 18.
149. Coleman, *The Heart*, 72.
150. McFayden, *The Call*, 42.

humanity" even after the fall.[151] According to Gen 5:1–3 and 9:6, it is considered that "the image [of God] can be passed on and passed on to an individual."[152] All human beings are, however, born in a distorted relationship with God because of the fall. Although man seeks to base his identity in what is ultimately meaningless, such as himself, people, possessions, etc., the true identity of humans can be found in the relationship with God. The image of God, therefore, stands in need of renewal and restoration (Eph 4:22–24; Col 3:10).[153]

Although human beings failed to obey God's commands, God's love for humans enabled him to have a plan for our redemption. "But because of his great love for us, God, who is rich in mercy, made us alive together with Christ even when we were dead in transgressions—it is by grace you have been saved" (Eph 2:4–5; cf. Col 2:13). Jesus Christ shows a complete divine and human nature. Jesus is "both fully human and fully divine, the true image of God, the redeemer of humanity, and the theological focus of all creation."[154] John 1:1, 14 says "In the beginning was the Word, and the Word was with God, and the Word was God... The Word became flesh and made his dwelling among us." Jesus has the proper relationship with God and others as a human person, and "therefore properly for Himself—both his relations and his identity are undistorted."[155]

The Apostle Paul also links Jesus to the true image of God (2 Cor 4:4; Heb 1:3), "who makes the invisible God visible in creation (Col 1:15)."[156] He even develops the concept of the image of God further to connect "with the concept of the divine glory (*doxa*) and points out that people who recovered the image of God in Christ should live "in such a manner so as to be God's Glory (1 Cor 10:31)."[157] Paul claims that the glory of God is visible in the face of Christ (2 Cor 2:4–6).[158] Christ is the true image of God and with his glory he is the true divine image.[159]

---

151. Grenz, *The Social*, 185.
152. Evans, *Woman*, 13.
153. Cortez, *Theological Anthropology*, 17.
154. Ibid., 5.
155. McFadyne, *The Call*, 46–47.
156. Cortez, *Theological Anthropology*, 17.
157. Grenz, *The Social*, 205.
158. Ibid., 209.
159. Ibid.

From creation to Christ and then on to the new creation the biblical narratives of the image of God is extended.[160] The true identity of human beings can be only found in the relationship with Jesus Christ. McFadyne states that: "In Christian faith, Christ is the meeting point between God and humanity, the person in whom God's Word and obedient human response are conjoined."[161] In Christ, the image of God for human beings is recovered as a new creation. When a sinner is born again, he becomes a new creation and recovers his relationship with God. He is able to find his new identity as originally intended. "As God intended in the beginning, this new self is 'created after the likeness of God in true righteousness and holiness' (Eph 4:24) . . . [and] the new sense of belonging to God is another aspect of salvation."[162] Cortez affirms that "indeed, in the NT, the divine intent for human persons is to conform 'to the image of his son' (Rom 8:29; cf. 1Cor 15:49)."[163] Christ grants "his glory to restore fallen humanity (Eph 4:24; Col 3:10)."[164] In this new creation, humanity has the image of God through its participation in Christ's resurrection by union with Christ as "a present reality."[165] Paul believes "that assimilation to Christ as the image of God results in a renewed person who exhibits a Christlike character and life to the watching world (2 Cor 3:18; Col 1:18; 3:10)."[166] Therefore, believers in Christ are "in the process of becoming the image of God and hence of fulfilling their divinely given, human destiny (2 Cor 2:14; 3:18; 6:10)."[167] All human beings are united as one in Christ Jesus: "There is neither Jew nor Greek, slave nor free, male nor female, for you are all one in Christ Jesus" (Gal 3:28).

Furthermore, by the indwelling of the Holy Spirit, one is able to abide in Christ and the Holy Spirit helps us to find our identity in the being and doing aspects of our lives. Coleman describes three personal dimensions of Christlikeness as the result of the indwelling of the Holy Spirit, and states that "upwardly, we can worship God; internally, Christ's character flows in

---

160. Ibid., 240.
161. McFadyne, *The Call*, 60.
162. Coleman, *The Heart*, 173–74.
163. Cortez, *Theological Anthropology*, 17.
164. Weng, "The Image," 13.
165. Grenz, *The Social*, 240.
166. Weng, "The Image," 13.
167. Grenz, *The Social*, 240.

our life; outwardly, we participate in evangelism and world mission."[168] The Holy Spirit grants "the organizational energy of communication open to others and to self-transformation which, through co-inherence with the Word, the ordering logos, produces open forms of individual and communal life."[169]

Overview of Status of Women in the Old Testament

As aforementioned, in Gen 1:27–28 God created male and female in his image and gave the right to rule nature to both of them equally.[170] Therefore original personhood and identity of women given from God cannot be limited by "culture, tradition, and society."[171] It is, however, considered from some conservative, evangelical Christian traditions that a woman is secondary to a man because Eve is created after Adam, made from a rib of man, taken from the man, named by the man, and created to be a "helper" for man.[172] These accounts of woman's creation, however, should be understood by mutual perspective as equal persons.[173]

Mary J. Evans strongly asserts that the "temporal priority of creation does not mean superiority" and the woman's creation from the rib of man was "the direct creative act of God in building up the rib that gave the woman her being, not the rib itself."[174] Harrison suggests another possibility to understand the concept of being made from the rib. The rib is also translated "side" in Hebrew and Greek, and it predicts that woman is another side of man.[175] Considering that Adam was asleep during Eve's creation, it also means that "it is God's and not Adam's work. Her creation from one of his ribs is a sign of their common nature, of their interdependence."[176] Evans also adds that comparing Gen 4:25 to the naming of woman in Gen

---

168. Coleman, *The Heart*, 173–74.
169. McFadyne, *The Call*, 63.
170. Fof, *Women*, 51.
171. McNeal, "Contextualisation," 145.
172. Evans, *Woman*, 14.
173. McQuilkin, *Understanding*, 209.
174. Evans, *Woman*, 15.
175. Harrison, *God*, 96.
176. McFadyen, *The Call*, 35.

2:23 is different from the naming of animals as an exercise of authority and "something other than an official naming."[177]

Furthermore, the meaning of 'helper' means woman is man's counterpart, his complement, his partner, his companion and his associate, bone of his bone, and flesh of his flesh.[178] Helper is a calling given by God of a woman before the fall. The Hebrew verb-help (*ezer*) is not subordinate, but complementary in meaning. It is used to mean God's help in Ps 121 and Eccl 4:9–10. *Ezer* "carries the idea of mutual support, which in turn forms one of the central characteristic[s] of true human community."[179] The meaning of suitable (*kenegdo*) also translated "alongside" or "corresponding to "identifies an additional aspect of the mutuality that is crucial for human community."[180] Therefore, human sexuality has importance for the image of God in the perspective of mutually created and composited.[181] Man and woman have "the closest physical and spiritual mutuality of 'help and understanding, joy and contentment in each other'" and humans are created to need each other.[182]

After the fall however, the Old Testament society showed a tendency of an androcentric society and in general regarded men as having a higher position than women.[183] In the culture of the Old Testament, women were considered lower than men, but God also called and anointed women as his servants to lead the Israelites in diverse ways, for example Miriam, Huldah, and Deborah.

New Identity—New Creation

As aforementioned, in the Old Testament the image of God is a fundamental principle which shows human identity. In the New Testament Jesus Christ, the Son of God, is the starting place for Christians to find their identity. Mostert states that the identity of Christians is God-given: "their identity in life and death is in the merciful and gracious action of God the

---

177. Evans, *Woman*, 16.
178. Ibid., 16–17.
179. Grenz, *The Social*, 275.
180. Ibid.
181. Ibid., 279.
182. McFadyen, *The Call*, 33.
183. Evans, *Woman*, 21.

Identity Crisis

Holy Trinity in the crucifixion and resurrection of Jesus Christ."[184] Therefore, to be a Christian means to have "a sense of belonging to God *through* Christ or *in* Christ."[185] In Gal 2:20 Paul declares that Jesus died for us, and Christians live by faith in Christ who died for them: "I have been crucified with Christ and I no longer live, but Christ lives in me. The life I live in the body, I live by faith in the Son of God, who loved me and gave himself for me." Jesus redeemed and owned believers by his death. Therefore, Christians' belonging is only to Christ not to themselves and "their being is in Christ."[186] This new finding of ourselves in Christ overcomes all our weaknesses and sins after the fall.[187] In that sense, baptism is a sign for Christians to have "faith in Jesus Christ and participate in his baptism, his own death and resurrection." It is also "fundamental to Christian identity"[188] and "an identity forming ritual act" to show believers' ultimate belonging to God in Christ.[189]

The basic identity of a Christian is based on being a new creation in Christ. 2 Cor 5:17 also contends that anyone saved by Christ is a new creation in him: "Therefore, if anyone is in Christ, he is a new creation; the old has gone, the new has come." Regardless of gender, if one is in Christ, one's identity is based on Christ. Because one's old identity has gone, now one enters a new stage of life and belongs to a new spiritual world. Abraham van de Beek describes the identity of Christian believers as follows:

> They no longer belong to the world of sin and death, and they no longer belong to their self-created identity—but they are the children of God [Rom 8:1–17], heirs of an eternal kingdom [Jas 2:5], in which they are kings and priests [1 Pet 2:9]. That is not only a promise for the future. It is far more a reference to the reality of the present identity of Christians. They have clothed themselves with Christ [Gal 3:27]. They are in Christ. They are citizens of heaven [1 Pet 2:9].[190]

The terms of old self and new self in John's gospel and the Pauline letters are expressed as a spatial category such as inner and outer, and above

184. Mostert, "Christian," 55.
185. Ibid., 51.
186. Beek, "Christian," 17.
187. Kim, *Women*, 22.
188. Borght, "Introduction," 3.
189. Mostert, "Christian," 54.
190. Beek, "Christian," 19.

and below.[191] According to Joel Green, "To substitute chronological for spatial images is the embodied metamorphosis of the old person into the new, a transformation instigated in 'new birth' (John) or 'new creation' (Paul) by the work of the Holy Spirit."[192] These two concepts "articulate the formation of 'self' as a journey from previous self-identity to a new identity arising from the work of the Spirit."[193] When human beings are reborn in Jesus Christ, they are able to find their new recovered identity originally given by God from creation. In this journey, the Holy Spirit (Eph 3:16) strengthens the Christian inner man.[194]

Christian identity is also communal identity. For the relationship with others, Paul in Gal 3:26–28 affirms that in Christ everyone becomes a child of God by faith in him, so there is no longer discrimination based on gender, race, socioeconomic level for as Paul says: "You are all sons of God through faith in Christ Jesus, for all of you who were baptized into Christ have clothed yourselves with Christ. There is neither Jew nor Greek, slave nor free, male nor female, for you are all one in Christ Jesus." Through Gal 3:28 Paul confirms Gen 1:26–28 that God created man and woman according to his image and made them as representatives of God. In Jesus Christ God rectifies the distorted and broken human fellowship, and overcomes discrimination of race, sex, class, and status.[195] In this equal unity, Christians have a communal identity as the body of Christ: "The body of Christ is the community of people who are identified by their belonging to Him."[196] "Now you are the body of Christ, and each of you is a part of it" (1 Cor 12:27).

Furthermore, "this community is an eschatological community."[197] By faith in Jesus, believers "have been transferred to his eschatological community in which we are called to sanctification of growing in our true identity as citizens of heaven."[198] Our being a part of an eschatological community means that we have a heavenly identity. Christians have inherited a pilgrim

---

191. Green, *Body*, 11.
192. Ibid.
193. Ibid.
194. Theron, "Devastating Grace," 48.
195. Ibid.
196. Beek, "Christian," 18.
197. Ibid., 19.
198. Borght, "Introduction," 2.

Identity Crisis

principle.[199] Because Christians are "conditioned by a particular time and place, by our family, group and society, and by culture,"[200] their faith has a vernacular nature.[201] But all Christians throughout time and place belong to the full body of Christ and have assured hope to participate in the glory of God in heaven (1 Pet 5:1).

Women and Jesus

In the New Testament, we can see that Jesus treats women equally to men. Against the culture of Judaism and the Roman Empire in the New Testament, the attitude of Jesus towards women was contrasted. Jesus encountered women, made women comprehend their own self-worth, and served them. Evans confirms that "Jesus related to women primarily as human beings rather than as sexual beings, that is, he was interested in them as persons, seeing their sex as an integral part but by no means the totality of their personality."[202]

Like Islam, in Judaism the woman was a danger for men, causing sexual sin.[203] From his birth to resurrection, however, women were important and valued in Jesus' life and ministry. Some examples where this is shown are in Matt 5:28; 15:21–28; 26:6–13; Mark 7:24–39; Luke 3:16;10–38–42; John 4:7–12; 11:20–33, Jesus treated women as "subjects in their own rights, as fellow human beings, fellow disciples, and not just the objects of men's desire."[204] Jesus also approached women as also being responsible beings for their life and sins. In theological conversation, synagogues, and the announcement of his resurrection and on other important occasions, women were with Jesus (Mark 16:7; Luke 10:42, John 4:25–6, etc.).[205] Jesus always encounters women with compassion, and overcomes barriers "that would divide these women from their society, religion and from himself."[206] In divorce, Jesus taught mutual responsibility between husband and wife in marriage (Mark 10:12).

199. Walls, *The Missionary*, 8.
200. Ibid., 9.
201. Walls, *The Cross-Cultural Process*, 29.
202. Ibid., 44.
203. Ibid., 45.
204. Ibid., 47.
205. Wood, *Theology*, 185.
206. McNeal, "Do Muslim Women Really Need Saving?," 84.

Although women's status of leadership in churches and in other place is still contested, it is clear that Paul declared in Gal 3:26–28 that in Christ Jesus everyone is equal and one. When Paul deals with relationships, he emphasizes "unity, mutual responsibility, mutual love and mutual submission."[207] He does not say just to be uniform, but to recognize others and be united in Christ. Thus, in Christ, human beings can overcome gender, social status and ethnicity. However in marriage (Rom 7:2; 1 Cor 7; Eph 5:21–33; Col 3:18–19; 1 Thess 3:4; and Titus 2:4–5) and behaviors at the gathering of the church (1 Cor 11:3–16; 14:34–35; 1 Tim 2:8–15), he brings up basic principles and considers the cultural values. Therefore, in the New Testament, the relationship between men and women can be understood as unity with diversity and mutuality.

New Identity of BMB Women through Women's Narratives in the Bible

Hagar

In the process of BMB women finding their new identity, there are good examples of women who have similar backgrounds to them in the Bible. Hagar's story in the Old Testament shows similarity and continuity of lives with women in Jordan, by virtue of the fact that they, like Hagar, often are neglected and live "behind" others. Miriam Adeney also compares a woman in Islam to Hagar. "While cultural expressions of patriarchy in Islam seek to hide women away in the 'private' sphere, the story of Hagar in Genesis reveals she was not hidden from God . . . Being the servant of a woman in a world where social structures meant that she was out of sight, God saw her."[208]

Hagar is not the only female Christian figure who could show "what it means to interact with God" along with the Abraham and Sarah narratives.[209] But she is also a vital figure for Muslims regarding the importance of Ishmael in Islamic religious narratives. Although Hagar's name is not mentioned in the Qur'an, the Hadith, and other Islamic oral traditions state that she is "the mother of all Arabs who are the followers of the Prophet

---

207. Evans, *Woman*, 64.
208. McNeal, "Contextualization," 145.
209. Adeney, *Daughters*, 15.

Identity Crisis

Muhammad, a descendant of the Prophet Ishmael,"[210] and "a symbol of Islamic identity" in Muslims' hearts.[211] She is also known as being full of "faith, love, fortitude, resolution, and strength of character."[212]

The story of Hagar from Islamic narratives is similar in some parts, but her status is quite different from the Biblical narrative. In Islamic narratives, Sarah, her mistress, was very jealous of Hagar, because of Hagar's pregnancy and later her son, Ishmael. Sarah even desired to cut "three limbs" off Hagar.[213] After being expelled by Sarah, Hagar encountered the angel Gabriel in the wilderness. The angel commanded Hagar to return to Abraham and Sarah, and assured her that she will deliver a male baby, Ishmael, through whom God would work much good and who would come to own the lands of his brothers. When Ishmael was thirteen years old, Hagar and he were expelled again from Sarah. On the way to leave Hagar and Ishmael in the wilderness, Abraham faced the Ka'ba and prayed for them (4:37). When Hagar and Ishmael were about to die from thirst, she encountered the angel Gabriel again and she found a small pool (*thamila*) of water lying in a hole in the sand.[214] That is the well of *Zam Zam* which is located inside Haram or the Holy Place in Mecca.[215] She made Ishmael drink the water and she built a dam to contain the water.[216] One day a caravan approached this area and the people in the caravan asked her if they could live near the well of *Zam Zam*. Finally, they settled there and she found a woman to be Ishmael's wife from the Jurhum tribe.[217]

According to Islamic interpretation, the conflicts between Sarah and Hagar and the expulsion of Hagar from Sarah's authority were a divine plan mentioned in1 4:37 "to reestablish God's true sanctuary and its pure rituals in the wilds of a barren valley far away."[218] In the Qur'an 14:35–41 Abraham in prayer was sure that "in order to fulfill the prophetic mission of building the Sacred House of God (which Muslims believe to be the first House of God at Mecca), it was necessary to leave a part of his family [Hagar and Ish-

---

210. Hassan, "Islamic Hagar," 154.
211. Stowasser, *Women*, 44–49.
212. Ibid.
213. Kathir, *Qisas*, cited in Stowasser, *Women*, 47.
214. Dickson, *The Arab*, 294.
215. Ibid.
216. Stowasser, *Women*, 48.
217. Ibid.
218. Ibid., 44.

mael] in the uninhabited, uncultivated land."[219] Thus, in 2:124–29, Ibrahim and Ishmael built a new cornerstone by the will of Allah (the Ka'ba, 2:127, cf. 4:100) and became Muslims (2:128). Furthermore, Hagar's running away from the persecution of Sarah is also connected to the idea of "Hijra" [the Prophet Muhammad and his companions exiled twice from the persecution of Meccan non-Muslims] or "going into exile for the sake of God."[220]

In the Bible, the Hagar and Ishmael story starts in Gen 16. Sarai asked Abram to go in to her Egyptian maid named Hagar to give an heir to Abram. Later Hagar had problems with Sarai. Hagar's pregnancy made her boastful and she looked down on her mistress (v. 4). This caused problems resulting in Hagar fleeing from her mistress' maltreatment.

Hagar encounters the Angel of the Lord in the midst of desolation.

> Now the angel of the LORD found her by a spring of water in the wilderness, by the spring on the way to Shur. He said, "Hagar, Sarai's maid, where have you come from and where are you going?" And she said, "I am fleeing from the presence of my mistress Sarai." Then the angel of the LORD said to her, "Return to your mistress, and submit yourself to her authority." Moreover, the angel of the LORD said to her, "I will greatly multiply your descendants so that they will be too many to count." The angel of the LORD said to her further, "Behold, you are with child, And you will bear a son; And you shall call his name Ishmael, Because the LORD has given heed to your affliction. He will be a wild donkey of a man, His hand will be against everyone, And everyone's hand will be against him; And he will live to the east of all his brothers" (Gen 16:7–12, NKJV).

Some believe that when "the Angel of the Lord" or "the Angel of God" is mentioned in the Old Testament, the article "the" specifically denotes "a pre-incarnate appearance of the Eternal Son of God, our Lord and Savior Jesus Christ."[221] The Hebrew *matza'* (find, or its derivatives) has a particular meaning as well: "When the direct object of 'find' is a person with God as the subject, it implies going well in English and includes elements of encounter and of divine election" (cf. Deut 32:10; Ps 89:21).[222] After the Angel of the Lord found Hagar, he called her by her name (v. 8). Yahweh wants to communicate with her. "Hagar is one of only a few characters who

---

219. Hassan, "Islamic Hagar," 153.
220. Ibid., 155.
221. Hamada, *Understanding*, 62.
222. Maalouf, *Arabs*, 62.

have a dialogue with Yahweh" in the Old Testament.²²³ Before departing, the Angel told Hagar to go back to Sarai and submit to her again. It was necessary "since Ishmael was to be born in the house of Abraham, reared in the godly patriarchal family, and circumcised in Abraham's home (Gen 17:22–27) before being ultimately led to his divinely appointed land."²²⁴ Finally, the Angel of the Lord gave Hagar a message of hope: her seed would multiply exceedingly, a blessing that only the Lord could provide (v. 10). This promise to Hagar is parallel to the same promises given to the patriarchs, which has huge implications (cf. Gen. 17:2; 22:17; 26:24).²²⁵

Sometimes Ishmael and Hagar's narrative is understood by Christian commentators negatively as opposite figures of Isaac and Sarai. Although the covenant promise was to come through Isaac's line, the first Abrahamic blessing would be for "all the kinship groups of the earth."²²⁶ Since God promised that Abram would be the father of many nations (Gen 17:5–6), Ishmael and his descendents appear as a part of God's plan for human history.²²⁷ Louis Bahjat Hamada, a Lebanese theologian, believes that "Hagar and her son, Ishmael, were chosen to fulfill their historical roles and also to receive willingly God's gracious gift of everlasting life."²²⁸ Through care for the predicament of Hagar and Ishmael in the narratives, God shows compassion "for the human race in general and the disinherited and despised in particular."²²⁹ Wright demonstrates that Ishmael is a clear example of God's blessing with universal implications: "It is noteworthy that both God and Abraham speak warmly of Ishmael."²³⁰ God also ordained his lifestyle that he will live as a wild donkey of man and in hostile relationships with others. Hamada states that "the great majority of Western biblical scholars and others have been unknowingly mortifying and vilifying the Arabic world by appealing to Gen 16:12."²³¹ Tony Maloouf clarifies how this description

223. McKeown, *Genesis*, 96.
224. Maaloouf, *Arabs*, 64.
225. Okoye, "Sarah," 170.
226. Wright, *The Mission*, 216.
227. It is believed that southern Arabians descended from Joktan (Gen. 10:25–30), northern Arabians from Ishmael (Gen 25:12–18), central Arabians from Abraham's wife, Keturah (Gen 25:1–6). Some also include descendents of Cush, son of Ham (Maaloouf, *Arabs*, 21).
228. Hamada, *Understanding*, 60.
229. Ibid., 61.
230. Ibid.
231. Ibid., 88.

should be interpreted considering Middle Eastern cultural practices and perspective in those days.

> Ishmael is called *peré adām* (a wild donkey of a man or a wild colt of a man) . . . While in the present-day culture referring to someone as a wild donkey of a man seems to be a negative attribute, animal imagery was used extensively in the nomadic culture of patriarchal times. In fact, the wild donkey was a valued and admired animal in the ancient Near East . . . This is a fine image of the free intractable Bedouin character which is to be manifested in Ishmael's descendants.[232]

Historically the Hebrew word wild (*pere*) denoted one who was free-spirited and unrestrained, and it was not used to mean savage or untamed as it is commonly understood in modern times.[233] The prophecy that Hagar's son will be like a "wild ass" or "donkey man" does not imply a strictly negative meaning in the Middle Eastern culture. Nomads and nomadic life are different from the village or city life. Considering the dangerous nomadic way of life, "the image chosen for Ishmael is perfect."[234] In Gen 49:14, when Jacob blessed his sons, he called Issachar a rawboned donkey.[235] Therefore, it can be interpreted as "Ishmael would never be a slave like his mother but a freeman who roams the desert and who is answerable to no one."[236] Furthermore, in the last part of prophesy (v. 12) the term "*al-pené*" (dwell, live) is translated variously in English translations.[237] *Al-pené* literally means "before the face of" or "in front of."[238] When it is translated "at odds with," or "in hostility with," it has to depend heavily on contextual considerations.[239] He will not be under the hand of any one. Although many would like to subdue him ("everyone's hand upon him"), he will always be able to maintain his freedom ("his hand upon everyone").[240] This emphasizes "the

232. Maaloouf, *Arabs*, 70–71.

233. Hamada, *Understanding*, 88–89.

234. Noort, "Created in the Image," 35.

235. Issachar is a rawboned donkey lying down among the sheep pens (Gen 49:14, NIV).

236. McKeown, *Genesis*, 97.

237. KJV translates into "he shall dwell in the presence of all his brethren." NASB and NKJV translate into "he will live to the east of all his brothers." However the NIV translates into "he will live in hostility toward all his brothers."

238. Maaloouf, *Arabs*, 73.

239. Ibid.

240. Ibid., 75.

Identity Crisis

unshackled and unrestrained desert life of Ishmael and his descendents."[241] It has also proved true in Middle Eastern history regarding Bedouins' raids to "obtain food and valuables using hostile methods during the times in which social systems break down and the interrelationship between areas is disrupted."[242] Therefore in these promising words God gives Hagar hope in the midst of her miserable circumstances.

Hagar is the first and only person in the Bible to give God a name.[243] She receives "both an epiphany of God and a promise of progeny although the promise lacks the covenant context and the possession of the land of Canaan in the Old Testament."[244] When she encountered Yahweh, Hagar declared the name of the Lord who spoke to her, and named the well where she experienced him. She found herself who is seen by God and sees him. She found her primary and ultimate belonging. "'You-Are-the-God-Who-Sees'; for she said, 'Have I also here seen Him who sees me?' Therefore the well was called Beer Lahai Roi; observe, it is between Kadesh and Bered...'" (Gen 16:13–14, NKJV). In Gen 21:17 when God heard Ishmael's crying and comforted Hagar by confirming his promise again, Hagar's title and her identity was also changed. She was longer a maidservant of Sarai. Hagar was free from her past, thus the command to return was made obsolete. Instead of "submit yourself under her [Sarai's] hand" (Gen 16:9), now she was told to "Hold him with your hand" (v. 18).[245] She can be portrayed as a "matriarchal figure" from that moment.[246] In encountering God, we concurrently encounter ourselves.[247] Through Hagar's story, BMB women, daughters of Hagar, know how God loves Arab people and meets their needs. They also find their new identity as children of God through encountering him. Thus they are no longer under the hand of law, but are free as new creations in Jesus Christ.

---

241. Hamada, *Understanding*, 89.
242. Noort, "Created in the Image," 35–36.
243. James, *Lost Women*, 94.
244. McKeown, *Genesis*, 96.
245. Noort, "Created in the Image," 41.
246. Nikaido, "Hagar," 220.
247. Theron, "Devastating Grace," 34.

Rahab

The narrative of Rahab also shows how to choose for God even when one's culture does not approve. In Josh 2, Rahab in Jericho decided to choose Yahweh and to hide the Israelite spies. When she faced soldiers looking for the Israelite spies in her house, she had to make a decision. Although there is no record that the two Israelite spies asked her to hide them before the men from the king of Jericho came to her, Rahab had taken the two men and hidden them (v. 4). Alice Mathews explains that this decision "came out of who she was and what she believed about herself, about her world, and about God. What she believed gave her the courage to go against her people and her government when she was faced with a split-second decision."[248] Rahab knew that the Lord had given the land to the Israelites and via many miracles led the Israelites out of Egypt (v. 8–10). She realized and confessed that "the Lord your God is God in heaven above and on the earth below" (v. 11). Only when we are convicted of the sovereignty of the Lord can we have the courage "to confront our culture or go against the time of society around us."[249] In the end her decision saved her life and family and all who belonged to her (Josh 6:25). She was a prostitute and of the lowest social status, but her decision made her an ancestress in the genealogy of Jesus (Matt 1:5). Rahab also is one of two women mentioned by name as women of faith in Heb 11:31: "By faith the prostitute Rahab, because she welcomed the spies, was not killed with those who were disobedient."

The Bible calls her decision an act of faith. She had built her identity as a woman of faith. For BMB women, to make a decision on accepting Jesus as their Savior and becoming Christians brings shame upon their Muslim family. Therefore the BMB women's choice is like a betrayal of their own family and people. They only make a decision to believe in Jesus and to hold onto their new faith when they truly know who God is and who they are.

The Samaritan Woman

The New Testament account of the Samaritan woman displays clearly that encountering Jesus brought changes to her understanding of herself. These changes made her the first evangelist (John 4:1–30). Her narrative shows

---

248. Mathews, *A Woman*, 39.
249. Ibid., 41.

Identity Crisis

that if we are to face ourselves as we are,[250] we find our real identity and new life through encountering Jesus. There were many barriers trying to stop her from believing in Jesus.

She was a Samaritan woman and Jesus was a Jew (v. 9). In that time most Jews and Samaritans avoided all contact with one another. They were "bitter enemies, much like Jews and Arabs today."[251] It is difficult to imagine that a Samaritan woman would be able to meet and have a conversation with Jesus, but it happened. There were not only ethnic, social, and sexual barriers, but religious barriers in this encounter. She was a shameful woman who brought shame on herself as well as her community by her immoral personal behavior (v. 17–18). She followed the religious traditions and place of worship of her ancestors (v. 12, 20) and community and considered Jesus as only a prophet (v. 19). She focused on external religious worship, which are the same tendency Muslim women having towards religious practices. Jesus, however, made her understand a different kind of worship, an internal worship, and face the object of worship, God.[252] Jesus moved her away from ethnic tradition, religious places, and rituals, and through this she encountered and then saw him as Messiah (v. 21–26). Jesus gave her hope to be a real worshipper in truth and in Spirit. She overcame internal shame and all her limits. She became a new person and understood herself as a new person. Therefore she could go back to her community. Her life and view of herself "had undergone a profound change that saw both her and her community in a new relationship."[253] For BMBs in these days, it is certainly difficult to overcome all the barriers which they have to come and follow Jesus, but they can experience of transformation of understanding themselves through encountering Jesus as Messiah, not just as prophet, and this will challenge their community after all.

---

250. Ibid., 209.
251. Ibid., 210.
252. Ibid., 220.
253. McNeal, "Do Muslim Women Really Need Saving?," 86.

3

Women in Jordan

THIS CHAPTER WILL DESCRIBE the general context of Jordan in order to understand the milieu that Jordanian women live in and how they are influenced by the political and sociocultural perspectives. I will also investigate Jordanian women's identity based on these Jordanian contexts.[1]

The official name of Jordan is the Hashemite Kingdom of Jordan and it is neighbors with Israel and Palestine, Syria, Iraq, Egypt, and Saudi Arabia. Hashemite is the name of the Arab *Quraysh* tribe who are descendants of Abraham's son, Ismail (Ishmael), and also direct descendants of the Prophet Muhammad through his daughter, Fatima al-Zahra, and her husband, Imam Ali bin Abi Talib, the fourth caliph of Islam.[2]

General Context of Jordan

Historical Context

During the fifteenth and sixteenth centuries, the majority of the Muslim world was located in three great empires: the Ottomans, the Safavids, and the Mughals.[3] The Ottoman Empire ruled over all the Arabic-speaking countries, except for parts of Arabia, Sudan, and Morocco. The Ottoman

---

1. In the Bible, Jordan is one of the main regions in history where we see works of God, and is referred to as the land of Moabites, Ammonites, and Edomites.

2. "Ali ibn Abi Talib."

3. Hourani, *A History*, 207. Cf. "The Mughal Empire was an imperial power in the Indian subcontinent from about 1526 to 1757" ("Mughal Empire"). "In the early sixteenth century, Iran was united under the rule of the *Safavid* dynasty (1501–1722), the greatest dynasty to emerge from Iran in the Islamic period" (Yalman, "Art").

Empire was a bureaucratic state, ruling over different regions within a single political and economical structure, but at the same time keeping its Islamic values.[4] It lasted for more than 300 years. The locations of modern day Jordan, Syria, and Palestine belonged to the Ottoman Empire and were called Great Syria.

During the first half of the nineteenth century, European powers reached these areas, and after the First World War (1914–1918), the Ottoman Empire was divided up into various parts. Several areas were handed to France and England as "mandate territories": England colonized Palestine, Jordan, Iraq, and Egypt; France ruled over Syria and Lebanon.[5] Therefore, the invasion of the Western powers brought changes to Great Syria, whose inhabitants were previously able to maintain unity in political and Islamic religious lifestyles under the Ottoman state's umbrella for a long time.

The Modern History of Jordan

After a short period of colonialism by the British in Great Syria and Palestine, Britain carved out a semi-autonomous region of Transjordan in the early 1920s,[6] and Jordan gained independence on May 25, 1946 as the Hashemite Kingdom of Jordan. Jordan established itself as a monarchy once it became independent and Emir Abdalla, from the lineage of the Saudi Arabian royal family, became the first king of Jordan. The background of the royal family, which traces its lineage to the Prophet Muhammad, has helped to legitimize Hashemite rule and to lead the Islam practiced in consolidating the country.[7] "In 1959 the land west of the river which was not part of the state of Israel was annexed to Jordan," however in 1967 Israel took the West Bank and the eastern part of Jerusalem from the victory of "the Arab-Israeli war."[8]

Philip Robins in *A History of Jordan* categorizes four periods in the creation of the Jordanian state: the period from the post-First World War settlement to the post-Second World War settlement, from the end of the 1940s through to the beginning of the 1970s, the early 1970s through to the late 1980s, and then the period of liberalization and founding of democratic

4. Ibid.
5. Ibid.
6. Central Intelligenc Agency, "Jordan."
7. Brand, "Women and the State," 104.
8. Braswell, *Islam*, 171.

reform.⁹ During the first span, Jordan as a modern state attempted to be forged from desolate circumstances by "a small band of British officials on the ground and the dependent administrative elite they introduced from outside."¹⁰ The second phase was the turbulent period especially for the West Bank through the 1950s and 1960s.¹¹ The third phase of development for Jordan's modern state was established from "the secondary benefits of oil wealth recycled in the form of Arab aid and remittances."¹² The fourth phase began with King Hussein's resolution to make peace with Israel in 1993.¹³

Undergoing an upheaval of political circumstances, Jordan has a constitutional monarchy but with absolute power residing in the king. The parliament acts democratically, but its autonomy has been limited.¹⁴ Mansoor Moaddel calls this form of the Jordanian state as "authoritarian pluralism" in which monarchy allows diverse ideologies to be expressed such as "Arab Nationalism, Islamic conservatism, pro-Western modernism, and tribalism."¹⁵ In particular the alliances of various tribes and the Muslim Brotherhood have been critical political agents in the development of the state of Jordan. The Bedouins in the army have been loyal to the king at the beginning of the establishment of the state and served to sustain the monarchy. Later they have "enjoyed a strong political and sociocultural role" in Jordanian society.¹⁶ The Muslim Brotherhood emerged with the economic depression and political issues of the Palestinians.¹⁷

Since the late 1990s, the Jordanian government has developed "Jordan First" as its national slogan. This tries "to weaken traditional [tribal] power" and to encourage personal achievement not as a member of a tribe, in this "new beginning of the political liberalization process."¹⁸ The diverse political situation within the Jordanian state is characterized as "rentierism, patrimonism, authoritarianism, bureaucratic expansion, and military

9. Robins, *A History*, 1.
10. Ibid.
11. Ibid.
12. Ibid.
13. Ibid.
14. Al Oudat and Al Shboul, "Jordan First," 65.
15. Moaddel, "Religion," 559.
16. Al Oudat and Al Shboul, "Jordan First," 70–72.
17. Moaddel, "Religion," 528.
18. Ibid., 77.

and political dependence on forces outside the country."[19] The political development of Jordan, however, still has difficulties of lacking political legitimacy between its traditional institutions based on tribalism and its secularized modern political legitimacy.

Demographics

Today, Jordan's population is approximately 7,588,954 (March, 2014 estimate)[20] and the GDP per capita is around $6,100 (2012 estimate).[21] The urban population is 82.7 percent of the total population (2013 estimate).[22] Ethnic composition consists of mostly Arabs (95.4 percent): East Bank Jordanians (31.3 percent), Palestinians (33.2 percent), Iraqis (13.8 percent), Bedouin (4.0 percent); and non-Arabs (4.6 percent): Circassians (1.6 percent), Chechens, Armenians, Turkmen, and others.[23] In the aspect of religion, Islam is the majority religion. Ninety-two percent of Jordanians are Sunni Muslims (official). Shi'a Muslims, Baha'i, and Druze are an estimated 2 percent of the population.[24]

Most Shi'a Muslims are Iraqi refugees from the Gulf War crisis (1991) and the 2003 invasion of Iraq. The UN High Commissioner of Refugees reported approximately 32,000 Iraqis residing in Jordan.[25] Because of the Syrian civil war in 2012, Syrians registered refugees are around 600,000 (April, 2014).[26] There are no available statistics regarding the number of Sufi Muslims in Jordan. Christians make up 6 percent, with the majority being Greek Orthodox, but with some Greek and Roman Catholics, Syrian Orthodox, Coptic Orthodox, Armenian Orthodox, and Protestant denominations.

19. Ibid., 529.
20. "Jordan Population 2014."
21. Central Intelligence Agency, "Jordan."
22. Ibid.
23. Mandryk, *Operation World*, 495.
24. Ibid.
25. Bureau of Democracy, "Jordan."
26. Beaumont, "Jordan Opens."

Religious Context

Islam

Orthodox Islam

It is believed that in the vast region east of Jerusalem, present-day Jordan, Syria, and Iraq, the majority of people were Christian by the seventh century.[27] Islam came to Jordan during the lifetime of the Prophet Muhammad. He himself "led the expedition to northern Hijaz and southern Jordan between years 629 and 630."[28] The majority of Jordanians are now Sunni Muslims following the *Shafi'i* (or *Hanafi*) or *Madhhab* Schools, which Syria, Lebanon, Iran and Egypt follow and adhere to the same legal traditions.[29] For the *Shafi'i*, there are four sources from which to draw on to make legal decisions: the Qur'an, the Sunnah of the Prophet, which includes the Hadith (or sayings attributed to him as well as his actions), analogy (or *qiyas*), and finally consensus (*ijma'*).[30] In Sunni Islam, *ijma'* is an important factor to rule over everything and to keep one from departing from the traditions; if "someone argues that the Quran doesn't advocate *hijab* [veil] and that the relevant Prophetic reports/traditions (*hadith*) that require wearing of the *hijab* are false, the authority of past consensus continues to be critically important."[31]

Jordanian Muslims believe in six fundamental Islamic beliefs: one and only Allah as the Creator; invisible beings as angels, Satan and *Jinn*; the Scriptures; Messengers and prophets of Allah; Judgment Day; and fate.[32] They practice Allah worship in both broad and specific meanings. In its broad sense, they worship (*'ibadah*) Allah by obedience to all the commandments laid down in the Qur'an, including all institutional and extra-institutional rules of conduct. In a more limited sense, they also worship Allah by observation of the "five pillars": the pronouncement of *shahada* (or declaration of faith), payment of *zakat* (or an alms tax), *siyam*

---

27. Wilken, "Christianity."
28. Shoup, *Culture*, 12.
29. Ibid., 29–30.
30. Ibid., 30.
31. Esposito, *The Future*, 124.
32. "A Brief Illustrated Guide."

Identity Crisis

(or fasting during the month of Ramadan), *salat* (or prayer five times a day) and *hajj* (or a pilgrimage to Mecca once in their lifetime).[33]

Islamic rituals in regular practices of Jordanian Muslims' lives enhance group unity. Erving Goffman mentions that these ritual offerings give an individual "a sign of involvement in and connectedness to another."[34] Paul Hiebert also affirms that "religious rituals provide people security and comfort in times of crisis and opportunity for people to express and demonstrate their oneness and social cohesion."[35] Therefore, Jordanians through Islamic rituals and traditions are deeply connected as the *dar ummah* (the house of Islamic brotherhood).

The religious educational system is designed for the whole life of Muslims. The first stage is at home instructed by parents along with the Qur'anic schools (*al-Kuttan*), which correspond to elementary school, to enable the child to read and write the Qur'an. Then the children attend the *Madrasah*, which corresponds to secondary school, to study the Quran, the Hadith, linguistics and theology.[36] According to Jordanian I. H.,

> From kindergarten, they [Muslims] are taught to memorize Qur'anic verses and songs about the Qur'an. When they go to school, all the textbooks are from the Qur'an. Grammar and vocabulary are from the Qur'an and Muhammad's life story. There are also religious classes to teach Islam throughout every school year. Outside the schools there are activities in mosques and special classes for memorizing the Qur'an (jammaiye-hefed il Qur'an) in summer clubs.[37]

Folk Islam

Bill Musk describes folk Islam as popular religious activities used to deal with the problems of immediate, everyday life of Muslims.[38] Jordanian society includes the great tradition of orthodox Islam as well as the lesser acknowledged traditions of popular Islam. The most popular and

---

33. Ibid., 31.
34. Goffman, *Relations*, 63.
35. Hiebert, *Cultural Anthropology*, 376.
36. Jawad, *The Rights*, 19.
37. I. H., interviewed by the author, Jordan, March 4, 2013.
38. Musk, *The Unseen Face*, 181.

representative form is the fear of "*Jinn*"[39] or simply "*Shaytan* (Satan)", and it is found more among women. In the Jahiliyya period, Arab people believed in over 300 idols, and after the introduction of Islam, even Muhammad could not eradicate the folk beliefs and practices, and these idols' names are recorded in the Qur'an: the goddesses *Allat, Manat,* and *al-Uzza* (53:19–20).[40] People also worshipped stones (Ka'ba in Madina) and nature. The *Jinn*'s power and works are recognized as one of the important components of Arabs' lives and also are mentioned in the Qur'an and Hadith.

Jordanians believe that *Jinn* can change into animals, such as cats, so they do not strike cats on the street during the night. They are also scared to fall down at night, because they might land on *Jinn*, and if someone grinds her/his teeth, *Jinn* could be afflicting that person. If a person's stomach does not feel full after eating, it was probably because *Jinn* ate the food inside him, and *Jinn* can kill or make people crazy and cause natural disasters.[41] People ask for protection from Allah when they go to sleep. They believe that *Jinn* live wherever one relieves one's self even in the desert, so when they go to the restroom, they say, "I take sanctuary" or "I seek refuge in you, Allah, from male and female Satan."[42]

Charms and amulets are used for protection from evil spirits and evil eyes. They are composed of bone, shells, beads, silver and gold. They may be worn around the neck, or arms, stitched on clothing, carried on the car dashboard, or placed in an obvious place in the home. Prominent on the charms are inscriptions from Qur'anic verses, and many people frequently chant the names of Allah. The hand of Fatima is a very popular symbol, and is believed to protect one from the evil eye, which is written about in the Qur'an.[43]

Dreams and reading coffee grounds are easy ways to predict what will happen to their lives, in particular for women. When they have an unusual dream, they go to the local interpreter to ask its meaning.[44] Reading

---

39. *Jinn* are beings created with free will from smokeless fires (Surah 7:12, 15:26–27, 55:15), living on earth in a world parallel to that of man, and are invisible to human eyes in their normal state (Philips, *The Jinn*, 1).

40. *Manat* was the goddess of fate, *al-Uzza*, the Arabian Venus, was the chief deity of the *Quraysh* tribe, and *Allat* was a mother-goddess figure akin to the Babylonian Ishtar (Brown, *A New Introduction*, 25).

41. Lee, "*Jinn*," 15.

42. Lee, *The Gospel*, 243.

43. Azban, *Diwan Baladna*, 61.

44. Dickson, *The Arab*, 329.

Identity Crisis

the cup is a kind of "divination or fortune-telling method that interprets patterns in tea leaves, coffee grounds or wine sediments."[45] Most women "enjoy getting together to read their fortunes in coffee cups," and search for their future.[46]

Christianity[47]

Orthodox

As aforementioned, the ancient churches have existed in this Levant area for almost two thousand years. In these areas, "there are Eastern (Byzantine or Greek) and Oriental (non-Chalcedonian-Armenian apostolic, Coptic Orthodox, and Syrian Orthodox) Orthodox churches, Catholics of Latin and Oriental rites, the Assyrian (Nestorian) Church of the East, Anglicans, various Protestant denominations, and a large number of sectarian groups."[48] Nowadays, the Greek Orthodox Church is the largest Christian group. Parish priests and laity are, for the most part, Palestinian Arabs, whereas the patriarch, bishops, and monks are Greeks. The patriarchs of the churches sponsor schools, orphanage, and homes for the elderly.

Protestant

At the beginning of the nineteenth century, Protestant missionaries from various churches entered the Middle East to carry the teaching of the Reformation from America and Scotland, as well as from the Anglican Church in Britain and the Lutheran Church in Germany.[49] American and British missionaries were particularly influential in starting the Protestant mission in Great Syria. It consisted of the Evangelical and Episcopal groups who were under the Church of England in Palestine and Jordan, and of the Reformed Presbyterian Communities in Syria and Lebanon, which belonged to the American Presbyterian mission.[50]

---

45. Ibid., 77.
46. Ibid.
47. There is no distinction for most Muslims between Orthodox and Protestant Christians. For Muslims, they are all Christians.
48. Horner, *A Guide*, 6.
49. Badr et al., *Christianity*, 713.
50. Ibid., 730.

The Christian and Missionary Alliance (C&MA) Church was built in the 1930s in Kerak, and Protestants then had a stronger presence in this area. Furthermore many of the ancient Christian tribes in Salt, Ajloun, and Mafraq became Protestants. These tribes continued to maintain their Christian tribal identity and solidarity, which still exists to this day. This phenomenon is commonly called the "North Palestine Revival."[51] Besides the Anglican, and C&MA Church, there are Baptists, Free Evangelicals, Nazarenes, and other missions with small commitments in Jordan, including the Assembly of God (seven churches) and the Lutheran Church (three).[52] Theological education has taken place through the Jordan Evangelical Theological Seminary, and the PTEE program.[53]

Relationships among Jordanian Religious Groups

CHRISTIANS AND MUSLIMS

Operation World reports that Christians in Jordan represent 2.25 percent of the population (evangelicals 0.3 percent), but the percentage is declining annually at a rate of 0.4 percent (2010).[54] In general, relationships between Muslims and Christians in Jordan are good, and the Jordanian government helps sustain "Jordan's image as an open and tolerant place."[55]

For a long time, Muslims and Christians have coexisted and Christians know how to live with Muslims. But in making concessions to the majority community, Christians experience problems of duality in the religious and social spheres of life. Fr. Joseph EL-Zahlaoui, an orthodox priest, states that "Too many Christians, accustomed to their situation as a minority, conceive of their religious life as being only with the church."[56]

---

51. Kong, *Revival*, 248.

52. Ibid.

53. It is a program for Theological Education by Extension which began in Jordanian in 1981.

54. Ibid.

55. Allen, "Even in Jordan." "For example, eight percent of the seats in Jordan's parliament are reserved for Christians, even though they represent only about three percent of the population" (ibid.).

56. EL-Zahlaoui, "Witnessing," 102.

Identity Crisis

THE ANCIENT AND THE PROTESTANT CHURCHES

Under the Islamic governments, the ancient churches were treated as a "millet" or sect, of religious communities in the Ottoman State. Michael C. Hudson expounds that "under the system local communities of a particular sect were autonomous in the conduct of their spiritual affairs and civil affairs relating closely to religion and community, such as church administration, marriage, inheritance, property, and education."[57] It was only at the end of the eighteenth century that the centralization of churches around the patriarchs was reinforced. Before that period, the local communities lived independently, only nominally recognizing any head of the church.[58]

As a second-class citizen, the ancient churches had a certain level of stability in their lives by upholding their duties under the Islamic State. However, the progressive disintegration of the Empire fundamentally changed Ottoman Christians' circumstances and the intervention of European states in the affairs of the Ottoman Empire increased after the 1840 treaty between Britain, Prussia, Australia, and Russia.[59] As a consequence of the European powers and Protestant missions entering this region, many of the ancient churches started to lose their church members to Protestant churches. In addition, the Muslim authorities, who responded to the pressures of British and American consuls, ignored the complaints of Eastern Christian church leaders who objected to missionaries' stealing their church members.[60] Therefore, both the ancient and Protestant churches share the same milieu as minority religious sects, but historically, the ancient churches' members have harbored bitterness toward the Protestant churches.

Image of Christians in Jordanian Circumstances

Christians in the Qur'an

In the Qur'an, Christians and Jews are referred to as the "People of the Book" or "followers of the Book," because "they believe in the Torah and the

---

57. Hudson, *Arab Politics*, 58.
58. Badr et al., *Christianity*, 759.
59. Ibid., 728.
60. Sharkey, "Empire," 45.

Evangel, the Books revealed to Musa and 'Isa respectively."[61] In the Qur'an, Christians are considered in differing ways: very positively or argumentatively or highly hostile. Generally speaking, though, Christians in the Qur'an are not perceived as favorable. It has been noticed that even some positive statements of Christians are often related to when Christians do good deeds for Muslims or believe in Muslims' beliefs, i.e., the revelation of Allah and righteous deeds. Many times Christians in the Qur'an are viewed as wicked, deceiving the truth, and supposedly going to hell unless they accept Islamic truth.

Positive or Neutral Image

- The Qur'an 5:82 praises the Christians and mentions they are closest to the Muslims in affection. According to the Pooya/Ali Commentary, these early Christians in the Qur'an were particularly indicated as the followers of *'Isa* (Jesus) and they were not Trinitarians.

   > It is impossible to exaggerate the formidable quality of the Jew as an enemy. The Jews and idolaters were most excessive in hatred of the believers, but those who said: "We are the followers of Isa," were closer to the Muslims because the priests and monks among the early Christians were not Trinitarians.[62]

- Sincere Christians are also said to not be worthy of hell (2:62; 5:69), because they believe in God (Allah) and the Last Judgment Day. Youngil Choi, a Korean Islamist scholar, comments that these people, however, need a true faith which follows the revelation of Allah to the Prophet Muhammad in order to go to paradise (heaven).[63] The Pooya/Ali Commentary also emphasizes that

   > This verse (2:62) refers to those Sabeans, Jews and Christians who, as sincere faithful, followed the original teachings of their respective prophets, without ever corrupting the true message, and believing in the prophecy of the advent of Muhammad made known by Musa, Isa and other prophets.[64]

61. Chapman, *Cross*, 104.
62. The Pooya/Ali Commentary
63. Choi, *The Holy Quran*, footnotes 110–12.
64. The Pooya/Ali Commentary.

Identity Crisis

- Some Christians also do good works and have faith (3:110,113–15).
- Some are trustworthy with money (3:75).
- Some verses suggest that the followers of the Book keep doing righteousness and holding on to the Law (5:65–66; 61:14).
- Allah gives mercy and compassion to the followers of Jesus (57:27).

Negative Image[65]

Transgressors and Wicked

- When Christians reject the Qur'an, it is said to be due to unreasonable wickedness and deceit (3:21,110; 5:49, 59, 66; 57:27; 98:6; 62:5).
- Christians are charged with knowingly concealing the fact of the Qur'an's truth. Questioning the authenticity of the Qur'an proves one's wickedness (2:146; 3:71; 5:15).
- Christians are also accused of using deception to proselytize Muslims even to the point of misrepresenting their own scriptures and using seductive tactics that misrepresent Islam (2:120; 3:78; 3:99,100; 4:44; 5:49).
- Some Christians will steal if entrusted with money (3:75), and Christians compete with one another to make illicit profits (5:62).
- Christians have a great hatred for Muslims in their hearts which they deceitfully hide (3:118, 119) and rejoice when disaster befalls Muslims. They also act toward Muslims with guile (3:120).
- Christian priests don't forbid their people's sins and instead commit them themselves (5:63), and Christian monks devour wealth and hinder people's way to the truth (9:34).
- Christians display pride, enmity and hatred in their factionalism among themselves (5:14; 30:32).

65. "Muslims Befriending."

Deceiver

- To these are added accusations that Christians teach perverse doctrines: Christ's Sonship (9:30–31; 3:79, 80; 4:48, 171; 5:17), crucifixion. (4:157–58), and any reference to the Trinity (2:116; 5:73), which Muhammad misunderstood as a "trinity" of the father, Jesus Christ, the son, and Mary, his mother is included. Christian's doctrines such as the above present are the greatest sin possible, the unforgivable offense of "*shirk*."
- Muslims believe that Christians disobey their own Book, stress falsehoods in their religion, and exaggerate in their teaching (5:66, 77; 4:171). Monasticism and saint worship are condemned (57:27; 9:31).
- Before Muhammad came, Christians were lost in error. Christians are those who go astray (1:5). Islam and the Qur'an are the only remedies (98:1–6). If they don't come to the truth, they will be in Hell.

Warnings[66]

- Don't make friends with Christians: in view of accusations about Christians' wickedness and deceptions, the Qur'an warns Muslims about friendship with Christians. As a general rule Muslims are not to take Christians for friends, especially over Muslims (3:118; 4:144; 5:51, 57).
- The only exception given is if one needs to have Christians as one's friends to guard one's own security (3:28). This last part means that the Muslim is allowed to feign friendship if it is of benefit. Renowned scholar Ibn Kathir states that "believers are allowed to show friendship outwardly, but never inwardly."[67]
- Allah's curse and warnings are on Christians:"Christians should not make exaggerated claims for Jesus" (5:66; 4:171; 9:29, 30–31; 5:72–73).[68]
- Convince Christians to accept Islam (29:46; cf. 22:20; 16:125).[69]

66. Huda, "What does the Quran say?"
67. "Christians in the Quran."
68. Chapman, *Cross*, 262.
69. Ibid.

Identity Crisis

Christians in Jordanian History and Culture

Jordanians have a complicated mixture of feelings towards Christianity beyond thinking of Christianity as a foreign religion. Historically, the Crusades have left serious scars in Christian-Muslim relations. Politically in modern history, Arab people regarded the Protestant churches as a tool of imperialism. While the Ottoman Turks ruled Levant areas, "Arab nationalists were found [in] both Moslems and Christians."[70] When Western powers invaded these areas however, according to Antonie Wessels, many Muslim nationalists were assured that "the missionaries were using local Christians with whom they worked as gears for the foreign powers in a divide-and-conquer politics that was intended to weaken national movements."[71]

Moreover, because church members were converted by Western Protestant mission enterprises, Orthodox Christians along with Muslims resisted the activities of the Protestant missions in the Middle East; "both Muslims and Orthodox were often anti-colonial, anti-Western, and anti-Missionary [that is, against the Western missions] by disposition."[72] In his article, Heather J. Sharkey also claims the following:

> Those days, missionaries were helped by "Western intervention" (through colonial authorities or consuls) whenever they felt threatened on the ground in pursuing their work. At the same time, as foreigners, they enjoyed a privileged status under the Capitulations, a system of legal prerequisites and exemptions that reflected the strong political and economic position of the Western powers in the region.[73]

In particular, Lisa Taraki points out that this "historical antagonism between Islam and Christendom created an area of cultural resistance around women and the family, which came to represent the inviolable repository of Muslim identity."[74] According to her, civilizing mission activities by colonial administrators and Christian missionaries tried to liberate and reform the "sexual mores and family traditions of Muslim."[75] Therefore, Muslims consider feminism as an influence of cultural imperial-

70. Wessels, *Arab*, 39.
71. Ibid.
72. Ibid.,183.
73. Ibid., 46.
74. Taraki, "Islam," 645.
75. Ibid.

ism. Especially fundamentalist Islamists have emphasized the modesty of women even stronger in contemporary days. They believed that to "change the position of women [was] viewed as tainted with cultural in authenticity if not outright betrayal."[76]

There exist still political and cultural antipathies toward Christianity in today's Jordan.[77] Zionism is another important issue which causes Muslims to acknowledge Christianity as a foreign and hostile religion. Palestinians make up half the population of Jordan. For them, Christianity is connected to Western countries' desire to protect Israel. Culturally, Christianity as a Western religion represents individualistic and free lifestyles for Jordanian Muslims. Some Muslims regard the church as the place where men and women freely meet and do immoral things. Harvie M. Conn also states that Muslims identify Christianity "not simply with theological *kufur* (blasphemy) but with colonialism and Western culture."[78]

Muslim Women in the Sociocultural Context of Jordan

Muslim women in Jordanian society face multifaceted situations. The society of Jordan has been built on complicated interwoven aspects between strong religious conservatism and secularistic liberal modernism. For a long time, before the formation of the Arab countries, the Arabs throughout the Peninsula were divided into numerous local tribes or clans. With the tribes, unity was kept by sharing the same bloodline and traditional sentiments and not by political bindings.[79] The Arabs consisted of homogeneous kinship groups. The kinship of tribal structure in Jordan represents a patrilineal descent, patrilocal residence, patriarchal authority, and patrilineal kin group endogamy.[80] The lineage structure is important as a social unit among Jordanians. Based on the strong bond of kinship, Jordanians have a sense of mutual dependence among members of their tribe and collective responsibilities inwardly, and have *ummah* to the religious community outwardly. To intensify solidarity of family, tribe and society, honor and other traditional values are emphasized as the primary ideals to maintain the collectivism among Jordanians.

76. Ibid., 645–46.
77. Weiss, "A Jordanian Complains."
78. Conn, "The Muslim Convert," 64.
79. Zwemer, *Arabia*, 159.
80. Al-Oudat, *Tribal Identity*, 14.

Identity Crisis

Manifestations of Islam in Jordanian Society

Religious Revivalism in Modernity

Modernity has brought about a chain reaction of events in many sociopolitical settings worldwide. In Western nations, it led to the secularization of society. The response among Muslim societies, however, has been different and unexpected. Modernity in Islamic societies has showed up as a widespread Islamic religious revivalism.[81] The quest for identity for the contemporary Muslims is pursued in terms of Islam and in the reaffirmation of the Islamic values.[82] The Jordanian society like other Arab countries went through an Islamic revival in the 1980s. The revival movement featured the rising of more religious social structures, as well as a greater adherence to Islamic customs and beliefs. At the same time, modernity brought tension to women between the pressure from traditionalism and the opportunity of self-realization.

One of the main reasons for the Islamic revivalism is due to the fact that finding an authentic identity in postcolonial societies has meant that the majority have returned to their Islamic Arab culture and heritage. Many Arabs feel that even though political colonialism finished, "economic and cultural colonialism" has been replaced, so adherence "to indigenous culture and tradition" is the right way to overcome Western influences.[83] In the same vein, Muslims consider redefining women's roles in society as an influence from Western cultural domination.[84]

> The increased interest in associating Islam more fully into daily life was expressed in a variety of ways. Women wearing traditional Islamic dress and head scarves were seen in the streets of cities as well as rural areas. Attendance at Friday prayer meetings rose, as did the number of people observing fasting during Ramadan.[85]

The Islamic revival also resulted from the "economic recession and the failure of nationalistic politics to solve regional problems."[86] In the late 1970s and the beginning 1980s, Jordan suffered a severe economic depres-

---

81. Keskin, "The Sociology," 7.
82. Minces, *The House*, 24.
83. Hijab, "Islam," 48.
84. Ibid.
85. Library of Congress Country, "A Country Study."
86. Hijab, "Islam," 48.

sion because of their oil-producing neighbor countries' economic collapse and Iran.[87] Jordanian foreign debt reached one of the highest per capita debts in the world in the middle of the 1980s.[88] During those days, many Jordanians had to go to work in other countries, such as Kuwait, the United Arab Emirates, and so on. They sent remittances back to Jordan to support their families.

This socioeconomical situation provoked conservative people to focus on recovering their religious value to overcome all the difficult situations faced. The Islamist slogan was "Islam Is the Solution."[89] In this process, they also were concerned about the traditions of women's modesty and other virtues, and laid emphasis on appropriate women's dress and conduct.[90]

On top of that, Jordanian political situations between the beginning of the Jordan state and the tribes in the process of establishing Jordan as a state brought more pressure on women. According to Brand, this alliance has operated unfavorably for women's status.

> Beginning with 'Abdallah and continuing with Hussein, state subsidies as well as state employment (often in the army) were used as a means of cooptation or reinforcing loyalty, and they were generally directed at Jordan's tribes. In addition to building support for the state, such practices by extension strengthened the role of the *shaykh*, tribal structure, and tribal laws. As we shall see, the continuation of the state's support for the tribes and its tolerance of traditional law (*'urf*) as opposed to civil law has had a negative effect upon women's inclusion as full citizens in the kingdom.[91]

Jordanian women did not gain suffrage in general parliamentary elections until 1974, and have exercised that right from 1989.[92] The emphasis on the military and Bedouin culture as the traditional heritage of Jordan has reinforced traditional gender roles, which as a new state was needed to develop cultural continuity.

---

87. Moaddel, "Religion," 528.

88. Gallagher, "Women's Human Rights," 212.

89. The Islamist deputies from the Society of the Muslim Brethren (*Jama'at al-Ikhwan al-Muslimin*), Islamic Liberation party, and Dar-al-Qur'an were principal agencies to engage society as an Islamist movement in the late 80s and 90s (Goodwin, *Price*, 282).

90. Taraki, " Islam," 648.

91. Brand, "Women and the State," 102.

92. Ibid., 119.

Identity Crisis

Sharia Law

Islamic doctrine is tightly intertwined with Muslims' sense of identity and with community life.[93] According to Kraft, *tawhid* or *shahada*, the confession of oneness of Allah, has been used in diverse forms in Muslim society to affirm religious adherence and to bind society members to each other.[94] On the other hand, *sharia* law shapes and guides the community both in religious and ethical perspectives.[95] It is considered to guide the appropriate lifestyles of members of the society by pointing out to them how to manifest good conduct in their lives in Jordanian society.[96] Tariq Ramadan compares *shahada* and *sharia* in "The Way (Al-*Sharia*) of Islam."

> Just as the *shahada* is the expression, in the here and now of individual faithfulness to the original covenant by means of a testimony that is a "return to oneself" (a return to the *fitra*, to the original breath breathed into us by God), so the *Sharia* is the expression of individual and collective faithfulness, in time, for those who are trying in awareness to draw near to the ideal of the source that is God. In other words, the *shahada* translates the ideal of "being Muslims," and the *Sharia* shows us "how to be and remain Muslim."[97]

The Jordanian government has a secular constitution and guarantees human rights. Its constitution stipulates that Jordan's state religion is Islam but allows the freedom of religions "unless they violate public order or morality," and gives equality "in the rights and duties of citizens on grounds of religion."[98] The legal system, however, is based on a combination of Islamic *sharia* and French codes, so Islamic values and *sharia* law are used to sustain and control Jordanian society.[99]

In regards to apostasy, nearly a century ago, Zwemer pointed out that "one of the reasons of small visible results in Muslim Evangelism in spite of great sacrificial endeavor is due to the Muslim law of apostasy."[100] Although

---

93. Kraft, *Searching for Heaven*, 35.
94. Ibid., 36–42.
95. Mahameed, *The Justice*, 13.
96. Ibid., 7.
97. Ramadan, "The Way," 66.
98. Ibid.
99. Ibid.
100. Zwemer, *The Law of Apostasy*, 17.

many years have passed since Zwemer's statement, the situation today is not different in most Islamic countries regarding the apostasy law for converts. Following *Hanafi* and *Shafi'i* schools of legal interpretation, the *sharia* law of apostasy in Jordan does not allow anyone to convert away from Islam to any other faith, and regards converts as apostates who betray family and community.[101] There are several verses in the Qur'an related to apostasy (2:214, 217; 3:86–90; 4:88–91, 137; 5:59; 9:66, 74; 16:106–9; 47:25–27). The Qur'an 47:4 and other Surahs (4:4–6, 34, 90; 16:106–7) state that Muslims are to treat apostates like other *kufa*r, whose treatment varies from kindness to killing depending on the circumstances and on the degree of hostility they show towards Islam and Muslims.[102] Although both *Hanafi* and *Shafi'i* schools state that apostates should be given the death penalty, it has never been officially applied in Jordan and converts often leave the country.[103] About a woman apostate, "she is not put to death, but is imprisoned, until she returns to the faith."[104] By leaving Islam, the convert loses one's identity in relation to his/her local community and the house of Islam (*dar al-islam*) and is seen as a part of *dar al-harb* (house of the infidels). "Judges have annulled the convert's marriage, transferred child custody, conveyed property rights to Muslim family members, deprived them of civil rights, and declared converts wards of the state and without any religious identity."[105] Also if couples are apostates, their children and grandchildren belong to the state.

> If a husband and wife both apostasize, and desert to a foreign country, and the woman becomes pregnant there, and brings forth a child, and to this child another child afterwards is born, and Muslim troops then subdue the territory, the child and the child's child both are plunder and the property of the state.[106]

Along with Apostasy, *sharia* courts also handle "matters of personal status for Muslims—marriage, divorce, child custody, and inheritance—while special tribunals of the respective religious communities exercise jurisdiction over personal status matters for non-Muslims."[107] Nadia Hijab

101. Chapman, *Cross*, 284.
102. Shafaat, "The Punishment.""
103. Marshall, *Religious Freedom*, 231.
104. Ibid., 41.
105. Bureau of Democracy, "Jordan."
106. Marshall, *Religious Freedom*, 42.
107. Ibid., 230.

states the "family laws" in *sharia* are a good example of "subjugation of women under [a] male-oriented structure of society."[108] Because *sharia* law as well as Islamic customs of Jordan are formulated and continued by the influence of patriarchal structures and men's hegemonic presumption of dominance and superiority,[109] "it regulates all kinds of rights and responsibilities related to family issues, but [it] does not provide any fairness for male and female members of the family."[110] Mernissi also asserts that there is no ideology of female inferiority in Muslim societies, but laws and customs make women subjugate to men.[111]

Honor killing is a good example of the subjugation of women. Honor is highly valued in Jordan, and the conservation of family honor is regarded as a male responsibility, which requires that a male family member kill a woman whose honor is questionable. Such a murder is called an honor killing (*Jarimat al-sharaf*) and generally results in a light prison sentence. Between fifteen and twenty women each year are killed in Jordan as victims of honor crime.[112] The public awareness campaigns launched in 2001 were welcomed as members of the royal family took the lead, but it was an insufficient force for major change.[113] It is reported that in order to protect women form honor killings from their families, some "women who were raped, assaulted or had relationships outside marriage were being kept at Qafqafa, northern Jordan."[114]

New Challenges in Society

Although the Islamic revivalism required women to be limited in the framework of Islam, economic recession brought Jordanian women to have wider education opportunities. In addition, they could join the wage-based labor force not only from the higher classes, but also from the middle and

---

108. Hijab, "Islam," 46.
109. Esposito, *The Future*, 119.
110. Ibid.
111. Mernissi, *Beyond the Veil*, 11.
112. "Jordanians kills."
113. Arsu, "Turks."
114. Moran, "Honor Killing."

lower classes.¹¹⁵ A lot of Muslim women are increasingly found in professional workplaces and are active administrators of organizations.¹¹⁶

It is true that most Jordanian women are still considered second-class citizens and are limited by traditional patriarchalism. This changing milieu of education and anticipation of economic forces, however, increases women's awareness of their basic rights as member of society.¹¹⁷ With this trend in today's society, Jordanian women, however, have started to realize their status and have made their voices heard for women's rights, such as opposition against honor killing. It also has raised the voice of feminists even though feminism is still not a powerful force of the society.¹¹⁸

Globalization is also a critical element for Jordanian Muslims which exposes them to other ideas and beliefs in the world in diverse aspects. Therefore, current changes in the economic levels, high educational levels and the successive social interaction have greatly influenced Jordanian lives.¹¹⁹ The majority of people in the capital Amman have become Westernized and have risen as a new power of change in Jordanian society. With the increase of satellite television and the internet, people have more opportunities to contact other places in the world. Although the Jordanian government controls the major forms of media, Jordanians are able to access "information on a wide range of topic[s]."¹²⁰

One of the important responses of many Muslims has been to begin to separate religion and politics, similar to separation of church and state in the West.¹²¹ Social relations and changes caused by the economic recession challenged "the underlying principles of Islam as a social order."¹²² Many young people experienced influences outside their family and this challenged their traditionalism by working outside of their tribes' business or abroad. Later, these young people became the middle class who are modernized and more actively involved in the social changes of Jordan. John Shoup, an Islamic scholar, states that the emergence of a middle class

---

115. Taraki, " Islam," 648.
116. Esposito, *The Future*, 119.
117. Brand, "Women and the State," 112.
118. Mernissi, *Beyond the Veil*, 11.
119. Shoup, *Culture*, 100.
120. Ibid, 49.
121. Kraft, *Searching for Heaven*, 52.
122. Mernissi, *Beyond the Veil*, 83.

challenges the older traditional social customs, in particular to younger Jordanians.[123]

The middle class is the agent that is leading Jordanian society in democracy and internationalization, while many of them have become nominal Islamic believers and more secularized. Cultural nominalists, or secularists, among the middle class have spread throughout the country since the 1990s. Cultural nominalists are "the Muslims whose link with Islam is purely through cultural heritage and not through the meaningful practice of Islam," according to Saeed's categorization.[124] Notwithstanding a strong identification with Islamic orthodoxy, religious practices differ among different segments of Jordan's population. This asymmetry in religious practices does not correlate with an urban–rural division or differing levels of educational background. Despite this, most people try to give the impression that they are devout Muslims, although many people still do not fast during Ramadan. They are affiliated with Islam as "a cultural connection to Muslim ancestors and families and friends," rather than active religious beliefs and practices.[125] Peter Berger argues that a decline in individual religious beliefs is just as important as this macro-level of secularization: "The process of secularization has a subjective side as well. As there is a secularization of society and culture, so there is a secularization of consciousness."[126]

Jordanian Women's Identity in the Sociocultural Dimension

In constructing one's identity, an ideology of a specific society has great influence on those who belong to it. In her book *Revising Herself: The Story of Women's Identity from College to Midlife*, Josselson, a psychologist, defines identity as "what we make of ourselves within a society that is making something of us," and asserts that this particular society binds us to construct our identities.[127] Identity is also "at the centre of any form of social interaction and social interactions help us to make sense of how people behave and relate to each other within communities."[128] In Middle Eastern

123. Shoup, *Culture*, 106.
124. ASaeed, "Trends," 400.
125. Woodlock, "Many Hijabs," 397.
126. Berger, *The Sacred Canopy*, cited in McGuire, *Religion*, 288.
127. Josselson, *Revising Herself*, 28.
128. Marranci, *The Anthropology*, 94.

societies, where community and family are central to people's daily lives, it is not easy for a person to change his or her own personal conviction to the point where he/she leaves his family, social, economic, and political life behind.[129]

Muslim women in Jordanian society also format their identities within Islamic and Arab cultural boundaries. These sociocultural factors work as "powerful agents in shaping identity."[130] Jordanian society has both traditional conservative as well as modernized trends. Ahmad Kamal Azban distinguishes the current Jordanian Arab culture by variation and contradictions:"We are simultaneously mimicking and renewing, conservative and modern, constricting and free, proud and humble, internal and external, local and global, old and new."[131] Jordan, however, still has a strong tendency towards the traditional Arab society based on Islam as not just religion, but also a sociocultural foundation to tie women down.

Classification of Jordanian Women

A social researcher and activist Suhayr al-Tall divides her analysis on Jordanian women into three categories according to place of residence (town or village), socioeconomic status, region of origin, religion, and so on: Bedouin women, village women, and urban women.[132] Women in each category show a different quality of life both economically and educationally.

BEDOUIN WOMEN

Whereas the proportion of Bedouins is small in comparison with the total population of Jordan, Jordanian society respects the Bedouin's mythical ideal for many Arabs. Honor and bravery are symbols of the Bedouin's culture. For women, modesty and honor are critical, because these factors are considered "for the protection of women, on the one hand, because they are seen as weak and, on the other, because they bear the offspring."[133] Among Bedouins, a woman's status is due to where she belongs (tribe and lineage)

129. Badr et al., *Christianity*, 714.
130. Ibid., 30.
131. Azban, *Diwan Baladna*, 16.
132. al-Tall, *Muqaddimah*, 40.
133. Brand, "Women and the State," 103.

and the procreation of male descendents.[134] In order to keep honor (*sharaf*) of family and herself, a woman should be a virgin at the time of marriage.[135] In traditional Bedouin law, a bride has no say concerning her own marriage and is sold to the highest bidder.[136]

Village Women

In rural areas, traditionally women are regarded as an important labor force in the agricultural sectors.[137] In the villages, most women engage in unpaid labor for the family, often in the fields.[138] Moreover, this labor is regarded by most rural dwellers as managing the household and does not constitute "work." Conservative people in rural areas still think that "a women's worth derives from two things: her chastity and her production of male children."[139] At the same time these days, more girls are being educated even to tertiary level and work outside. According to family traditions and situations, some village women live in strong conservative circumstances or at the beginning of modernized phases.

Urban Women

In general, women in the cities such as Amman, Zarka, and Irbid, have access to a range of services such as schools and health clinics. The education rate and percentage of women in the paid labor force outside the home is higher in these cities than in rural areas.[140] Lately educated women, represented by Queen Rania, are continuing to fight for women's rights.[141] Educated women are actively involved in politics and societal affairs such as the Jordanian National Commission for Women (JNCW). According to JNCW (with HRH Princess Basima as president), "representation of Jordanian women in political decision-making positions is around 12 percent, which

---

134. Ibid.
135. Ibid., 104.
136. Ibid.
137. Ibid.
138. Ibid.
139. al-Tall, *Muqaddimah*, 40.
140. Brand, "Women and the State," 104.
141. "World's Most Powerful Women."

does not meet the international percentages."[142] JNCW wants to enlarge the women's contribution "in political life and to empower the leadership of women and their participation in public life."[143] Asma Khader, a lawyer and human rights activist, is also one of the representatives for women's rights as a president of Sisterhood Is Global Institute/Jordan (SIGI/J) and Secretary General of the Jordanian National Commission for Women.[144] At the same time, it can be said that the vast majority of Jordanian women see their lives as simply wives, daughters and mothers.

Cultural Values

Traditionalism As a Cultural Continuity

Traditionalism is one of the crucial characteristics of Arabs. Raphel Patai, in his book *The Arab Mind*, describes this traditionalism among Arabs in this way: "In modern Western culture, the new is considered better than old, and thus change in itself is considered a good; in tradition-bound Arab cultures, the old is regarded as better than the new, and thus the retention of the existing order is considered a good."[145] Lewellen articulates that "within traditional societies, family, kinship, and community are the primary relations" in comparison with modern societies in which individuals build more often "impersonal relations based on jobs, clubs, sports teams and government agencies."[146] Hence, Jordanians have a group personality and show traditionalism which highly appreciates cultural continuity in their value and lifestyles.[147] Although the modernization of Jordan has made people Westernized in their modes of life and some cultural values, they try to preserve a conservative cultural identity.

Jordanian traditionalism characterizes that it is associated with parochialism, subsistence agriculture, economic systems based on reciprocity, social division that is based on rank rather than class, and the structuring of society around religion.[148] This traditionalism within a hierarchical struc-

142. Emam, "Jordanian Women."
143. Ibid.
144. "Asma Khader."
145. Patai, *The Arab Mind*, 279–80.
146. Ibid.
147. Lewellen, *The Anthropology*, 101.
148. Sharify-Funk, *Encountering*, 136.

Identity Crisis

ture is supported by the traditional religious interpretations of the Qur'an with "inherent preference for patriarchal authority" of Islamic interpretative schools.[149]

It is also expressed in strong tribalism in Jordan. All Jordanians of the East Bank have tribal (*'ashirah*) roots.[150] According to Ghazi bin Muhammad in *The Tribes of Jordan: At the Beginning of the Twenty-First Century*, Jordanians belong to a tribe not only because of genetic relationships but also by sharing the same worldview and lives.

> A person and his/her tribe think the same way; believe the same principles; assimilate the same values and ethos; act according to the same unique rules and laws; respect the same hereditary *Shaykh* (Tribal Lord); live together; migrate together; defend each other; fight together and die together.[151]

The sense of mutual dependence among members of the tribe and collective responsibilities are central dynamic factors of tribal solidarity, reinforcing the cohesion within the tribal structure. Although the establishment of the Jordanian government has brought a change of lifestyle and traditional political structure, cultural loyalty to their tribes and clans is embedded in the lives of Jordanians. Craig Storti, in *Figuring Foreigners Out: A Practical Guide*, articulates that "one's identity is in large part a function of one's membership and role in a group."[152] He points out that "harmony and interdependence of group members are stressed and valued" in a collectivistic society.[153]

Silman Khawalde and Dan Rabinowitz also mention that "hierarchical society emphasizes continuity while ascribing deep value to blood ties and descent; their lives are more accurately described as a constant race from the bottom."[154] Within the tribal system, the extended family is a basic unit of Arab family rather than a nuclear family. Therefore, the extended family is a more influential and significant part of Jordanian society rather than individual choices or decisions. According to Eugene Nidar, traditionalists feel "the comfortable emotional security of their 'extended family,' which

---

149. Ibid.
150. Muhammad, *The Tribes*, 9.
151. Ibid., 13.
152. Storti, *Figuring*, 25.
153. Ibid., 26.
154. Khawalde and Rabinowitz, "Race," 227.

maintains itself primarily by resistance to ideas from the outside world, [and] cannot be pushed into making quick decisions."[155]

In the Arab society, the concept of genealogy and marriage shows the tendency of traditionalism. Muslims regard the bloodline as a way to bind to the past and connect them to the present: "As a link to the past, through genealogy, blood is essential to the definition of cultural identity."[156] Thus, even though marriage is a secular unit and not a divine one initiated by Allah, Muslims consider "marriage as an essential of life," and regard it as a foundation of Islamic society.[157] In marriage, although it is not a legal requirement, parent's consent and blessings are absolute elements for the marriage. According to the Qur'an and Hadith, parents have almost sacred status for their children.[158] First-cousin marriage is also a more preferable and critical tradition of Arabs, and in particular the Bedouin heritage. Traditionally among Arabs, a girl is considered to belong to the son of her father's brother (*ibn 'Am*).[159] Therefore, normally Muslim women learn "their identities from their patriline."[160] It is natural to keep family genealogy and fortunes to hold on to the father's family line. In patriline, the role of uncles from the father's side is very powerful, and sometimes they work as agents to encourage honor killing if their nieces bring shame on the family by misconduct.[161]

Karin Ask and Marit Tjomsl also define patriarchalism as a basic structure of contemporary Islamic societies, and see that it is shaped "by the institutionally enforced authority of males over females and their children in the family unit."[162] Therefore, at home female family members are required to submit to male authority within the "extended, patriarchal . . . and occasionally polygamous familial structure."[163] Muslim women are used to living behind the veil and under male family members' protection. Mernissi strongly asserts that modern Muslim societies should recognize "that the traditional family mutilates the woman by depriving her of her

155. Nida, *Message*, 178.
156. Abu-Lughod, *Veiled Sentiments*, 41.
157. Roald, *Women*, 213.
158. Muhammad, *The Tribes*, 35.
159. Dickson, *The Arab*, 140.
160. Abu-Lughod, *Veiled Sentiments*, 54.
161. S. R., interviewed by the author, Jordan, February 25, 2013.
162. Ask and Tjomsl, *Women*, 192.
163. Patai, *The Arab Mind*, 281.

humanity."[164] In spite of this fact, the traditionalism and strong genealogical solidarity in Jordanian kinship lines still define women's identities and strongly "tie [them] to a code of morality, that of honor and modesty."[165]

COMMUNALISM: *UMMAH* AND PRIMORDALISM

It is true that if any Muslim wants to find "Self," it can be found within community. It is impossible for one to understand oneself without connecting with others in the Islamic community. Haddad stresses that one's identity is established between individualism and communalism, but, ultimately, is for community.

> . . . for Islam exists as the intersection of the individual and the communal. What this means in practical terms is that one cannot be a Muslim outside of the context of the community . . . God's word, the Quran, was not made manifest to redeem the individual as an individual and set him free; its primary goal was the establishment of a community living under the law and guidance of God, a community committed in prayer and obedience to His will.[166]

Ummah (a brotherhood of Islamic society) is considered as "the primary source in Islam,"[167] and is the ideal social community of Islamic societies. Mernissi also defines *ummah* as the structure of "the totality of individuals bound to one another by [the] tie" of Islam.[168] Before the advent of Islam, Arabs were loyal to only their clans and tribes, but Islam developed a new type of broad conception of religious allegiance to the Islamic community.[169] Marranci explains the character of *ummah* as community and communal identity, and quotes that "*ummah* is the unique principle of social identity valid in Islam, and it makes for the only Islamic Community, of which any Muslim is a member simply by virtue of being Muslim."[170] He

---

164. Mernissi, *Beyond the Veil*, 81.
165. Abu-Lughod, *Veiled Sentiments*, 40–41.
166. Haddad, "Traditional Affirmations," 67–68.
167. Wadud, "Alternative Qur'anic Interpretation," 16.
168. Mernissi, *Beyond the Veil*, 18.
169. Kraft, *Searching for Heaven*, 48.
170. Marranci, *The Anthropology*, 109–10.

also acknowledges that emotions and feelings are central to the conceptualization of the *ummah* in contemporary use.[171]

Considering that Islamic society is male-dominated, the *ummah* is a favorable community to male members of the society. Anwar points out that the notion of *ummah* functions by "the male concept of what is good."[172] She states continuously that female sexuality is regarded as one of the factors that causes the corruption of society and needs to be controlled for men and the community.[173] Thus, the public world is under the reign of men, and the private world of home and family is the women's place, though bounded by the walls of fathers or husbands.[174] For the establishment and maintenance of *ummah* with a communal aspect, hierarchy is necessary for Muslims, so "the women's position in the *ummah* is ambiguous and [it seems] Allah does not talk to them directly."[175] Mernissi points out in today's society in the domestic realm such as the family system, Muslim women's duty is to be subordinated to men.[176] She also mentions that women are the second nationality in the public sphere, the domain of religion and politics, as well as the domain of power in the management of the affairs of the *ummah*.[177]

Based on the aforementioned strong bond of genealogy, primordialism is another character of Jordanians. Lewellen defines it as "ethnicity that is based in some deeply inscribed, long-term group cohesion, with shared claims to blood, soil, language and a mythologized history."[178] Geertz points out the attachment of primordialism.

> By a primordial attachment is meant . . . one is bound to one's kinsman, one's neighbor, one's fellow believer, ipso facto; as the result not merely of personal affection, practical necessity, common interest, or incurred obligation, but at least in great part by virtue of some unaccountable absolute import attributed to the very tie itself.[179]

171. Ibid., 112.
172. Anwar, *Gender*, 145.
173. Ibid.
174. Lindholm, *The Islamic Middle East*, 228.
175. Mernissi, *Beyond the Veil*, 107.
176. Ibid, 139.
177. Ibid.
178. Lewellen, *The Anthropology*, 106.
179. Geertz, *The Interpretation*, 259–260.

Identity Crisis

'Assabiyya (loyalty) is a prominent characteristic of primordialism among Jordanians. Arab historian Ibn Kaldun in the fourteenth century said that "*Assabiyya*" was the basic bondage of human society and the energy to move history in Arab society.[180] In their article, Khawalde and Rabinowitz explain this Assabiyya in detail.

> . . . Originating in the root *'asab* (nerve). *'Asabiyya* denoted a strong sense of "us": a self-evident solidarity and intimacy most cultures associate with the immediate family, extended to apply to the wider kinship group. It promotes cooperation and mutual dependence, conflating the experience of belonging to an agnatic blood group with commitment to loyalty and solidarity, in daily routines as well as in emergencies.[181]

Strong solidarity in *ummah* and primordialism binds Jordanians with closed communal sense.

Along with '*Assabiyya*, the code of fatalism, honor, and hospitality are also critical characteristics and their practice keeps communalism in Jordanian society. Influenced by religion, Jordanians accept all their life affairs as the "will of God" (*In sha' Allah*). This natural acceptance of destiny makes them more able to submit to authority in their kinship or their agreements. This fatalism comes from the Bedouin's cultural heritages: "Previously, when a family fortune might be uncertain, being governed by acts of nature and the successes and failures of intertribal raiding, the Bedouin developed a fatalism which left almost everything in the hands of God."[182] To intensify solidarity of family, tribe, and society, honor is the important ideal that maintains the value of collectivism among Jordanians. Strong hospitality also maintains communality of them. Jordanians have "extensive information networks among family, friends, colleagues, and clients involved in close personal relationships."[183] Therefore, building relationships is a primary virtue for them and is expressed by their hospitality. Hosting a guest well is a critical aspect of their hospitality. When the host honors the guest, it means "he honors the guest's whole kin group, which explains why sheep are slaughtered for women guests or individuals who are not especially important personally."[184] Along with hosting the guest

---

180. Kong, *Understanding*, 265.
181. Khawalde and Rabinowitz, "Race," 235.
182. Keohane, *Bedouin*, 70.
183. Hall and Hall, *Understanding*, 6.
184. Abu-Lughod, *Veiled Sentiments*, 66.

with food, "complimenting based on oral communication culture, is used for many different purposes" in greetings and so on.[185] Jordanians believe that appropriate complimenting is one of the best ways to show honor and respect for others.[186]

Women's Virtues

In the sense of the contribution of tradition as resources of developing one's identity,[187] traditional Arabs' cultural conception towards women substantially influences the concept of Jordanian women's virtues. In particular, the Bedouin nomadic tribal traditions have been considered as essential Arab's cultural heritages. Because the ideal image of Bedouin ethos is considered the cultural root of Jordanians,[188] conservative aspects are required of women.

Honor and Modesty

The code of honor is an essential factor to understand Jordanian society and its culture. Shoup discusses the meaning of honor for Jordanians as a standard of individual's behavior related to his or her entire family.

> Honor is connected with the behavior of individuals and the honor of a family can be ruined by the so-called bad behavior of an individual. The entire family is judged by the actions of an individual, as the actions of the individuals reflect the general moral level of the whole family. While much of this comes from tradition, religion is often used to justify the traditions around values such as honor.[189]

Because the sense of honor is very critical for Jordanians, if their honor is threatened, they try to keep it or regain it through retribution.[190]

Men's honor is related to braveness, courage, and hospitality, but women's honor is expressed as modesty. Women keep their honor through

185. Azban, *Diwan Baladna*, 43.
186. Ibid.
187. Schrieter, *Constructing Local Theologies*, 105.
188. Patai, *The Arab Mind*, 73.
189. Shoup, *Culture*, 40.
190. Braswell, *Islam*, 104.

Identity Crisis

sexual purity. Hence, a woman's modesty, as a way of keeping her honor, is strongly required. In the Qur'an 33:32–33, the "special commandments addressed to women are: to be modest and steadfast in prayer, to give alms, obey God and His apostles."[191] Furthermore, a woman's honor in Arab society is not hers alone, but is strongly connected to direct and extended family members. Patai expounds the reason as follows: "In the Arab world, the greatest dishonor that can befall a man results from the sexual misconduct of his daughter or sister, or *bint' amm* (one's father's brother's daughter)."[192] Therefore, if a woman loses her honor, she also loses her brothers' and father's honor.[193]

Submission and Obedience

Submission is a cardinal code for Muslims. In Arabic, primarily Islam means submission to the will of Allah, and Muslims should be totally committed to Allah. This code of submission is not only practiced in the aspect of religion towards Allah, but also in relationships with people. Hence, it is often expressed as submission to Allah and *ummah*, which is given by Allah among men, as submission to Allah and to male authorities among women. In the relationship between male and female, "female self-determination, feminine initiative, whether in the home or the outside world, is the very embodiment of the absence of order, the absence of Muslim laws."[194]

The obedience of women is necessary to hold order for the Muslim family and society. A wife should obey her husband, therefore, a husband disciplines his wife if she disobeys his word with beatings (4:34). Children also need to be disciplined in order to be obedient toward their elders.

> Since the Arabs are convinced that it is primarily the early childhood influences that form character and personality, and since subordination of one's ego to the authority of the father (and/or the actual head of the family) is a corner stone of the Arab social edifice, the children are disciplined, if necessary severely, in order to make them accept, and acquiesce in, paternal rule. As a result of Arab child-rearing practices, the children learn to subordinate

---

191. Patai, *The Arab Mind*, 99.
192. Ibid., 119.
193. Ibid., 95.
194. Mernissi, *Beyond the Veil*, 84.

their own personal interests to those of the family as represented by the father or grandfather.[195]

Within the extended family structures and clan systems, women are always, to some degree, dependents. They are to be "ruled" by men and should be obedient.[196]

Belonging

In regards to communalism and the concept of genealogy, Muslim women build their identities related to the idea of "belonging." This sense of belonging is "essential because there is no life outside the group, no alternative social group other than the community of agnates into which one is born."[197] Women are beings dependent on their father, brothers, husband, and sons. Diane King asserts that "belonging can mean fitting in, feeling at home, feeling a part; this kind of belonging is profoundly social. Belongings can be possessions, objects closely associated with one's deepest notions of identity."[198] Muslim women have to be more sensitive to this understanding of belonging in order to maintain their security and dignity within this communal and familial tradition.

Identity of Jordanian Women As Women

Jordanian Muslim women have Islamic features of their identities, but at the same time they have specific features as women. In the sense of communalism, their self-understanding is built on their relationships with others within the frame of religious and cultural requirements.

Types of Women's Identities

As aforementioned, Josselson categorizes four characteristics of women's identities: Guardians, Pathmakers, Searchers, and Drifters. Guardians make their identity "without a sense of choice, carrying forward the plans

---

195. Patai, *The Arab Mind*, 27.
196. Abu-Lughod, *Veiled Sentiments*, 104–5.
197. Ibid., 237.
198. King, "Middle Eastern Belongings," 261.

for their life mapped out in childhood or designed by their parents."[199] Pathmakers format their identities based on their own exploration or crisis, so they could say that "I've tried out some things, and this is what makes most sense for me."[200] Searchers stay "in an active period of struggle or exploration, trying to make choices but not yet having done so."[201] Lastly, Drifters do not have any concerns on finding their identity—"These people are likely to say, 'I don't know what I will do or believe, but it doesn't matter too much right now.'"[202]

It can be said that most Jordanian Muslim women have the Guardian type of identity, because Islam is always with them from their birth and the people surrounding them are all Muslims as well. How parents instill values, as well as the education system, are guided by Islamic beliefs and traditional Arab cultures. One of the characteristics of Guardians is that "their self-esteem had all their lives rested on submission to exacting regulation."[203] They do not want to change their identity, so they close "the possibility of forming an independent identity by seeking to preserve ways of thinking, responding, and valuing that had always been. Preoccupied with security, they chose what felt safe."[204]

When Muslim women change their religion or try to become independent from traditional values or norms, they move for a period to being a Searcher. Searchers often feel guilty and fear, according to Josselson, because they have "forsaken the values of their childhood" and they are not "quite sure what they [are] doing with themselves."[205]

OTHERNESS-RELATEDNESS OF JORDANIAN WOMEN IDENTITIES

Muslim women can construct their identities according to preexisting cultural or ideological expectations which are projected onto women by others.[206] Ask Karin and Marit Tjomsl articulate "relatedness" as one of the unique characteristics of women's identities, because "women's boundaries

---

199. Josselson, *Revising Herself*, 35.
200. Ibid.
201. Ibid.
202. Ibid., 36.
203. Ibid., 46.
204. Ibid., 45.
205. Ibid., 38.
206. Berger and Luckmann, *The Social Construction*, 150–51.

of self are considered to be more permeable than men's in many cultures."²⁰⁷ From interviews with Muslim women in diverse Islamic countries, Sharify-Funk also suggested that "many Muslim women are seeking to form their identities in the midst of various processes of 'othering,' or in other words, in cultural environments in which the possibilities for self-definition are sharply constrained by stereotypical categories."²⁰⁸

Muslim women are placed under the care and authority of men.²⁰⁹ Hence, a young girl should be "an obedient daughter" and "exhibit modest and chaste behavior."²¹⁰ Later, she finds her true identity in the roles of a wife and mother, and all other aspects of her "intellectual and social life should be directed toward that dual end."²¹¹ Haddad also persists that roles of women are limited and restricted by their traditions, namely "wife and mother," and asserts that this is not only their role, "it is to be [their] sole identities."²¹² Peter Berger and Thomas Luckmann stress the importance of others: "The significant others in the individual's life are the principal agents for the maintenance of his subjective reality."²¹³ In the Arab Bedouin tradition, maleness is represented as autonomy and femaleness as dependency.²¹⁴ Jordanian women project their identities within dependent relationships upon male members of society, generally their family members. In the sense of understanding "Self," Jordanian women have the concept of belonging in an Arab family cohesion rather than as independent agents of their lives. Therefore, Jordanian women's identity is "not a matter of being but fundamentally of being with."²¹⁵

---

207. Ask and Tjomsl, *Women*, 81.
208. Sharify-Funk, *Encountering*, 135.
209. Beck, "The Religious Lives," 34.
210. Ibid.
211. Ibid., 17.
212. Haddad, "Traditional Affirmations," 63.
213. Berger and Luckmann, *The Social Construction*, 150–51.
214. Abu-Lughod, *Veiled Sentiments*, 118.
215. Ask and Tjomsl, *Women*, 81.

4

Narratives of Banaat al Urdun (Daughters of Jordan)

THIS CHAPTER WILL DESCRIBE three kinds of interviews I have conducted with Jordanian Muslim women, BMB women, and workers for BMB discipling ministry in Jordan respectively. Simple and informal interviews were conducted with forty-five Muslim women from various backgrounds and three different cities in Jordan to investigate their understanding of women's general life and their understanding of themselves. Among them there are thirty-two under thirty years of age and thirteen over thirty.[1] Thirteen live in villages, four are nomads from Bedouin tribes, and twenty-eight live in urban areas. The interview questions I asked the Muslim women were directed at finding out their opinion about the life of women, important virtues of women, the ideal Muslim woman, the image of Christian women, and the concept of honor and shame for women.

For BMB women the interviews were carried out in semi open-closed interviews. Some of these women called themselves "people who are crossing." One of the interviewees explained to me the phrase refers to people crossing from darkness to light. All of their circumstances were different, but there were similar threats directed to them when they crossed over to a new faith.

---

1. In general, Arabs traditionally considered fifteen years as one generation. In the past when women were in their mid-teens, they got married. It has always been true in villages that when a married woman reaches her late 30s or early 40s, she usually becomes a grandmother. This is still prevalent today according to places.

Narratives of Banaat al Urdun (Daughters of Jordan)

In order to focus on their identity issues, the interviews investigated what kind of difficulties they faced and the changes they noticed before and after conversion. I divided the interview questions for BMB women into three parts: Background, Before Being a Christian, and After Conversion. To understand their backgrounds, I interviewed their general situations such as age, educational background, family and marital status, social status and class, and conversion experiences. In the section on Before Being a Christian, I asked about the general life of a Muslim woman and the image they had of Christian women. I also asked them to share their opinions about what their largest difficulties and hindrances were when they made a decision to become a Christian. In regard to finding out about After the Conversion Experience of BMB women, I purposed to know what happened inside of them at the beginning stage of their conversions and at what period they felt assured about their new faith. I also additionally asked these BMB women's views on the differences they had noticed between the difficulties male BMBs and female BMBs had faced in order to distinguish BMB women's circumstances from those of BMB men's.

Another type of interview I conducted was with foreign and local female workers who have been involved in discipling BMB women over the years. One interviewee is a Jordanian who has been committed to evangelizing and discipling BMB's for over fifteen years. The others are Westerners, but spent much of their lives in Jordan: 50, 39, and 25 years respectively. I interviewed them on their observations about general life of a Jordanian woman, Muslim women's identity and self-understanding, and the image of Christians among Muslims. I also asked these female workers about their opinions and understandings of the most difficult hindrances and challenges BMB women face at the beginning phase of their search for Christianity, and the reasons BMB women go back to Islam or step back from their new faith. I have also included my personal experiences with six BMB women to analyze and investigate the lives of Jordanian BMB women.

Interview with Muslim Women

The questions for Muslim women I asked were aimed to figure out their general view of women's life and identity in Jordan. Along with questions about general life and the image of a woman in Jordan, I included a question about honor and shame in my interviews, because this honor and shame concept is very critical and representative of Jordanian thinking related to women. The interviews took ten to twenty minutes depending on the person. I interviewed Jordanian women who have been dwelling in the desert, villages, and urban areas including Syrians, Yemenis, and Iraqis living in Jordan.

Most Muslim women I interviewed had similar answers to the questions. Regardless of their education or ages, being a good wife and mother is the most ideal identity a woman can have. The Qur'an and Hadith were the main, nonnegotiable resource for them to form their identities. These religious standards and cultural customs were the basic foundations of constructing their identities. With carrying on religious duties, following the instructions required of them as women was the basic groundwork for their identities. As for important virtues of women, most interviewees had similar answers giving characteristics of being a good mother and a good wife. Although many of the interviewees were unmarried, many of them understand that they are in the process of creating their identity to be a good mother and wife in the future. They have focused on who they should be rather than who they are, in their identity formation. Regarding their image of Christian women, all interviewees had the same answer that they respect other religions according to the Qur'an. Many of them answered that they have never seen or thought of Christian women in their lives. When I asked them to describe the differences between Muslim women's and Christian women's lives, there were diverse opinions on their perspectives of Christian women's lifestyles, most of which were perceived as negative. The concept of honor and shame for them was based on modesty and what others thought of their behavior to maintain their family's reputation.

Summary of Interviews

In order to give a general summary of interviewees' answers, I use the following abbreviations because many answers were repeated.

- W, M, and/or D is an abbreviation for: the aim of their life is to be a good wife and mother, and if she is not married, to be a good daughter. It includes the idea that a woman should cook, clean the house, bring up her children well, and obey her husband or father or brothers in her home. These abbreviations will be found in categories: "General Life of Women" or "Virtue of Women."

Narratives of Banaat al Urdun(Daughters of Jordan)

- RD is an abbreviation for: doing religious duties (Five pillars) such as *shahada* (confession of faith), prayers, fasting, going on pilgrimage, and almsgiving. They call it *multajim* (the necessary things). This abbreviation will be found in the category: "Ideal Muslim Women."

- T is an abbreviation for: being tolerant and respectful of other religions according to the Qur'an. This abbreviation will be found in the category: "Image of Christian Women and Life."

- C is an abbreviation for: customs that do not allow talking or walking with strange men, not to have a relationship with other men except her husband, not to show her hair, and not to wear short clothes. This abbreviation will be found in the category: "Honor and Shame."

Table 1: Interview with Muslim Women

No	Interviewee Information			Interviewee Views				
	Age, Nationality, Residency	Marital Status, Education Level, Work Status	General Life of Women	Virtue of Women	Ideal Muslim Woman	Christian Women and Their Lifestyle	Honor and Shame
1	60s, Syrian villager	Widow, Uneducated, Housewife	Work as well as W and M	Beauty, W and M	RD	No relationship	According to C.
2	23, Iraqi villager	Unmarried, Secondary, Unemployed	Work as well as W and M	Good W, M and D.	Pure heart, RD	Normal	According to C.
3	17, Syrian villager	Unmarried, Secondary, Student	Study and D at home	Morality, Religious person	Good W and M	No relationships	Honor: Obey family and be religious.
4	25, Jordanian villager	Unmarried, Tertiary, Employed	Women have no right to decide their own life.	Beauty, Good M	RD, Obeying everything according to the Qur'an.	No thought	According to C.

			Knowing Allah Good M				
5	21, Jordanian villager	Unmarried, Tertiary, Employed	Men control and decide everything for women.	Wearing *hijab* & long clothes	Good W and M	Good people	According to C. Keep her honor.
6	45 Yemeni Bedouin	Married, Illiterate, Housewife	Women are happy as W and M.	Beauty; Good behavior	RD	No relationship	According to C.
7	23, Yemeni Bedouin	Married, Uneducated, Housewife	Work as well as W and M	Bravery and strength	RD	No relationship	According to C.
8	32, Jordanian villager	Divorced, Tertiary, Employed	Work as well as W and M	Patience because of children	Take care of her home, children and husband	They believe Jesus Christ is the son of Mary.	According to C.
9	20s, Jordanian urbanite	Unmarried, University Student	Women are free. The law of Jordan is equal for men and women. Women can have high positions in society.	Patient. Wearing long dresses. Be reasonable and generous.	RD, Morality. Good behavior with people.	T Muslim women are more comfortable than others. Other religious people separate their religion and their life, but we don't.	According to C.

10	40s, Jordanian villager	Married, Secondary, Employed	Work as well as W and M	Patience with her husband and care for children	RD Do not mingle with other men.	Good people	According to C. Be quiet and kind with her husband and others.
11	30s, Syrian villager	Married, Secondary, Employed	Normal	Good M and W	RD, Do not leave her home by herself. Wear long clothes.	No relationship	According to C. Obey husband and do duty.
12	23, Jordanian villager	Unmarried, Tertiary, Employed	Work as well as W and M	According to her education & culture, these things make her become a good mother & good woman.	RD Good behavior	Arab traditions & culture are more important than religion.	According to C.
13	20s, Jordanian urbanite	Unmarried, University Student	Women have boundaries They have many roles. Working lives.	Family should be first.	Getting a college certificate.	Religion is a personal choice.	Muslims have boundaries. According to C.

14	20s, Jordanian urbanite	Unmarried, University Student	In the past, the life of women was difficult, but now it is open.	Trust-worthy Be educated	Obedience to the Qur'an.	Customs are more important than religion. If a Muslim is not allowed, neither is a Christian.	Her honor is based on acting acceptably in the society. Her honor is related to her reputation.
15	20s, Jordanian urbanite	Unmarried, University Student	Work as well as W and M	Be aware of responsibility for home and family.	Wearing *hijab*. Praying.	T. Christian women have more freedom, but Muslims have restricted freedom.	One must do her role according to her status. A woman faces many challenges
16	20s, Jordanian urbanite	Unmarried, University Student	Jordanian society sometimes puts pressure on women and sometimes not.	Morality, Religion, Education	Wearing long clothes and covering her body.	T They must follow Arab traditions.	Respect and keep the boundary according to religion and the traditions of society.

17	20s, Jordanian urbanite	Unmarried, University Student	Normal But women must obey the tradition. There are boundaries and women must not go beyond them.	Should be respected by people. Not doing anything wrong that makes people misunderstand her.	Living according to Islam	T Clothing is different.	According to C.
18	20s, Jordanian urbanite	Unmarried, University Student	Women are respected and in Amman are more important than men.	Honest and loyal to her husband.	Wearing *hijab* is not important. She has to keep her way according to her decision.	T	According to C.
19	20s, Jordanian urbanite	Unmarried, University Student	Women must live according to the tradition. She cannot do whatever she wants, because she is constantly being judged. Working W and M.	Honesty, Morality, Beauty	Praying, Wearing long clothes.	T Their traditions and clothing are not good. They are ignorant and not organized and not clean like Muslims.	According to C.

20	20s, Jordanian urbanite	Unmarried, University Student	This is a male society. When a woman does anything wrong, the society does not forgive her.	Family. Shyness. Quiet behavior. Do duties for family.	Praying. Good behavior.	T Other religions are not complete and miss something.	According to C. Respect husband. Do whatever Islam asks you to do.
21	20s, Jordanian urbanite	Unmarried, University Student	The society is bad.	Wearing clothes according to Islam.	RD, Good behavior	T. Many things in Islam do not exist in other religions.	Keep the boundaries regarding family and tradition
22	20s, Jordanian urbanite	Unmarried, Secondary, Unemployed	Work as well as W and M	Morality	Respect-able	Muslim women do not need to work, but Christian women work a lot.	Our religion is easy to follow.
23	30s, Jordanian villager	Married, Secondary, Employed	Everything is available to women. They are free.	Patience and strength	RD	No relationship	According to C.

24	45, Jordanian villager	Married, Secondary, Housewife	Work as well as W and M	Morality	RD and reading the Qur'an. Beauty is only for her husband.	Normal	Loyalty to her husband and follow C
25	50s, Jordanian urbanite	Unmarried, Tertiary, Employed	In the past, women's life was only about marriage & children. Now it includes education and work.	Education, Beauty, Treatment of Others	RD But in reality we don't follow Islam well.	No difference	The meaning of shame changes according to societal rules. Honor is to keep your word.
26	20s, Jordanian urbanite	Married, Secondary, Ex-employed	Islam should be reflected in her home and herself, for ex. wearing *hijab*. W and M	Patient Deep faith. Keep customs. The correct nature of women is in *Sharia*, Sunna, and the Qur'an.	RD Education for children.	Muslims do not drink alcohol. In Islam there are a lot of restraints, but Islam is stronger than their religion.	According to C.
27	30s, Jordanian urbanite	Married, Unknown Educational Level, Housewife	Work as well as W and M	Wearing *hijab*. Learning religion and culture.	Wearing *hijab* and prayer. Everything should be done inside the boundaries and not go outside.	Muslim women wear the *hijab* and pray at home. Christians do not wear the *hijab* and pray at the church.	According to C.

28	40s, Jordanian urbanite	Married, Secondary, Employed	Beautiful and simple practice	Take care of herself. M and W	Take care of children. Follow religion in right way. Morality and good behavior.	We are all human beings. Muslims have more freedom.	According to C.
29	21, Jordanian urbanite	Unmarried, University Student	Freedom to work but boundaries from religion and family & society.	Strong, Modest	*Hijab* and wearing long clothes. Open minded. Accept other	Christian women do whatever they want. people.	According to C.
30	25, Syrian Villager	Unmarried, Secondary, Unemployed	Work as well as W and M	Keep smiling, Speaking good words.	RD, Good M	Normal No differences	Keep family honor. Follow C
31	30s, Jordanian urbanite	Married, Secondary, Housewife	Beautiful, Most of women are educated and have a high social status. But we have to be good W.	Keep culture. Wise thinking. Take care of children. Women must learn how to bring up children in the right way.	Appropriate clothes. Our body is for our husbands; not people in the streets.	We must deal with these people with respect and love. We are higher class than those in other religions. We respect and live together, but we have laws from Islam we should follow.	She should not come home late at night. But if she has a car, it is ok.

32	20s, Jordanian urbanite	Married, Secondary, Housewife	RD Keep herself and take care of herself and live within the boundaries of religion and good morality.	Be trusting and be shy/quiet.	Prayer and fasting. Keep herself well and take care of herself.	We respect them.	C.
33	22, Jordanian urbanite	Unmarried, University Student	Simple	Polite, Morality, Being a good woman.	Obey all religious obligations. Wearing *hijab* is a personal freedom of choice.	Muslim women have some things they are not allowed to do. Christians have more freedom.	All people are different.
34	21, Jordanian urbanite	Unmarried, University Student	Normal. Study, Work and marriage	Morality Appropriate clothes	Being religious. Covering your body. Normal Muslim women and conservative Muslim women are different.	We are the same, except for religion.	According to C.

35	23, Jordanian Bedouin in Urban Area	Unmarried, University Student	Women are working, studying and have more freedom than the past. She has rights, but she should do something for it.	Morality M	According to the law, she should be very organized and systematic in everything.	Muslim women have rules and boundaries from religion, the Qur'an and the family, that Christians don't have.	According to C.
36	20s, Jordanian urbanite	Unmarried, University Student	Everything is open to and allowed for women.	Bravery Morality Tradition Everything should be done within the boundaries.	To follow religion and *Sunna* and RD Not to follow the natural human way.	T	According to C. She must be careful to not say anything wrong within the boundaries of family and Islam.

37	20s, Jordanian urbanite	Unmarried, University Student	Jordanian society is open & without restrictions. Normal life includes study, marriage, & doing what she wants to do within limits. Different religions require different behavior.	Morality RD	RD She must do everything according to religious rules.	community Everyone's life and behavior is different according to and environment.	Honor: Women act according to allowed things and should not give reason to be criticized. Shame: the opposite of what is valued by community and religion.
38	20s, Jordanian urbanite	Unmarried, University Student	Education and certification are women's weapons, especially in Arab society.	Morality Education	She should have a pure inside and do good things.	Not everything is different. But some people wear different clothes and behave differently.	Morality In Jordan, there are things women are not allowed and there are boundaries.
39	20s, Jordanian urbanite	Unmarried, University Student	Women are free. The law of Jordan is equal for men and women. They can have high positions in society.	Patient. Wearing long dresses. Be reasonable and generous.	RD Morality. Good behavior with people.	T Muslim women lives are comfortable. We do not separate our religion life.	According to C

40	20s, Jordanian Bedouin in Urban Area	Unmarried, University Student	The way of dressing, speaking, and behavior of Bedouin is very conservative.	Beauty Honor Tradition Morality	RD Bring up children Modest	Traditions are different. As we are family, we have love for them.	According to C. We have boundaries: tradition, choosing good people and friends, learning religion.
41	20s, Jordanian urbanite	Unmarried, University Student	In the past, women weren't educated. There is improvement in the society. Women are free.	Be strong, She should make decisions. She is responsible for everything.	What is inside is important. Understanding religion, *hijab* and wearing appropriate clothing. Religion should be practiced; not just thought about but used in society.	The religious practices are different.	She should not cross the boundaries and should keep her honor. She should do women's role in the society.
42	20s, Jordanian urbanite	Unmarried, University Student	Jordanian society is open, but traditions & customs still exist. The new generation is normal and not strict with boundaries	Marriage Education	Religion and morality do not change wherever she goes.	All of us are bound by tradition and religion. They are more open and different than Muslim women.	According to C.

#						
43	20s, Jordanian villager	Unmarried, University Student	Women have rights in society such as participation in elections.	Religion Morality	RD, Be conservative. Keep a pure heart. There is a boundary so she cannot cross the red line.	T, Christians' clothing is different and it is not necessary for them to keep our tradition. Muslim women have traditional boundaries.	Shame: happens when women cross the boundary. Must keep morality of religion.
44	20s, Jordanian Urbanite	Unmarried, University Student	Women are respected in society. She participates actively as a member of the community.	Be feminine. Respected. Polite.	Islam gives her the best image. Live with the best status. Freedom within boundaries.	Most Muslim women can do anything but within the boundaries of Islam. Other religions do not protect women. Christian women should work and are very tired, but Muslim women are protected.	Honor: Keep a good reputation and be polite. Shame: Acting against Islamic morality.
45	35, Syrian, Villager	Married, Tertiary, Teacher	Work as well as W and M	Good M	RD, Memorizing the Qur'an. Obey husband.	Normal	Keep her honor by being loyal to her husband & following C.

Narratives of Banaat al Urdun(Daughters of Jordan)

Synopses of Varied Views of General Life of Women

In the village, most of the women answered that taking care of their families was the general feature of the lives of women in Jordan. Some working women in rural areas mentioned the working lives of women, but being a good mother and wife was the primary and the most important status in all of their lives. On the other hand, in urban areas only one woman described a woman's life as only cooking, cleaning, and bringing up children. For them, working outside the home was depicted as part of the status of women's lives. Women in urban areas, however, still acknowledged clearly the importance of a woman's life as wife and mother, and stated certain limits that are not allowed for women in women's life of Jordanian society. Some examples of what the interviewees said follow.

> *With her husband, a woman brings up children and takes care of the house. This is what is important* (a working woman in a village).
>
> *How do I have a good life? I have to take care of my family and be a good wife and mother to my family* (a working woman in a village).
>
> *Women have boundaries, but also have many positions in this society* (a university student in an urban area).
>
> *Women used to not work a lot, but recently they have started to work. So you can find women everywhere now* (a university student in an urban area).
>
> *This is a male society. When women do something wrong, the society does not forgive them* (a working woman in a village).
>
> *Naturally, tradition is here. One must obey the tradition. There are boundaries and women must not go beyond them* (a university student in an urban area).

Synopses of Varied Views of Virtuous Women

There are two clear categories in the thinking of the ideal characteristics of women by the interviewees: one is related to being a good mother and wife, and the other is related to others' opinions and how they are viewed based on their behaviors.

> *Be patient with your children and your husband even though he is bad. Because of your children, you have to be patient* (a working woman in a village).
>
> *Be respectful and you will be respected by others. Deal with others in the right way. Do not do wrong things and people will understand you correctly* (a university student in an urban area).

Synopses of Varied Views of the Ideal Muslim Women

In general, many older women believe to have an ideal life as a Muslim woman, one must complete the religious duties such as prayers, fasting, going on pilgrimage, helping the poor, and worshipping Allah (*shahada*). Religious rituals and practices are critical for them. Most of the younger generation, however, did not emphasize the necessity of religious practices; rather, they stated the importance of outlook, for example, appropriate wearing of clothes and respectful behavior according to the Qur'an. It should be noted that since these notable things were from the interviews with young or working women in urban areas, there were liberal and nominal Muslim voices among the answers. For them, even wearing the *hijab* and practicing religion is considered a personal choice. Some young students differentiated between ideal Muslim women and normal, general Muslim women. Those students classified themselves as normal Muslim women. They answered that even though they wear the *hijab* and *abaya* (long dress), they were not good models of Muslim women. According to them, ideal Muslim women should commit to religious duties sincerely.

> *Normal general women and good [ideal] Muslim women are different* (a university student in an urban area).
>
> *Religion is a personal choice* (a university student in an urban area).
>
> *We don't want to hear "do this and do that"* (an employed woman in an urban area).

Synopses of Varied Views of the Image of Christians and Their Lifestyle

According to Islam, Muslims should respect other religions and be tolerant of them. Therefore, almost all interviewees answered that they respect Christians. In regard to the differences between the two religions in women's

Narratives of Banaat al Urdun (Daughters of Jordan)

lifestyles, some interviewees said that both Christians and Muslims are bound together by traditions and customs rather than religions. At the same time, negative views of Christian women's lifestyles were expressed as well. The mainly negative answers were due to their perception of Christian women as wearing provocative clothing and exhibiting a free lifestyle.

> *Our religion says to accept each other and be tolerant of other religions* (a university student in an urban area).

> *In the Middle East, customs are more important than religion. If a Muslim is not allowed to do something, then a Christian is not allowed as well* (a university student in an urban area).

> *Muslim women are spoiled. If she needs anything, the family will give it to her. Muslim women do not need to work because her family takes care of her. But Christian women work more for their family. They like working* (a university student in an urban area).

> *Our religion is from Allah. Everything about how one should live is written in the Qur'an. Other religions are from people so they are not completed and miss something* (a university student in an urban area).

> *Other religions have no protection for women. Christian women need to work and that must be very tiring. But Muslim women are protected* (a university student in an urban area).

> *Some traditions and clothes [of Christians] are not good. These people don't recognize the correct way to live and stay clean like us* (a university student in an urban area).

> *Christian women have more freedom, but we have restricted freedom. You have choices according to religion and circumstances* (a university student in an urban area).

Synopses of Varied Views of Honor and Shame

Generally the concept of honor and shame among Muslim women was perceived according to their own religious practices and customs, which stretch across a spectrum from very conservative Muslims to quite nominal. Shame (*'ayeb* or *'aar*) happens largely when one does something that is *haram* (disallowed). *'Ayeb* is a more cultural term which is something the society cannot accept, but *haram* is a religious term which means Allah

Identity Crisis

does not allow a certain behavior. Therefore, most interviewees in villages recognize this concept as nonnegotiable. Modesty of women is essential to distinguish between honor and shame. On the other hand, the younger and more educated generation recognized the concept of honor and shame as requirements of society and understood why they should keep these customs.

> *Appropriate wearing of clothes is important. Our body is for our husbands not the people in the streets* (a housewife in an urban area).
>
> *Do not talk with strange men. Do not walk with strange men. Do not laugh loudly in front of people* (a girl in a village).
>
> *Honor means to be respectable and to maintain boundaries according to religion and the traditions of society* (a university student in an urban area).
>
> *There are traditions and rules here. Each society has rules. You can see a wide variety of girls' lifestyles according to where they are from and where they live now* (a university student in an urban area).

Interview with Women Who Are Crossing

All BMB women's stories are different and unique in how they encounter God and what kind of difficulties they have gone through. All interviews were conducted in Arabic except for Latifa's. It took thirty minutes to over one hour to interview each woman. The questions focused on the hardest difficulties for themselves and other BMB women in Jordan rather than motives and experiences of their conversion. Some interviews were carried out by me alone, while others were with informants who introduced the interviewees to me and have a very close relationship with them. One interview was performed by a foreign female worker who studies the Bible with Mariyam. I was not with her when she was interviewed.

General Backgrounds of Interviewees

What follows is general background information for each BMB interviewee.

Table 2: Interview with BMB Women

Name (age)	Highest Education Level	Marital status	Social status/job	Years to believe	Time to adjust
Fatima (54)	University	Divorced	Ex-computer programmer, Housewife.	13 years	4–5 years
Hiyam (50s)	University	Unmarried	Non	5 years	3 years
Maha (72)	Elementary	Widowed	Non	10 years	5 years
Mariyam (50)	University	Divorced	Professional job	13 years	3 years
Ruqiya (20)	Secondary	Unmarried	Secretary	16 years	12 years*
Amal (60s)	9th grade	Divorced	Housewife	20 years	1 year
Aliya (50s)	9th grade	Unmarried	None	20 years	until present
Kaula (25)	10th grade	Married with a BMB	Ex-factory worker Housewife	5 years	1 Year
Latifa (25)	College	Married with a BMB	Housewife	17 years	4 Years
Khaldiye (51)	Secondary school	Married with a BMB	Housewife	37 years	14 years
Amani (33)	Secondary school	Remarried with a Christian	Employed	6 Years	one month

*Ruqiya became a BMB at the age of four years old when her parents became BMBs. She experienced the love of Jesus for herself in 2009.

Identity Crisis

Narratives[2]

Fatima[3]

Fatima grew up in an open-minded Muslim family. Many of her neighbors were Christians, and she played with Christian children when she was young. Because of her childhood memories, she did not have any negative feelings toward Christians. After she got married, she was not able to become pregnant for thirteen years. At that time she was working in a company. One day a Christian colleague at the company prayed for her to get pregnant, and then she had a dream in which a baby was coming from Jesus into her womb. She found out she was pregnant soon after. She became a Christian through this miracle.

In the past, she always had fear, in particular of death: "When am I going to die?" "Will I be in heaven then?" "What should I do to go to heaven?" She felt everyone who practiced Islamic activities was better than her. Secondly, as a women she always felt bound by society and people. In addition, as a mother she felt a heavy responsibility to take care of her children.

Now she finds peace inside herself. She knows where she is going not by outside influences like prayer or activities but inside herself by the work of Jesus Christ. Slowly she has increased in her faith in Jesus through the fellowship and Bible studies she has with a Christian helper. When she meets this person, the meeting place is far from her house, so even her neighbors don't know about her meeting.

She has believed in Jesus for thirteen years. When she first began to believe, it took four or five years to completely decide to follow Jesus. She felt fear. However, she didn't know why she felt fear at the beginning when she wanted to believe in Jesus. Furthermore, she also faced difficulties from her neighbors and the society. If she did not wear the *hijab*, and perform her religious duties, people would be suspicious of her. When she didn't use specific Islamic expressions in her speech, people asked her why she didn't say "*biismillahi arrahman* . . . [In the name of Allah, the merciful . . .]"[4]

---

2. I chose five interviews with six people to represent BMB women's situations.

3. Fatima, interviewed by author, Jordan, February 12, 2013.

4. People use many Islamic phrases frequently in their conversations. From my (the author's) experience in a language center of an Islamic university, a professor encourage us to say "*biismillahi* . . ." at the beginning of all activities such as reading the book, giving a presentation, and writing a composition.

Narratives of Banaat al Urdun (Daughters of Jordan)

> I never want to return to be a Muslim, but I fear my society. So I wear the hijab. The thing that upsets me is that I feel I say things that aren't true to my Muslim neighbors. I feel like I deny Christ. We are weak human beings like Peter who denied Jesus three times. I am not able to say the word "Jesus" in front of people, so I pray to Jesus to put a word in my mouth. I am afraid to say the word "Jesus." But when I die, I want to say "Jesus," so people can hear and know that I am a Christian.

Another difficulty she experiences is that nobody from her family knows about her faith. She cannot share even with her children, who are teenagers, because she is afraid that they will tell others about her sharing. However, the dilemma is she wants to talk about Jesus with people, sing hymns, and pray. She wants to share the gospel with her children in the future.

Amal and Aliya[5]

Amal and Aliya are sisters. Their family is very famous and considered a big Muslim family in Jordan. They also have six brothers. These two sisters have believed in Jesus because of a spiritual experience they had over twenty years ago. Aliya had a mental problem and there were many other family issues, so their family had a very difficult time.

> Evil attacked our family a lot. We felt like we were being chained with many chains. We didn't know anything about Christianity. We were like drowning people in the water and wanted to hold onto even a small thing to live. We wanted someone to free and save us. We thought we would go to hell if we stayed like this.

One of their brothers' wives practiced magic. The family believed that the magic brought many bad things and affected their family badly. They believed that the many broken engagements were caused by this. Therefore they went to many people to help them break free from these bondages, but it got worse and worse. They even tried putting charms from exorcists who could expel bad spirits on Aliya and the family, but nothing helped.

One day, a female Christian neighbor came to their house and saw Aliya's situation. Amal shared her family problem frankly with her and

---

5. Amal and Aliya, interviewed by the author, Jordan, February 26, 2013.

Identity Crisis

then this Christian woman suggested going to a conference at the church.[6] Because their mother knew of the bad situations, she allowed them to go to church. She thought that going to the church was like going to the supermarket and taking whatever they wanted. She figured that after the situation got better, they would stop going. She didn't think they would become Christians by going to church once. Their mother and younger brothers went to church with them. During the service, their younger brother's shoulder problem was healed, and Aliya was freed from spiritual weakness by prayer with the pastor. From these spiritual experiences, Amal and Aliya became Christians, but their mother and brother did not.

In the past, Amal said that she could not sleep well because of lots of worries both about the future and life concerns, but now she feels peace. She considered herself someone who did not know about anything and needed help from her father and brothers. Because only men have authority in the Islamic world, she had grown up being told that women did not know anything, could not do anything, and could not manage money and life issues by themselves. But she knows now that she is with Jesus and that he helps her to live and manage her life well. Aliya also said that she now has peace and joy from God since she has known Jesus and has the power of the Holy Spirit.

Although they felt freedom and peace when they prayed with the pastor and experienced rebirth with Jesus Christ, they needed time to have assurance of their new faith. Amal needed one year. In the case of Aliya, she had peace as soon as she prayed with the pastor, but she said that she still needed more assurance.

Satan was fighting against us, but we tried to hold on to Jesus (Amal).

After the pastor prayed for me, I felt peace, but this peace has come and gone. The change in my life happened in a very simple way, but

---

6. Amal and Aliya's family have two houses. One is in B where it is known that many Christians live. The other one is in Amman. They often stayed with their mother in the house in B because their father did not want to show his family problems to others in Amman. Up to this point, Amal and Aliya's family had not had any relationships with Christians. This Christian neighbor had a daughter who was working in a hair salon across the street from Amal and Aliya's house in B. When the neighbor's daughter went to work at the salon, she previously had to get there via a long way around. Amal and Aliya got to know her at the salon. So they opened their house to make a short cut for her. Because of this, they ended up becoming good friends which would have never happened before because of their different faiths.

> it is not complete. I want complete joy and power in my body from
> my heart (Aliya).

Both of them also feared persecution from their father and brothers and their paternal uncles, because their family is a very well-known *sheik* (elder in Islam) family. Their family members do not know about their new faith, except their mother, who noticed their faith. Although she did not become a Christian, she allowed them to read the Bible, pray, and go to the church. In Amal and Aliya's case, because they lived in a city far from where all the other family members lived in Amman, they could go to church and maintain their faith. Now that they are older mature women, they have more freedom to go wherever they want.

Mariyam[7]

Mariyam grew up with nine brothers and sisters. When she got married, she had a very difficult time. Her husband was not with her in the house because he travelled a lot. She had four young children, so she desperately needed help. When she asked for help, she saw visions on numerous occasions. Through this experience of seeing visions, she became a Christian in May 2000.

In the past she led a selfish life and did not care about others. She believed that the important things for a Muslim woman were only practicing religious activities, obeying her husband, and taking care of the children. After becoming a Christian, she has learned to love herself as a daughter of the Lord, and can also see inside people's heart and love them too. Now, her behavior is graced with wisdom and she speaks to people at work with both love and wisdom.

It took her three years to have full assurance in her new faith.

> Inside of me I had many thoughts—"You are a Muslim. How can you be a Christian?" I was confused a lot. However, every time God showed me and taught me how to become a believer. But I was confused a lot.

In spite of all kinds of confusion, she was able to overcome these questions, by God's grace and the Bible studies she had with good sisters who

---

7. Mariyam, interviewed by S. H., Jordan, February 19, 2013. Because of security, she did not want to be interviewed by the author. The author gave questions to S.H. and she asked the questions and recorded the answers.

had regular contact with her. Personally she noted that making the big decision to be a Christian is the most difficult thing a Muslim has to do in the conversion process.

> A Muslim woman never makes such a big decision by herself . . . She isn't allowed to have her own opinion. She has to ask her husband, brothers and father's opinion.

Another difficulty she acknowledges as a married woman is the relationship with her family. Because the husband controls everything at home, if she doesn't obey her husband, he will think she is a bad woman, even a sinner. If he knew of her change of religion, he would divorce her and she would lose her children. Moreover, if the children knew that their mother became a Christian, they wouldn't understand their mother's change. Because all people around them are Muslims in this Islamic society, they would consider her an *kafir* (infidel).

Latifa[8]

Latifa has a very unique family background in regards to her faith. She became a believer when she was eight years old because of one of her brothers. Her brother previously was a very sincere, strict Muslim. When he was young, he had seen some visions, but he did not understand what they meant. After meeting with other BMBs and foreign workers, he became a Christian. In her eyes, his life was totally changed after that conversion. When he was a Muslim, he seemed like he was living in a box. After he came to know Christ, it was as if his chains were broken. He also became a friend and like a father to Latifa. At that time, he was twenty-one years old. Because of his conversion, her mother at the age of fifty-one and two other sisters also became Christians.

Her mother's change also influenced her. Her parents were separated and her father left home when she was very young. Therefore, her mother was responsible for six daughters and two sons. Her mother was always angry and bitter because of what her husband had done to her life, and she could not forgive her husband. But when she turned to Jesus, she was able to forgive him. When she watched the film *The Passion of The Christ*, she pondered how Jesus forgave everyone including those who did very bad things and then declared her forgiveness for her husband.

8. Latifa, interviewed by the author, Jordan, March 14, 2013.

Narratives of Banaat al Urdun (Daughters of Jordan)

Another motivation to become a Christian for her was by comparing the lives of Muhammad and Jesus. She compared the views of Muhammad and Jesus on the topics of marriage, miracles, and death. She asked herself: why Muhammad married so many women; why he did not do any miracles; why Jesus died on the cross. These comparisons were needed to assure her that she was making the correct decision. Because of her brother's change and some other family members' conversions, she became a believer, but she only gained full assurance four years later in 2000. It took four years because it was acceptable to be a Christian in her home, but she had to pretend to be a Muslim in her elementary school.

> When I was young, I was very confused between home and school . . . My brother and sister took care of me as a believer. In contrast though, I went to Islamic public school and learned the Qur'an from school. I didn't know what I should follow. Sometimes when I talked with my teachers about something, the teachers asked me why I talked like this and where I got my ideas. Sometimes they told me I behaved like a Christian. I was very confused. So I prayed, "God, who are you?"

After experiencing the answer of prayer for her sister's pregnancy, she was assured that God answered her prayer. Her sister's miraculous pregnancy gave assurance for her, but not her sister. Her sister's reaction shows one of the difficulties a Muslim woman faces in their new journey.

> My sister knew that this was a miracle from Jesus, but was afraid of her husband, people close to her and the broader society. She didn't want to be someone different [from others]. So she blocked everything from us. She said that she does not want to hear anything about Jesus and she was happy with Islam. They [Muslims] do not think about eternal life, but just are afraid what would happen right now.

In the past, when Latifa was watching TV, she wondered how Christian women could do certain things, such as drinking, inappropriate sexual behavior, and wearing revealing clothes while wearing the cross as a necklace. She thought that the media gives a bad impression of Christians.

She also thought she herself was useless. Because even though she was young, she knew that living as a Muslim girl in this community, she could not do anything.

Identity Crisis

> You cannot live according to who you are if you are a Muslim woman. People want to use you and not treat you as who you are. Women are not valued here.

But now she has confidence in her life and herself, because she knows that she can do anything in Jesus Christ (Phil 4:13). The most difficult thing for Muslim women, Latifa mentioned, is making a decision (the turning point) on whether to be a Christian or not. Muslim women never make major decisions, so they believe they cannot make a decision about faith matters without asking their family members. Furthermore, when the family knows of their faith, they go through much more difficulties than men. Latifa thinks that men would not find it as difficult as women. She stated that, for men everything is easier than for women. A man can even leave his family to look for a place to live, but a woman cannot.

She believes there is a tendency in new believers to want to go back to Islam and try to be close to Islam in order to prove to themselves that Islam is right and their thoughts or interests in Christianity were wrong. Finally some will be assured that Islam is wrong and Christianity has truth, but others will fail to return to their new faith and continued to follow Islam.

> I see that many people at the beginning of inquiring about Christ have a lot of confusions. They want to go more towards Islam in order to try and justify that Islam is true. Even if they never went to the Mosque before, they now go. Many people start wearing the hijab even if they didn't do it in the past. My friend went to the Mosque and started wearing the hijab until she felt assured about following Jesus.

On the other hand, because her husband also is a BMB, they have difficulty raising their children as Christians.[9] They also struggle to mix with Jordanian Christians from a Christian background at the church where they attend. Many people at the church do not know that her family members are all Muslims officially.

> Here living with Christians is also difficult. People who know our background, they always look at me as a second-class Christian. They are the first class in their thoughts and are afraid of us. I don't know why they are afraid. They are always talking about us. For me my role is to just love them. The problem is for them. Actually it is not secure for us to be talked about by people. I can trust some

9. Both of them are BMBs, so their children are officially Muslims.

people and share everything with them, but some people do not want to talk with me or to come to me.

Although BMB women go past the first stage of questioning about who they are as Muslims, they still have to face another stage of asking who they are as BMBs.

Hiyam[10]

Hiyam's family roots are Circassian from Russia.[11] After coming to Jordan, the entire Circassian community became Muslims. Although her family roots are Christians, she had no knowledge of Christianity until she became a Christian herself. In fact previously she was not pleased with Christianity and did not like Christianity. For instance, she believed that divorced Christian women should not remarry. She thought that the problem of the women's desire could not be solved in Christianity, but Islam successfully solved this problem. She also perceived Christianity as only dealing with externals of one's life and not dealing with the inside of one's self and one's cleanliness.

She described her life before encountering Jesus that she was lost. Although she was rich and had everything, she was not happy and felt empty. She was always afraid of her future and worried about tomorrow that she would possibly hear bad news that someone important to her had died. She became a believer during the period from the end of 2007 and mid-2008, but was only sure of her new faith in 2011.

She had lived a stressful life from family and personal problems. One day, she felt a deep hole in her heart. In the night, she prayed to Allah, "if you want me to do more religious activities, I will. But give me a sign. I don't have peace." She wanted to hear God's voice, and she did not want it to be her own imagination or that she was persuading herself. When she prayed to ask Allah to show her a sign, she remembered her sins. She asked Allah, "What kind of prayer did I say to make me remember these things?" Then

---

10. Hiyam, interviewed by the author, Jordan, February 12, 2013.

11. The Circassians were Christian when they lived in their home country in the mid-1800s. There were great territorial wars between Russia, Persia, and Turkey. "The Circassians carried out a notably fierce and protracted resistance to Russian domination, and when they were finally defeated in 1864, some 400,000 among them—almost the entire population—chose to emigrate rather than to live in subjection" (S.v. "Circassian," http://www.britannica.com/EBchecked/topic/118238/Circassian).

she kept praying for Allah to answer her questions. After praying to Allah, she fell asleep and dreamed. In her dream, a Latin priest was standing at the door of her house and said, "The Messiah died in an accident." At that time, she didn't know anything about Christianity at all and did not know any Christians personally. When she heard this in the dream, she felt love and cried a lot as if she had known him for a long time. She knew of Jesus only in the Qur'an and didn't know his love at all. So she did not understand why she cried. When she awoke, she asked Allah what the relationship was between her dream and her questions to Allah. Then she came to the priest. He told her dreaming of Jesus is good, but he didn't tell her to read the Bible or anything, because she was a Muslim. She asked other foreign friends about her dream. But nobody answered her quite correctly. After six months, she understood the dream was about Jesus. She started to read the Qur'an about Jesus Christ a lot for one week, but it was not enough for her. During that time, she was going to a foreign language center and had made some foreign friends. One of these new friends gave her a Bible. When she read the Bible, she was very happy. She understood the Old Testament. She felt like she was living in the prophets' times. It was similar to the Qur'an, but the stories in the Qur'an are shorter and the Bible gives more details. When she read the story of the prophets in the Bible, she felt that she was like them in the story, but when she read about Muhammad in the Qur'an, she did not feel anything.

Then in the New Testament, she quit reading because of the verse "If your right eye causes you to sin, gouge it out and throw it away" (Matt 5:29). She did not like the Bible anymore. Later, she told her friend that she wasn't going to read the New Testament anymore. The next day, her friend came to her and read the story of Jesus meeting the Samaritan woman in the gospel of John. At that point, she felt she was like the Samaritan woman.

> I felt something inside of me. I said to her, "I want this water now!" . . . Even my friend told me it was very dangerous to believe in Jesus as a Muslim. She asked me, "Are you sure?" I really wanted it and answered "Yes!" Then I felt peace. I was with Jesus at 12 o'clock noon like the Samaritan women was at the well. I became crazy about Jesus, and prayed all the time. I wanted to scream out through the window that I have Jesus . . . Now I do not have any fear of death. I even want to die to see Jesus. All things from God are acceptable. I pray that God gives me power if there is any temptation, because I am a weak person.

Although she had great joy and peace, at the same time, she had a hard time deciding between Islam and Christianity. She wanted to know where the Qur'an came from. She decided to search to find out. After reading some books that explained the origin of the Qur'an, she realized that Islam is made by humans, and came after Christianity. Another point that helped her to be sure of her faith was a healing experience she had in 2011. She had severe chronic pains in 2009. For a long time, she had suffered from it and could not walk well. But one day she dreamed of Jesus and hugged him. The next day she realized the severe back pain was gone. This spiritual experience through dreaming made her have a strong faith in Jesus.

Interview with Women Workers

Interviews with Christian women workers were conducted to get general observations about the lives of both Muslim women and BMB women. The general questions I asked Muslim women and BMBs were repeated, such as a description of the general life of Jordanian women, self-understanding of Muslim women's identity, hindrances and difficulties of BMB women and the general image of Christians among Muslims. Their experiences of working with BMB women in Jordan show features of the life of Jordanian women.

S. H. (60s)[12]

S. H. has been in Jordan for thirty-nine years. She has been involved in BMB discipling with her husband for twenty-five years. Over all these years she has discipled five or six BMBs, including men, in her fellowship. She has noticed that Jordan has lately become more influenced by Islamic revivalism. According to her, when they came to Jordan, the population of Christians was approximately 10 percent; however, it has decreased to only 2 percent. In addition, at the beginning of her time in Jordan only around 25 percent of the Muslim women wore the hijab, but now almost 90 percent of Muslim women wear it. Because of problems of leadership and politics of Jordan, Islam has emerged as the solution for political problems and Western colonization.

12. S. H. interviewed by the author, Jordan, February 25, 2013.

Identity Crisis

Regarding Muslim women's self-understanding, she has observed that Jordanian Muslim women value outward appearances, and they are disciplined to always be ready to serve the male family members. According to the Qur'an, Muslim women are mandated to bring children up as good Muslims and form a good home. Therefore, a woman is the one responsible for modesty and takes charge of the home. If the family and her home are not going well, she is usually blamed. She is a mother and the caretaker of the house; these are her main identities.

> To see themselves for who they are is difficult for Muslim women. They don't have any idea who they are [how valuable they are and how to exercise their rights]. Self-examination for Arab women is rare. They need to look at the choices they choose although they are very limited.

She also agrees with the fact that making the decision to cross over to Christianity is the most difficult thing for BMB women. She understands that Jordanian women are living under the shelter of their fathers, husbands, or brothers.

> Making the decision is the most difficult. It is very big for them. Their decision will also have an effect on their future. This kind of fear to decide such a big question is not normal for them.

Another difficulty she stated are the limits of women's life in Jordan. If she remains single, whether unmarried or divorced, her father, brother, and uncles will forbid her to live freely and basically control everything. Or if she is married, because of the apostasy law, when she changes her religion her marriage is dissolved and then she will lose her children. She also mentioned the power of the extended family over women, in particular paternal uncles.

> In general, if a woman wants a divorce and to go back to her family, uncles sometimes force her to stay in the marriage. They do not want to take financial responsibility . . . Honor killing is encouraged or done by her uncles to keep their family honor.

Therefore, fear of family is the main difficulty. In addition, even though she becomes a BMB, her identity card says that she is still a Muslim. Inside of her heart, however, she is a Christian. That also makes her confused at the beginning stage of her new faith.

Narratives of Banaat al Urdun (Daughters of Jordan)

She believes that the image Muslims have of Christians is generally negative. Muslims look at the outward appearances. They look at a Christian woman's clothing (provocative dress) and think that Christian women are not modest and not as careful as Muslim women. Furthermore, S. H. pointed out the suspicious attitudes of Christians toward BMBs in Jordan.

> Many Arab Christians are wary because they see many bad things done by Muslims. So most Christians I know are quite suspicious. So I need to advocate for BMBs sometimes.

A. H. (80s)[13]

She came to the Middle East in 1955 and has been in Jordan since 1964. She has worked mainly with Bedouin women and village women. She has been able to see hundreds of women becoming believers over fifty years of her ministry.

She thinks that the general lives of Jordanian women now are so different from how they used to be. They are much more educated now than before. For women living in Jordan it is difficult. In particular, the Bedouin women work physically harder than other women to take care of not only the family, but also the herds of goats or sheep.

She understands that a Muslim woman's self-understanding is decided by having a son, and taking care of her husband and family. Therefore, most women's lives are completely dependent on their husbands for theprovision of food, especially among the Bedouins.

> A wife and mother is the reason why they are here. In the badiya [desert], they [women] sacrifice their own desires and give their lives for their family. They [women] don't have their own life. They belong to their husband and elder sons. But educated girls' lives will be changed in the future.

She also points out that making a decision is the most difficult thing for BMB women.

> They are not allowed to make a decision as a woman. Husband and adult sons make decisions for them.

---

13. A. H., interviewed by the author, Jordan, March 4, 2013.

Identity Crisis

And the fear of being cut off from the family is the largest reason which makes it difficult for them to decide. After becoming a Christian, loneliness is also a big problem for BMB women. One BMB lady she knew once told her that she returned to Islam saying:

> I have nobody to talk and encourage me. But God knows my heart.
> I will be with you when you go to heaven.

She anticipates that there are many unknown believers among Muslim women. She states that nowadays many people are Muslim culturally rather than religiously. She has observed many people who introduce themselves as Muslims but are not religious.

The image of Christians, she feels, has become worse. According to her, in her early days even nominal Christians were respected. But the way of some Christians who eat pork, drink alcohol, and women wearing immodest clothing have given many Muslims a bad impression about Christians.

I. H. (40s)[14]

I. H. is a Jordanian worker from a Christian background. She started to share with Muslim friends and Muslim women in 1997. Since then, seven or eight women have come to her and have been discipled.

Regarding the general life of Jordanian women, she emphasized that there are multiple types of lifestyles in Jordan. In her opinion, if a woman has a degree in a university and works, she can be more independent in reality. But generally speaking, Muslim women need to serve men at home and in the society. They cannot make decisions for themselves. Men always make decisions for them. For Muslim women to be honorable in front of the people and to have peaceful lives are very important. Being a wife and mother is their main identity. In this vein, single women have less value than married women, and married women who have children are more valued than married women without children.

The difficulty of BMBs, she stated, is a lack of Christian BMB community and the limits which bound Jordanian women's lives.

14. I. H., interviewed by author, Jordan, March 6, 2013.

> BMB women cannot talk about it and always hide it ... They don't have freedom to go out and to contact Christians to grow in their faith. A man has much more freedom to go out and meet freely. The family usually requires the wife or daughter to know where she goes, whom she meets and what time she returns home ... Because of limited spiritual follow-up situations, they [BMBs] do not eat a consistent diet of good spiritual food. They cannot provide spiritual food for themselves at the beginning. Christian women can go to the meeting and read the Bible freely. Muslim women cannot be free, because they are watched [by their family].

Regarding the image of Christian women in Jordan, Muslims think that Christian women are free and can do whatever they want. Muslims also think that Christian women rebel against their menfolk and disagree with them. Christian women are considered to have no manners, because they wear provocative clothes and have the freedom to do wrong doings, unlike Muslim women.

M. H. (50s)[15]

For twenty-five years M. H. has been involved with BMB women's groups or with their husbands in BMB ministries. She has been in regular contact with three families and several single women, but the total number throughout those years was less than ten.

She observed that Jordanian women's identities are determined by their homemaking skills, as well as fathers, husbands, and children. She narrated an episode of what she experienced from her neighbors. When her neighbor asked what she had done that day, she meant what she had cooked. By and large, Muslim women are good mothers and give everything to their family. Therefore, individuality is not a big concept here. She noticed that even women don't want to be alone. Being alone is not something they desire.

She described the difficulties of becoming a BMB for women as being the lack of freedom of women and of thinking for themselves. She believes that those three BMB women who she was in contact with have kept their faith because their husbands are BMBs. Individually, Muslim women cannot make decisions and only are allowed to follow the decisions of their husbands. In addition, women do not question their identity, because it

---

15. M. H., interviewed by the author, Jordan, March 12, 2013.

Identity Crisis

is not allowed. Basically, their identity is already set by the culture. It is not deemed necessary to think about it by the women themselves. She also indicated that the feeling of pressure inside BMB women and having no support or encouragement from outsiders makes it hard for them to maintain their beliefs at the initial stage as a new believer.

5

Analysis

In chapter 4, I discussed the foundations of Jordanian Muslim women's identities, and the difficulties BMB women face in the process of their conversion based on my interviews with women from both groups. The narratives of BMB women showed that they had already struggled emotionally, psychologically, and religiously before exposing their new faith to others. This chapter will discuss findings from the interviews and the reasons for identity crises when Jordanian BMB women seek a new faith, based on the research theories mentioned in chapter 1.

Josselson defines an identity crisis as a realization that "we do not have to continue to be as we have been; we consider revisions and try out our new possibilities on others to discover their reactions."[1] Islam for Muslims is not one sect of religion but "a quality in some men's heart."[2] When a Muslim woman changes her faith, she realizes that her values and traditions that are parts of her identity and life from birth, no longer work. Furthermore, she finds out that some of these elements are denied in order to have a new faith.

Karin Willemse describes the identities of women in Islam as "restricted and limited by normative dominant discourses."[3] Jordanian BMB women also have constructed their identities within these boundaries. In psychodynamic terms identity is not a fixed structure, but "a property of the ego

---

1. Josselson, *Finding Herself*, 13.
2. Smith, *The Meaning*, 124–25.
3. Willemse, *One Foot*, 44.

that organizes experience."[4] Conversion also brings many transformations in one's life on the social, psychological, and cultural levels.[5] The converts encounter new ways of relating to people and the wider community, of "seeing and feeling about themselves," of "integrating their new beliefs into their personal lives," and of "living in the world where they have belonged for all their lives."[6] When they enter the new realm of Christianity, coming from their familiar Islamic religious and sociocultural realm, they face feelings of strangeness and confusion from the new experiences happening inside of them. Jordanian BMB women, therefore, face challenges on whole aspects of their self-understanding.

Findings from Interview

Findings from Interviews with Muslim Women
Fixed and Required Identity of Women

Most Muslim women had a clearer understanding of who they should be rather than who they are. All interviewees recognized their identities as being a good wife and mother. If she is not married, she should be a good daughter at her home. At the same time, she knew what kind of self-identity she should have. Many of their answers were quite similar in the questions about the general life of women and the ideal Muslim women, sometimes repeating the same answers. It shows how religious identity of women in the formation of identity is very powerful to Jordanian Muslim women.

> *It is different according to each woman's situation, but for Muslims and even Christians, success of marriage is important. According to her situation and circumstances, some families prepare her for marriage and train her in culture and knowledge to be a good woman* (a working woman in a village).

> *Many families say that women have only two things to do: to satisfy herself [by keeping her honor] (working or not working) and to take care of her husband and children* (a working woman in a village).

> *My family says that I should be educated to take care of my home. I am ready to work at home and I have to be ready to take care of*

---

4. Josselson, *Finding Herself*, 12.
5. Hiebert, "Worldview," 24.
6. Ibid.

husband. I have to learn the relationship between men and women, so I want to read books about them (a working woman in a village).

According to Arab tradition, even though she goes to university and her education level is high, she has to know how to take care her family (a working woman in a village).

Family, being the basis of women's lives, is where they construct their identities. Since there is a strong tendency of communal perspectives of identity, obedience and harmony with family members are critical for women. Therefore, their understanding of a good woman's characteristics and the concept of honor and shame are related to external acts and this keeps her and her family's honor.

Ayeb [Shame] means doing wrong things such as walking with men. My father and brother would be angry and kill me [if I did that] (a girl in a village).

Ayeb is not to obey one's family (an unemployed girl in a village).

[I must] obey [my] husband because if I obey him, it is the same as obeying Allah. Through my obedience to my husband, I achieve my obedience to Allah . . . I may have all the features of a Muslim, but if I do not obey my family and husband, it's worth nothing (a working woman in a village).

My life is mine from Allah. But we should ask our father's opinion (an unemployed girl in a village).

If I don't reply when my family speaks, it is ayeb. Allah prevents us from acting like this because it is haram [not allowed thing]. We should obey our parents in everything [according to Allah] (an unemployed girl in a village).

Beauty is very important. Women want to be attractive, because we have to look at each other such as our friends and other people. I do not think that this should be the aim, but people still seek to look beautiful (an employed woman in an urban area).

The Power of Tradition according to the Area Where They Live

Most women are influenced strongly by the place where they live. The level of education challenges their thoughts, but the traditions of the place where they live are more powerful than individual education or beliefs. Cultural traditions and the general thoughts of people in Jordan have a clear distinction according to where they live. Women who live in rural areas and deserts have very similar ideas about women's lives. For them, being a good mother and wife is the most basic and important role for a woman. Many of them do not mention any other role of women at all. When I asked their opinions about the topic of working outside, most of them answered that it was not important.

> *Going to the store by herself is not good. She should be with her husband or her boys* (a housewife in a village).
>
> *I am afraid to go alone to the market or any other place* (a Bedouin).
>
> *The standard is our tradition not religion. Ayeb and the wrong things are the same for Muslims and Christians* (a working woman in a village).

In the urban areas, women have stated the importance of working outside for women's lives. Many women mentioned of the importance of education for women. Nevertheless, they still had the same thought that even though working outside is important for women to self-development and financial help for their family; women have rules to follow according to the Qur'an and the society.

Creating Negotiated Identity

When Muslim women in the young generation answer the questions, "boundary" is the most repeated word from their descriptions. They recognized the lines they cannot cross and the limits of shaping their own identities, because they are aware of the reality of the society in which they live. Many of them enjoy their freedom within these religious and traditional borders. Some mentioned the equality between men and women in the society and the high social status of women. At the same time, some of them described Jordanian society as a male dominated one. One even said women do not have rights to decide things in their own lives.

> *Most Muslim women can do anything but within the boundaries of Islam* (a university student in an urban area).
>
> *Men control everything and decide whatever they want. They do not let the mother make decisions for boys but only girls according to the families* (a working woman in a village).

She doesn't have a right to decide . . . Men are always higher and make decisions for her (a working woman in a village).

In the interviews, those in the young adult generation, in particular, were somewhat rebellious in regards to following social customs without question. They understood who they were and that they wanted to achieve something for their own lives. They fully understood the conservative traditions and customs regarding women, so they tried to make a balance between the traditions and their own wishes. They have begun to understand themselves as independent beings. The reward of their obedience and good behavior has been freedom in what they want to do or have.

If I obey my family well, then I can do what I want. I am the first nurse in my village. Because my behavior is good, my family has allowed me to study nursing and to work. My uncles didn't like me studying nursing and told my father that I would have night duties and would need to sleep outside of the home [if I became a nurse]. My father, however, told them that he knew how he had raised me and my behavior had been good (a working woman in village).

I have many things I want to do, but my father and brother have objected already. I want to go to university and buy a car. I have to gain their trust. If they don't trust me, they won't give me freedom (a girl in a village).

Religion and customs are mixed in regards to honor and shame. One should follow the traditions. Respect your husband, and do whatever Islam asks you to do (a university student in an urban area).

I cannot do whatever I want to do. I am a girl. There are limits for girls and I don't have a right to do what I want. I don't want to follow all the rules. However, other people do not understand you when you are educated and they or their family are not. I simply want a balance between what they want and I want. I do what they want me to do and then tell them what I want (a university student in an urban area).

The Power of New Era and Education

With modernity, the power of education has increased for Jordanian women, in particular for the young generation. In the past, and even today among Bedouins, some women have not been able to read at all or have only gone to elementary school. Women, however, want to learn and develop themselves. Furthermore, most of the young adult generation recognizes that education is very important to acquire strength and ability. Many of the young generation want to complete their tertiary level of education and to get some certificates in specific areas, because in many places women have only been able to finish secondary school level. One mentioned that education and certificates are weapons for women to survive in the male society.

> *Education and certification are women's weapons, especially in Arab society* (a university student in an urban area).

> *But we don't study at all and we are like blind people. Our family did not let me study and work outside at all. Our family is ignorant. I don't even know how to read any Arabic letters. I do not understand at all* (a Bedouin).

> *We have to change the thinking about family and traditions. We are required to work together. But I don't know how to do it. We don't have enough strength to say "No" when our family asks us to do something. Education gives us strength and it is a main source to help us gain freedom of mind and physical freedom. Without education, women cannot work* (a university student in an urban area).

> *Now that we are educated more, women have more freedom . . . A long time ago, the aim for life was being a wife and a mother because this brought safety for their lives. Now there is a big difference. A certificate from the university is your life. Of course family is still important. If you have a certificate, you can work and it brings safety for you whatever happens in your future* (an employed woman in an urban area).

In particular, women in urban areas and among the young adult generation are beginning to have new ideas about what an ideal Muslim woman looks like and the concept of honor and shame in today's society. One woman answered that honor is to keep her words and not to lie. This view of honor and shame is more internal, in contrast to the more external views of the past where, for example, it was shameful for women to be seen talking to strange men. This change in thinking is evolving now with the new generation.

> *In the past the life of a woman was difficult. She had to work hard to help her husband. Now the society, in regards to the economy and*

politics, is open. It's not like it was in the past (a university student in an urban area).

Ideal Muslim women must follow the religious duties. What Allah asks us to do is to be the best human beings. [Ideal Muslim women] follow what Allah said and Muhammad said. But many women don't want to hear "do this and do this." Our problem is that we don't do what we should do (a working woman in an urban area).

The concept of shame has changed. In the past it was a shame to talk loudly in front of your parents. Many things were shameful. But now even the meaning is different and not many things are shameful. Honor is to keep your word and not to lie, but some people think differently (a working woman in an urban area).

Findings from Interviews with BMB Women and Workers with BMBs

Difficult Adjustments at the Beginning

Most of the BMB women I interviewed have gone through difficulties at the beginning stage of new faith. In particular, when BMB women decided on being Christians, they struggled inside with how radical a change it would be. On average, it takes four or five years for them to be totally assured in their new faith. During that time, diverse phenomena happened inside of them. Some returned to Islam and then some came back again to their new faith. Some suffered from guilty feelings and fear without specific reasons.

Inside of me I had many thoughts:"You are a Muslim. How can you be a Christian?" I was confused a lot (Mariyam).

I was very confused between home and school . . . I saw that many people at the beginning of inquiring about Christ have a lot of uncertainty. They wanted to go back to Islam and tried to prove that Islam was true because of their confusion (Latifa).

It took four or five years for me to decide to follow Jesus because of fear. I didn't know why I felt fear. Then everything became clear. I believed in Jesus, and there is no fear now. But still [growing in my faith is] slowly, slowly (Fatima).

Identity Crisis

> *After believing [Jesus], I had a hard time between Islam and Christianity. So I wanted to find out where the Qur'an came from. I then decided to search for some answers* (Hiyam).

In another aspect, the fact that women cannot easily share their new faith with their family members or other people also gives them emotional difficulties.

> *The thing that upsets me is that I feel like I say things to my Muslim neighbors that aren't true . . . I feel like I deny Christ* (Marwaha).

Difficulties As Women

The cultural and social situations of Jordan cause many BMB women to have many difficulties as women according to the interviews. For instance, wherever women go out, they have to report to their family where they are going. Ordinarilly interviewees pointed out that women have a lower status than men and have restrictions on their freedom because of the social customs and traditions.

> *I have fear because of my family. They would kick me out, and I would have to leave my home. I cannot stay with my family if they found out my faith. One of my friends hid the Bible in the bottom of her knitting bag. So when she works out, she brings it and reads it outside, because if her family knows about her faith, she will die* (Khaldiye).

> *How can she study the Bible? If her house is small, her family is in her house and there is no [private] space for her. How does she go to church? She has to report wherever she goes every time to her family. The woman is also responsible for her children and house chores and so on* (Hiyam).

> *The society here is male dominated. Boys can do anything but girls stay at home and there is nothing she can do. She is from the Islamic culture. A woman is nothing in Islam. She has to stay at home and obey male members whatever they want. She cannot have her own faith, opinion and ideas. It is difficult for her to make a decision different from the society, extended family, and friends* (Marwaha).

> *Men have authority in this society. They always said that if they don't allow you, you can't do anything. You don't know. Men can*

do everything, but not women. Women cannot manage their lives. There is no freedom for women (Amal).

New Identity of BMB Women

Most interviewees had clear changes of understanding of themselves as women. In their personal lives, they perceived they changed from darkness, binding, and oppression to freedom, self-love and confidence in self. Two of them shared the same verse of Phil 4:13: "I can do everything through Him who gives me strength." Both of them said that it was difficult for them to understand the first time when they read it, but after some time, they could apply this verse to themselves. Previously, they had thought of themselves very negatively, but after the conversion, they loved themselves and recognized themselves as strong beings with Jesus.

> *You cannot live according to who you are . . . It took many years to look at myself. I thought that I could not do anything and I was weak. But now I discovered that I can do everything in Jesus. I am not a weak person because of God. He strengthens me and gives me power. I look at myself as of great value. God created me not by chance, but he has a purpose and a plan for my life* (Latifa).

> *My brother told me that I could not do anything and didn't know anything . . . In the past, I was ignorant and didn't know anything. I was lost. After I believed in Jesus, I know what is right and wrong for treatment of me as a woman and now I even know how to lead other people* (Amal).

> *I love myself now as a daughter of the Lord* (Mariyam).

> *My life is changed. Now I know who will help me. Now I do not tell lies anymore and I do not hate anyone . . . I didn't know anything, but now I know everything. I am walking a straight path with God. Now I am with Jesus and I experience peace with Him in my heart* (Aliya).

> *I experienced big differences. There was no hope when I was Muslim, but I have hope in me now. All things from God are acceptable. I am a weak human. I want to love myself and to stay with Jesus* (Hiyam).

> *Yes, there is a big difference. I feel freedom from society. As women, we are always bound. Phil 4:13 was not encouraging before, but now*

Identity Crisis

> it is a very influential verse in my life. I was so weak and scared. But with Jesus, I can do anything in my life (Fatima).

> I am worthy to God, and if I want to do anything, I can ask God for what I want. He lightened my mind and thoughts. He opened my eyes and my life became beautiful. In the beginning, there was no meaning in my life. After accepting Jesus there is meaning in my life (Khaldiye).

Common Experiences

SPIRITUAL EXPERIENCES: DREAMS AND VISIONS

It is a very well-known fact that many Muslims have dreamed of Jesus or received spiritual guidance in dreams that led them to seek Jesus. Through the interviews, I found out that many of their dreams were similar to the stories of the Bible and in some cases, brought healing. This is a critical way to listen to the voice of God, about where to go and what to do, and the dreams have even given assurances in helping BMBs adjust to their new faith at the beginning stage. Their prayers are often answered by dreams when asking for direction from God.

> That night I dreamed. In my dream, I was looking at the sky. Jesus was coming from the sky slowly. I hugged and kissed him. I asked him "What is this love and greatness with you?" Jesus was wearing a white dress and looked like he was in his 30s. The next day I was completely healed from my back and leg pain. I could walk well (Hiyam).

INDEPENDENT LIFESTYLE

Most of the women in my research are divorced, never married, or widows. If she has a husband, her husband lives abroad to work, or her husband became a believer before she became a believer. It shows how difficult it is for Muslim women to keep their new faith under normal family conditions. In contrast to other Muslim women who live under many family influences, they have freedom.

In addition, when women become older, they gain a higher status than when they were young in family. When their parents pass away and the male family members have their own families, they intervene less in women siblings' lives.

Questions about High Contextualization Related to Identity of BMB Women

Some people believe in Jesus secretly, introduce themselves as Muslim, but continue all their Islamic duties (C5 or C6). This is prevalent in some South Asian Muslim countries and many become "followers of Isa." In Jordan, BMB women I interviewed see that this kind of high contextualization causes more confusion in their identity..

> It is like they [C5 or C6] have two faces and put one leg here and one on the other side. This is confusing. For me it is weird. This is not good for me. Some people are afraid to be killed... In the Bible, Jesus says, "If you don't witness about me, I don't know you." It's a very clear idea of faith and it's completely different from what people have (Latifa).

> When I heard about them [C5 or C6], it is difficult for me to understand them. In the Bible, every tongue and every tribe confess that Jesus is the Lord of Lords... But I love them and try to accept them, because God's thoughts are much higher than ours (Amani).

Many of the BMB interviewees have a clear understanding of the differences between Islamic and Christian beliefs such as the Trinity, the redeeming work of Jesus, the wrong teachings of Muhammad and so on. All of them distinguish between Muslim and Christian respectively, and think that they are Christians and followers of Jesus. These interviewees have successfully adjusted to their faith. What this also means, though, is if a BMB does not have a clear identity between Islam and Christianity, they would not keep their new faith, because it causes much confusion. Kraft finds the same tendency among her interviewees of BMBs in Egypt and Lebanon towards C5 or C6 believers: "They [BMBs] are troubled with the conception of "High level of contextualized converts... They worry that those individuals have not experienced a full turning of the heart, which seems to necessarily entail a rejection of Islam."[7]

---

7. Kraft, *Searching for Heaven*, 101.

Identity Crisis

Analysis

Challenges of Discontinuity from the Past and Resistance to the New

When BMB women convert to Christianity, they face discontinuity from their acquired Islamic cultural heritage. They have to change from their old Islamic views to new Christian beliefs, and feel emotional conflict because of the differences in religious beliefs, rituals, and practices, as well as cultural clashes between Arab values and foreign Western values. Furthermore, although they seem to separate from the old and build new things, they construct new selves on top of their old selves.[8] They often have tensions between their old selves and their old beliefs and their new selves and their new beliefs.[9] Thus, as Bauman states, identity has emerged as an important subject for BMBs at the beginning stages, because they are confused as to where they belong.

> One thinks of identity whenever one is not sure of where one belongs; that is, one is not sure how to place oneself among the evident variety of behavioral styles and patterns, and how to make sure that people around would accept this placement as right and proper, so that both sides would know how to go on in each other's presence.[10]

---

8. Speelman, "Continuity," 304.
9. Rambo and Farhadian, " Converting," 40.
10. Bauman, "From Pilgrim," 19.

Table 3: Jordanian BMB Women's Theories and Challenges to Form a New Identity[11]

Theories (theorists claimed)	General challenges of Jordanian BMB women
Transitional States (Baumann, Castells)	Standing between traditionalism and modernism
Dis-Continuity — Change of religion, and Woman (Islamic literatures, Rambo, Leone, Spleeman, Josellson)	Traditional and religious concept of ideal women and women's life
Collectivity (Triandis, Gregg)	Social value of oneness from *ummah* Arab cultural value of family and tribe
Resistance — Resistance from new (Castells, Rambo)	Conception of Christianity as foreign and Western religion; Immoral image of Christians

11. These tables are explanations of how the theories I mentioned in chapter 1 apply to Jordanian BMB women in regards to their identity formation.

Table 4: Jordanian BMB Women's Challenges to Create a New Identity

Jordanian BMB Women's Identity	
Old—identity of Jordanian BMB women	New—identity challenged to create
Fixed and required identity	Negotiated and flexible identity
Dependent identity	Independent identity
Uniformed identity	Integrated identity

Transitional States between "Global Flow" and "Cultural Closure"

Jordanian women's milieus have been affected from primordialism to postmodernism, from traditional societies to high technology, and from Islamism to secularism, concurrently. This means that they face multifaceted situations in ontological, cognitive, and phenomenological aspects. Emphasis on Islamic identity makes people and society conform to Muslim values.[12] For Jordanian women, Islam and tradition are critical elements to building their identity. For hundreds of years, Muslim women have not been able to define their own identities independently or freely and have not been agents of social change in society.[13] Traditional values and social restrictions for women are still strongly practiced in women's lives. In daily lifestyles, women are instructed to be careful what they wear, report where they go and who they meet and so on. They must also speak quietly. All of their lives are under the supervision of family and society.

Furthermore, as noticed from the interviews, the legal milieus of women's situations are still tightly bounded to a hierarchical, social system.

> *Because of wars and difficult situations, only my brothers could study, but my sisters and I could not. We only studied until the third grade of school. My parents and brothers said that because we are girls, that was enough . . . My father who had a lot of land, didn't leave any inheritance to my sister or me, and wrote only my brothers' names on the document. My mother wanted to give part of the monetary inheritance to us girls, but she was scared of her sons and*

12. Abu-Lughod, *Veiled Sentiments*, xiii.
13. Sharify-Funk, *Encountering*, 134.

> husband. She also wanted to give some land to my sister or me but she was afraid. My brother told my mother that if she gave the land to my sister or me, my divorced husband would come back and take the land from me . . . After all the discussion, my mother gave the lands to my sister and me. We sold the land and put the money in the bank. But our brothers were angry and asked how we could have money, when we cannot even manage our lives. So one day my six brothers came to us, hit us, and took away our money (Amal and Aliya).

Sharify-Funk also points out a gap between the law and the reality of women's right in Islamic societies. She affirms that even though officially women's rights are guaranteed, its application is often the opposite.

> Governmental proclamations in support of women's rights often appear quite ironic when actual practices and social conditions are taken into account. Contradictions between word and deed are especially evident in Muslim-majority states, where claims to support reforms providing 'equal treatment for women' contrast unfavorably with conditions . . .[14]

On the other hand, modern and postmodern ideas from Western influences have an effect on women these days. Finding one's identity has become a problem for today's Muslim.[15] The emergence of the middle class is presently an agency of new social change in Jordan. This middle class is more influenced by secularism and challenges traditional values.[16] Sharify-Funk uses "civil society" as an example of this middle class activity.

> If traditional Muslim society generated and legitimated social norms through the agency of the *'ulama* [Scholars of Islam] and their relationship with the Muslim state, contemporary Muslim societies are increasingly debating the legitimacy of social norms and political institutions within the context of an expanded "civil society"(in Arabic, *mujtama al-madani*).[17]

Contemporary Muslim intellectualism also contributes to create polarized perspectives among Jordanian society. The middle class face two worldviews: the "traditional/religious" worldview which is a past-oriented system emphasizing Islamic authority and traditions, and the "modernist/

---

14. Ibid., 10.
15. Anderson, *Identity*, 6.
16. Halpern, *The Politics*, summary-A.
17. Ibid., 117.

secular" world view which is a future-oriented system seeking to re-conceptualize Islamic value and tradition for modern days.[18] Therefore, individual achievement and educational credentials become the critical foundations of personal identity, and people have recognized that "identity and value are constructed rather than inherited or revealed."[19]

Regarding the influence of postmodernism on Jordanian women's identity, it is easy to think that Middle Eastern societies are not yet postmodern, because postmodern is often understood as a Western concept. In fact, many Islamic societies in their cognitive aspects stand between traditional modernity (traditional society and technological modern society) and postmodernity. In *Feminism and Islamic Fundamentalism: The Limit of Postmodern Analysis*, Haideh Moghissi suggests postmodern views which conceptualize about women in Islamic societies such as:

> The emphasis on narratives and the rejection of metanarratives and grand theories; suspicion of classical notions of reason, truth, universal progress, and the rejection of the idea of the existence of a hidden essential meaning and direction in history, with the emphasis, instead, on discontinuity, difference and the celebration of the "local"; the concern over representations of the "other," both imagined and real, and over processes of marginalization of others . . . an engagement with questions of sexuality as a historical construct and with sexual diversity and difference; a preoccupation with identity and with the notion of identity as a choice not a destiny; a mistrust of power; an awareness that the way things are and are done is not the only way and that all beliefs and knowledge are cultural constructs, and hence contingent and conversable.[20]

These days, especially, Jordanian "young women have sought to create a new positive image for themselves by updating and upgrading"[21] Ask and Tjomsl argue that these challenges are combined with the opening of educational opportunities to women, a growing control over childbearing and over the reproduction of the human species, and the development of the feminist movement in the aftermath of the 1960s' social movements and a globalized culture.[22] Thus, intelligent working women in urban areas

---

18. Sharify-Funk, *Encountering*, 62.
19. Ibid., 64
20. Moghissi, *Feminism*, 50–51.
21. Jansen, "Contested Identities," 89.
22. Ask and Tjomsl, *Women*, 93–94.

and young educated Muslim women have freer and more progressive understanding of their lives. Their identities often can be described as "fluid," "hybrid," and "multiple.[23]

The young generation in Jordan is in the new process of socialization.[24] The construction of self-identity in these days cannot be limited to ascribed statuses and roles.[25] Many young Jordanian women are educated, and have connected new values and beliefs through diverse circumstances such as globalization and technological innovations. In addition, two wars in Iraq and situations like the Arab Spring in other neighboring countries challenge their assurance of traditional values.

Furthermore, these changes bring doubt about the cohesion of the family and general Arab culture because of influences of the generation and gender gap.[26] Jordanian BMB women stand between "'global flows' and 'cultural closure.'"[27] Globalization and the internet influences open young people to challenge their fixed ideas, but for conservative traditionalists, these global flows increase the threat of secularity and intensify cultural closure from those new challenges. Sometimes these tensions between globalization and traditional Arab culture and between "flow" and "closure" cause "violent implications in many parts of the present-day world," such as Islamic fundamentalism types of behavior.[28]

Therefore, Bauman's discussion about fluid identity in transitional times needs to be related to the Jordanian women's situation. It is true that they form a fluid and flexible understanding of self as Bauman suggests, but it is more water with viscose or flowage.[29] Today's BMB women in Jordan stand between traditionalism and modernity, but are going towards postmodernity in their personal paradigms.

23. Marranci, *The Anthropology*, 99.
24. Castells, *The Power*, 243.
25. McGuire, *Religion*, 53.
26. Jansen, "Contested Identities," 91.
27. Meyer and Geschiere, *Globalization*, 2.
28. Ibid.
29. "Flowage is gradual deformation of a body of plastic solid (as rock) by intermolecular shear" (s.v. "Flowage,").

Identity Crisis

Understanding Themselves As Women Between Two Religious Beliefs and Ideologies

Modern Muslims stand "'in between' their secular and religious ideas."[30] It is easy for people to introduce themselves as nominal Muslims in Jordan. Among the Muslim women interviewees, those in the younger generation distinguished themselves from religious Muslims. This secular tendency in modern Islamic society helps women to search for new faiths. Right after finding their new faith, however, they have to face another reality.

BMB women at the beginning of their conversion stage are challenged by the ideal image of women based on their previous religious teachings. According to the Qur'an, they have built an image of women, understood the ideal life of women, and spent their lives trying to reach these standards. They grew up listening to others telling them where they belong, what women should do, and how they should behave according to the Qur'an. The Qur'an does not explain a woman's identity any further than that. Although they have a new faith, as women they still aren't sure how to live. All she knows is how to follow her father, brother, and husband in the Islamic traditions.

> When I heard of her dream, I showed my sister the Bible. She was surprised and read it for two weeks. Then she decided to go to church. However after she got married, she stopped going to church. She told me that her life was very difficult and she did not know what to do. She was afraid that her husband would find out about her faith. She loved him a lot and said she could go any place if she was with him. Therefore, she returned to Islam and then she followed more Islamic practices than she ever had done in the past (Amani).

They also need a clear understanding of the differences between Islam and Christianity and the distinctions of each. They are in the process of denying their old beliefs which they strongly put their trust in from birth and accepting their new beliefs.

> At the beginning, I had a hard time [keeping my new faith]. I wanted to know where the Qur'an came from. I decided to search for answers. After reading the books, I understood it, and I knew that Islam was made by humans and came after Christianity. I am happy now because I know the truth of the Qur'an's origins after becoming a Christian (Hiyam).

30. Sharify-Funk, *Encountering*, 68.

Analysis

> *Confusions happen. Actually they [new seekers] try to get closer to Islam. They want to go to Islam and try to know if this is true or not, so they wear the hijab and pray in the Islamic way. Even though they never went to a mosque before, they then choose to go to the mosque. Many people wear the hijab even though they didn't do that in the past. My friend went to the mosque and wore a hijab until she felt assured of following Jesus. Actually some of them did not know about Islam, and sometimes they started their new faith because they saw a vision or had a dream. But they wanted to check out Islam again . . . Later, they were sure about Christianity and knew the differences by virtue of going through that time* (Latifa).

BMB women previously saw being a good Muslim as completing religious rituals. They find it difficult to understand a faith based on belief and what to them is perceived as not doing any religious rituals. Diana Colby calls Islam "an embodied religion."[31] Islamic rituals are essential to express Muslims' pious heart to Allah and simultaneously to maintain their Islamic faith. In particular, the five prayers of the day are the epitome of their faith in Allah. Islamic prayer was a part of life and inscribed on their heart.[32] The Qur'an 2:238 strongly commands women believers to pray: "Guard strictly your (habit of) prayers, especially the Middle Prayer; and stand before Allah in a devout (frame of mind)." However, when they change their faith to Christianity, religious rituals which they practiced throughout their lives have to change in regards to both prayer and fasting. The celebration of Ramadan and other rituals are closely related to cultural practices, not just religious ones.

The difference in religious pedagogy is another cause of discontinuity in Jordanian BMB women. Throughout their lives, they had learned Islamic teachings through recitation and performing rituals, but when they become Christians, it is difficult for them to easily understand the general Western question and answer style of Bible study. Miriam Adeney states that Jesus, in his earthly life, "learned a lot of his Scripture in the synagogue as he read it aloud, chanted it and memorized it. For Muslims, too, silent reading is not the right way to use God's Word."[33] Not only religious education, but also traditional education has a preference for memorization: "Most Muslim women are oral communicators. Some Muslim countries educate girls

---

31. Colby, "Islamic Reformation," 65.
32. Ibid., 66.
33. Adeney, *Daughters*, 160.

Identity Crisis

but do so in schools that teach by rote memory, which doesn't encourage thinking and analysis."[34]

Disjointing of Collectivity

Besides religion in Jordanian society, Arab and Islamic culture influence "the intellectual, moral and spiritual atmosphere of life" and give guidelines to Muslims for living.[35] Jordanian women develop their identities influenced by male religious and sociocultural perspectives.

Traditionally, Islamic society aspires to unite as a religious community. Mernissi states that one of the internal aspects of the *ummah* is "the totality of individuals bound to one another by tie, not of kinship or race, but of religion, in that all its members profess their belief in the one God, Allah, and in the mission of his prophet, Muhammad."[36] The *ummah* is the community and the collective identity of Muslims.[37] When one recognizes oneself as a Muslim, he/she becomes a part of it. Five times a day every Muslim confesses *tawhid* that declares that there is no god except Allah and Muhammad is a prophet. Muslim prayers are "the fulfillment of . . . a witness to the new allegiance."[38] Thus confession of tawhid provides Muslims their religious morality and community. They do not want to be different from others.

> *My sister when she became pregnant knew that this was a miracle from Jesus. But she was afraid of the society, her husband, and everyone around her. She doesn't want to be someone different [from others]* (Latifa).

"Identity," means to know "where one fits," and is a "product of interaction with others in social settings."[39] A uniformed society in religion gives specific boundaries to comply with its own rules. *Sharia* and other religious traditions are good examples from which to shape women's identity and appropriate behaviors. For BMB women, it is a very real challenge to cross

---

34. A. H. "Discipleship," 146–47.
35. Rambo, *Understanding*, 8.
36. Mernissi, *Beyond the Veil*, 18.
37. Marranci, *The Anthropology*, 110.
38. Cragg, *The Call*, 106.
39. Gillespie, *Religious Conversion*, 126.

Analysis

the boundary. This requires an enormous amount of courage, because they have never tried something as big as this in their whole lives.

> *I was scared of Allah. If I showed hair, I would go to hell. I obeyed my father and brother, because I wanted Allah to love me. I always submitted to them according to the law. Allah only has laws to obey according to the Qur'an. If I don't follow them, Allah would dislike me. He has only the law, not love* (Amani).

Kraft describes the identity crisis among BMBs at the beginning stage of conversion sociologically as a feeling of anomie.[40] According to her, this anomie is caused by their social deviance and breaking social taboos. She understands that feelings of anomie among religious converts in the Middle East are due to two reasons.

> First, conversion is in and of itself a form of social deviance, and so the feelings of anomie which accompany deviance may therefore be expected to be experienced by converts. In fact, one may suggest that feelings of anomie were a factor contributing to their conversion decision, which helps explain how disappointed they may feel when their anomic feelings continue or even grow stronger. Second, when they broke one of the greatest taboos of their community, that against apostasy, they rejected the social norms and arrangements which provided their lives with some stability, and they may no longer know what is expected. Their act of making their own choice leads to uncertainty.[41]

This social deviance and breaking taboos of their society gives BMB women a feeling of betrayal and emotional grief.[42]

> *Inside of me, I had many thoughts: "You are a Muslim. How can you be a Christian?"* (Mariyam).

Rambo states that apostasy inevitably brings "grief over lost relationships, ideas, beliefs, rituals, and connections with friends and family."[43] He also deals with the power of the past in one's life and how it is related to the experience of apostasy.

> We are simply told to let go of the past, as if there were some electronics switch that one can flip, jettisoning years of experience

---

40. Kraft, *Searching for Heaven*, 73.
41. Ibid., 75.
42. Carrothers, *Identity*, 13.
43. Rambo, *Understanding*, 53–54.

with a single gesture. Such attitudes do not acknowledge the powerful pull of the past—even if that past is perceived to be evil and destructive. The past is powerful because that is the world in which we dwelt for years, and it lives on in our minds and hearts.[44]

The law of apostasy in the Jordanian society, the possibility of divorce, and concerns of child custody are the primary matters in which BMBs' faith is exposed to others. For instance, although a woman's guilt of apostasy is not punishable by death, she is condemned to perpetual imprisonment, and is to be beaten with rods at the hours of prayer.[45] Thoughts of apostasy bring terror and emotional grief to BMB women.

Being a woman in a traditional society also brings difficulties. The relationship with one's family becomes strained before the BMB meets physical dangers. Choosing to become a Christian without notifying or receiving the permission of any family authority is a big issue and a challenge for them, because they do not normally make their own important, life-changing decisions. Debi Bartlotti asserts that, "A Muslim woman's essential identity is determined by her relationships with men—her father, her husband, and her family. She is not defined autonomously, but in relationship to males . . ."[46]

Thus, the father is the most important figure in the daughter's life in acquiring education or other life's choices.[47] Suad Joseph explains how male members (father and brothers) in family are important for women. She affirms that normally "women are considered to belong to their natal families even after the marriage," because Islamic marriage systems such as polygamy and the easy divorce process make women vulnerable.[48]

> *A woman has a lot of stress. First, the husband controls everything. If she doesn't obey her husband, he thinks she is a bad woman and a sinner. Second, if children know that their mother was a Muslim, but became a Christian, they don't understand their mother's religious change. All people around them are Muslims. They consider her as kafir. Thirdly, if people know her faith, they can beat her and accuse her. But if it is a man, he can leave home or the place where*

---

44. Ibid., 54.
45. Zwemer, *The Law of Apostasy*, 118.
46. Bartlotti, "Muslim Women," 23.
47. Haider, *Gender*, 57.
48. Joseph, "Brother–Sister Relationships," 113.

Analysis

> *he lives. Women cannot go out. Men can go anywhere. For women here, there is no freedom to leave home or go anywhere* (Mariyam).

The threats against their communal identity are not only limited to the decision-making process to choose to become Christians, but is also felt in the security concerns of women, whose legal status and personal honor are obtained from their patrilineal lines and community. In relationships with their family, their own personal honor affects the whole family's honor and vice versa. Honor is the value of both a person's own eyes and his/her society's eyes.[49] Christopher L. Flanders describes a shame culture as a culture built on what others think.[50] The individual conscience which is formed in one's sociocultural circumstances evaluates one's behavior as right or wrong. Shame is more profoundly related to self and a painful assessment of self.[51] Furthermore, shame makes one feel that one is no good.[52] BMB women face conflicts and dilemmas, and this causes emotional ups and downs. When BMB women realize they bring shame to their family by being a Christian, they feel anxious.[53] They began to blame themselves for choosing their new belief.[54]

New Challenges

Not even considering the new religious beliefs, just receiving a new identity or having a new idea challenges their tendency towards traditionalism and inherited identity from religious and cultural influences. The image of Christians held by Muslims is reflected in the identity crises BMB women experience. Castell proposes that the struggles happen within resistance identities that occur inside of them. According to him, it also creates a secluded feature such as an Islamic fundamentalists' identity that "the construction of contemporary Islamic identity proceeds as a reaction against unreachable modernization (be it capitalist or socialist), the evil consequences of globalization, and the collapse of the post-colonial nationalist

---

49. Pitt-Riverse, "Honour," 21.
50. Flanders, *About Face*, 58.
51. Ibid, 62.
52. Lewis, *Shame*, 35.
53. Gilbert, "What Is Shame?," 6.
54. Ibid, 19.

Identity Crisis

project."[55] Before becoming converts, one of their identities is that they are not like Christians seemingly oppose Muslims' behaviors. In particular, in Islamic beliefs and values, being a Christian means being an idolater and apostate.

> *They are kufar [infidels]. People told me not to speak with them ... Greeting them is haram [disallowed religiously] and it is not encouraged* (Mariyam).

The image of Christians throughout Islamic history, with crusades and colonialism, was that they were the enemy. In addition, culturally, becoming a Christian is becoming a member of a foreign religion and seemingly immoral. Provocative Christian clothes, such as sleeveless blouses and short pants, and the freedom of women in the eyes of conservative Muslims, leaves a bad impression on Muslims.

> *When I was watching TV, I wondered how they [Christians] could act [like they do] and wear clothes like that while wearing a cross necklace. The media gives a bad impression of Christians* (Latifa).

Hence, another challenge for BMB women is to accept themselves as Christians whose image is seen as immoral.

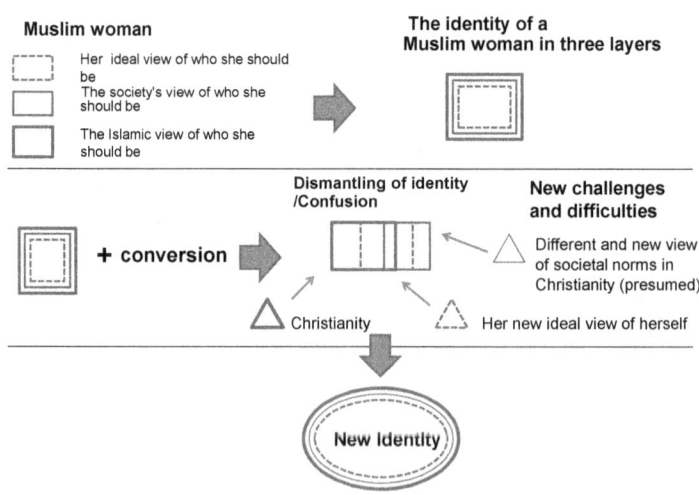

Figure 1: The Process of BMB Women's Identity Formation

---

55. Castells, *The Power*, 20.

Analysis

Challenges to Create a New Identity

According to Josselson's categorizations, the Guardian type represents very similar features to many Jordanian women, because this type of identity is constructed from their parents or other authoritative figures.[56] While she distinguishes this type of women as one category of North American women, most Jordanian women share this type of identity not only by family members, but by institutions of society regardless of educational and personal backgrounds. These women usually format their identities and values from childhood and don't have any doubt concerning them.[57]

The BMB women have been dependent on male family members and always considered those authorities' opinions when they made decisions. In the process of conversion, however, they directly face new experiences to be decision-makers, independent, and responsible without any family support. When Jordanian BMB women seek the Christian faith, there are lots of differences between Christian and Islamic beliefs, and becoming a Christian for them is to doubt what they have learned and believed as absolute truth. Spiritually, they are not their old selves anymore, but have become a new creation. At the same time, they are challenged in their opinion to be new beings to leave their traditional obedient Muslim past to become radical independent Christians. Jordanian BMB women are required to create new identities. They become Searchers who are on the road to finding their identities.[58]

Uniqueness of Women's Conversion

Women's approach to their new faith and making decisions is different from men's approach. Gillespie states that for women, conversion is understood in a unique way based on others' research of epistemology of women. He connects approaches of women to conversion with the fact that "women move toward subjective knowledge—a kind which is personal and almost intuited and constructed knowledge which views all knowledge in its context as it interplays with intuition and the knowledge of others."[59] Carol Gilligan also affirms that "the worldview of choice" is different between

---

56. Josselson, *Revising Herself*, 35.
57. Ibid.
58. Ibid., 106.
59. Gillespie, *Religious Conversion*, 56.

men and women: "They did not ask what was the ideal solution, [or] even the 'right' solution, but the least harmful solution for everyone involved."[60] According to research on women making moral decisions, there is a general tendency of woman to consider not endangering or hurting other people "in contrast to the man's notion of morality—as "having a reason . . . a way of knowing what's right, what one ought to do."[61] Thus if other people seem happy and the relationship with them is better, women usually think they have made a good decision.

Another tendency of women is: "As daughters, wives, mothers, sisters, and friends, women have been enmeshed in relational complexities that blur the boundaries of self and other."[62] In the patriarchal dyads, usually "women are thus prepared for the role of mother and nurturer in relational settings."[63]

Furthermore, women have a more affect-based and emotional approach to a new faith rather than analysis.[64] Therefore, without having supportive relationships in the conversion process, it is difficult to maintain one's new faith. From the interviews, many of the interviewees mentioned the critical help of one Christian person or persons who have spent time with and encouraged them. In that sense, the affection of Jesus Christ for women is a quite impressive point for BMB women to see who they are. Evelyne Reissacher, who researched the comparison between male and female conversion among fifteen North African women living in France, also supports the view of Jesus toward women which helps BMB women to find their real identity as a woman,[65] because it is more personal and shows love for BMB women.

Moving from Fixed and Required Identity to Negotiated and Flexible Identity

Jordanian BMB women already had an ideal and compulsory identity from religion and society which agreed. Evans suggests three aspects of a personal identity: core identity, who I am in my inner self; social identity, who

60. Gilligan, "Different Voice," 172.
61. Lyons, "Two Perspectives," 125–26.
62. Keller, *From a Broken Web*, 2.
63. Ibid., 133.
64. Kathryn Kraft, interviewed informally by the author, Jordan, Feb, 6, 2013.
65. Reissacher, "North African Women," 109.

I am in relation to my group or groups; and collective identity, who am I in my group identity and in the eyes of the world.[66] Thus, he understands that the impact of changing one's religious identity also impacts each of the other three identities, such as the confusion of worldviews at the core level, the unknown belonging sense at the social level, and the feeling of treason at a collective level.[67] In the case of Jordanian women, the ideal women's identity is found as the essence in the core, social and even collective identities and is formed as a coherent picture of these three identities.

When BMB women convert or seek a new faith, this brings a challenge to the existing concepts and creates a new identity. In fact, the resources and basics of the image of ideal women have existed since Islam started in the seventh century AD. In a negative way, women in a patriarchal and traditional society have internalized distorted inferiority images.[68] Islam has never asserted that woman is inferior to man, but it has only made the point that woman is different.[69] Although Jordanian women do not think they are inferior, it is true that the distinctions between male and female have existed according to religious beliefs and sociocultural conventions for ages. For instance, when women face unequal situations, many of them accept them, because they are women and different from men. This is why BMB women normally "find it more difficult than men to define their place in society after conversion and what their attitudes should be as female Christians living in a Muslim context."[70] So it is an unavoidable process to reflect on their concept of identity for BMB women in the process of conversion. BMB women face challenges to all the virtues of Muslim women, such as a sense of honor and modesty, submission and obedience and belonging, which is discussed in chapter 3. Kevin Robins claims that the change of a given identity to a person provokes feelings of anxiety and fear.[71]

Another fixed and required image of women in the society is that they become like icons in Islam. A pious and religious Muslim woman is a symbol of Islam. The best virtue of a Muslim man is to submit to Allah and follows the guidance of Allah. In a similar way, the best virtue of a Muslim woman is to submit to her male authorities given by Allah and be modest.

66. Evans, "Discipleship Session 1."
67. Ibid.
68. Taylor, "The Politics," 25.
69. Khan, *Woman*, 11.
70. Reissacher, "North African Women," 114.
71. Robins, "Interrupting Identities," 61.

Identity Crisis

This behavior symbolizes that this society or home are following the will of Allah. Davary states that Muslim women are the symbolic embodiment of tradition.[72] Bartlotti asserts that a Muslim woman "functions as a symbol of both honor and Islam."[73] Stowasser also points out that, "[The] Islamic community (*umma*)[74] is 'a symbol of the faith' in the Geertzian sense... Indeed, the role of women in Islam has itself achieved the status of a cultural symbol, (which is) seen to have far-reaching implications for the religion as a whole."[75]

As a mosaic puzzle picture, Jordanian Islamic society seeks a picture of the total submission to Allah and as a piece of it women should follow the rules or boundaries. Islam is a more law-oriented religion than Christianity.[76] When a Muslim woman becomes a BMB, she breaks this fixed and required rule.

> *A Jordanian woman has the most wonderful life of a Muslim. She can do anything, but only within the boundaries of Islam* (a university student in an urban area).

> *Yes we have a good religion. There is an important border in it. A woman should not cross the border, and must keep honor when she is a girl, a married, daughter, or mother. She has a role of woman in the society. But we have a boundary and we cannot cross the red line* (a university student in an urban area).

> *We have freedom to work and do whatever, but we have a boundary based on religion, family, and people* (a university student in an urban area).

> *In our religion, women are bound by religion and she cannot break it* (a housewife in an urban area).

Moving from Dependent Identity to Independent Identity

Another challenge BMB women face at the beginning period of seeking their new faith is being independent in their lives. This independent identity for Jordanian women does not mean the same as individuality as

---

72. Davary, *Women*, 142.
73. Bartlotti, "Muslim Women," 23–24.
74. *Umma* is the same word as *ummah*.
75. Stowasser, "Women," 23.
76. Schlorff, "Muslim Ideology," 174.

understood in the Western world. In Middle Eastern society, individuality is based on the extended family and *ummah*. Individualism in a Muslim context is discussed only on "a small community scale instead of community on a societal scale."[77] However, in collectivism on a large societal level, the freedom of individuals is less exercised for family and society. For women, as I mentioned already in previous chapters, being independent is a more feasible concept for them rather than being defined as an individual, because it is impossible for them to view themselves without referring to "otherness."

Wilhelmina Jansen states that in Jordan the most significant others are family and this relation to family defines individual identity.[78] Thus, "otherness," "relatedness," or "belonging" are the most primary description of characteristics of religious and sociocultural identity of Arab people particularly for women. "Relatedness" is the term that defines "women's boundaries of self."[79] Rolland Müller has observed Jordanian society for over thirty years and asserts that "nearness or belonging" is at the core in relationships of people.[80] Shrify-Funk also supports the significance of "otherness" in formation of Muslim women's identity.

> Whatever the way in which a Muslim woman activist attempts to define and project her identity, she faces the prospect of having this identity rejected in favor of a collective label that corresponds with expectations derived from a preexisting cultural or ideological tendency. Whatever choices she makes in life, she comes up against the alienating reality of existing as someone else's "Other."[81]

Anwar proposes "an extensional and reciprocal dependency" based on consideration of the "otherness" tendency among Arab women. She understands that "the self-relational dependency to the family and society" are made from the hierarchical gender system.[82] The authority of women "at the personal, familial and communal levels" is rarely found in their roles, and their fathers (and later husbands) "have the authority to decide

---

77. Kraft, *Searching for Heaven*, 55.
78. Jansen, "Contested Identities," 80.
79. Ibid., 81.
80. Müller, *The Messenger*, 100.
81. Sharify-Funk, *Encountering*, 135.
82. Anwar, *Gender*, 124.

what is best for women."[83] Jordanian BMB women come from an extended family structure where men are dominant and decisions are made by the eldest male member in the family and by the leadership in the *ummah* and society. They have grown up in this environment in which women cannot fully exercise their opinions and authority to decide.

With an independent perspective, decision-making is one of the most difficult things BMB women face at the beginning stage as a good example. Making a decision to believe in Jesus or to be a Christian is the most frequent response from BMB women when they were asked what the largest difficulty was at the beginning stage of their new faith. This process from passivity to subjectivity in the formation of women's identity brings conflicts inside them. Rambo asserts that decision-making often causes "an intense and painful confrontation with the self."[84]

Not only mental but also physical and emotional dependencies are needed. They are isolated from having fellowship in their Christian faith and cannot easily share their faith with others as well. It causes them to struggle about having a sense of belonging and of otherness. It is a devastating experience to lose one's whole support group as well as one's existed identity.[85] Horst B. Pietzsch, an overseas worker for BMBs, states that the difficulties of BMBs in traditional *ummah* society are the following. "Becoming a Christian usually results in becoming comparatively lonely. They have to take responsibilities for themselves and make many decisions alone; they experience this as a steep learning curve."[86]

Moving from Uniformed Identity to Integrated Identity

Anselm Strauss indicates in his *Mirrors and Masks: The Search for Identity* that the old identity often persists when it is challenged.[87] According to cases, it gives self-betrayal.

> If past acts appear to fit together more or less within some scheme, adding up to and leading up to the current self, then "they were me, belong to me, even though I have somewhat changed." . . . The subjective feeling of continuity turns not merely upon the number

83. Ibid., 31.
84. Rambo, *Understanding*, 126.
85. Müller, *The Messenger*, 105.
86. Pietzsch, *Welcome Home*, 20.
87. Strauss, *Mirrors*, 144.

of degrees of behavioral changes, but upon the framework of terms within which otherwise discordant events can be reconciled and related. Past purposes and dedications may be challenged and abandoned but when viewed as part of a larger temporal design they do not plague one by feelings of self-betrayal.[88]

According to him, this past identity is reconciled by an integrated interpretation that encompasses both old and new identities.[89] Gillespie affirms that one of the major roles in the religious conversion experience is identity formation itself.[90] He understands that "conversion causes heightened awareness and acute perceptions of danger to the self," because one needs to reorganize and integrate "on a deep level of consciousness."[91] Thus, this integration process between the old and the new identity brings confusion.[92] The identity crisis in this process of integration can be called various names as anomie, interrupting identities in-between places,[93] and double-faceted.[94] There was only one unified identity given by Allah and Islamic society as an ideal Muslim woman, but a BMB woman has encountered a new one and she has to hide this new feature of herself to other. Müller points out that many BMBs fail to integrate their two different identities (Muslim in the past and Christian in the present) and they develop two faces.[95] It often brings tragedy to their recognition of self-identity and makes them give up their new faith.

> The obvious quick solution to the issue is to develop two faces. With one face they welcome Christianity . . . This is where their heart is. With the other face, they live and relate to their family and community . . . This is also where their heart is. And so the tension builds . . . The convert may abandon his new faith and go back to what is familiar to him. This may be because of persecution or pressure, but often it is because he feels he cannot exist in a two-faced situation. As long as he has two faces there is always

---

88. Ibid., 146.
89. Ibid., 147.
90. Gillespie, *The Dynamics*, 188.
91. Ibid.
92. Leone, *Religious Conversion*, 79.
93. Robins, "Interrupting Identities," 65.
94. Müller, *The Messenger*, 100.
95. Ibid., 108.

the strong temptation to abandon the Christian face and assume the old one.[96]

Unless BMBs find ways to integrate old and new-selves, they are "distraught with the two faces that they eventually (make them) become mentally unstable."[97]

Another difficulty faced by BMB women in the integration process is overcoming failures from their expectations. Kraft understands this confusion comes from struggles between gaps of optimism and of frustration.[98] New expectations of belonging, relief from guilt, excitement, and stimulation are brought out when a person joins a new religion.[99] At the same time, emotional gratification of BMB women has been challenged by difficult situations after conversion as aforementioned. The inhospitable attitude towards BMBs from some Christian churches would be a good example of their disappointment.[100] As seen in the interview with Latifa, BMBs are often considered second-class Christians by some narrow-minded local Christians.

> *Here living with Christians is also difficult . . . They always look at me as a second-class Christian. They are the first in their thought . . . Some people do not want to talk with me and don't come to me.*

These disappointments are from unattained high expectations of BMBs, because they find a series of identity and community challenges after deciding to follow a new faith in reality.[101]

In order to lessen the gap, Kraft unifies the integrated identity of BMBs by accepting Islam as their ethnicity, but Christianity as their religion.[102] Because BMBs cannot abandon their identity as Muslims, she suggests that BMBs need to create two identities at the same time.[103] Kraft's terminology of using Muslim as their ethnic identity, however, gives confusion related to religious terms and all interviewees do not use Muslim to explain them-

---

96. Ibid., 109
97. Ibid.
98. Kraft, *Searching for Heaven*, 73.
99. Rambo, *Understanding*, 83.
100. Emetuche, "The Challenge," 6.
101. Kraft, *Searching for Heaven*, 75.
102. Ibid., 101.
103. Ibid.

Analysis

selves. According to the interviews, BMB women prefer other terms such as BMB, followers of Jesus people who are crossing, and Christians not Muslim.

6

Conclusion

THIS RESEARCH ON IDENTITY crises of Jordanian BMB women has provided a general overview of what kind of identity crises they go through at the beginning phase of new faith and the reasons for it. It is true that many new believers from Islamic backgrounds come to Jesus Christ and confess him as their Savior, but at the same time many of them do not adapt well to their newfound faith and return to their Islamic lifestyle.[1] This is because converts face a great deal of dilemmas and nonconformities, in comparison with their have previous with religious experiences and circumstances. Anto Karokaran expresses the identity of a new convert as an alien identity. "Converts get an alien identity. This in turn leads to their alienation from their native identity with family, ethnic community, larger society, nation, religion, culture, and finally from their own deepest self."[2]

Integrative Summary

Islamic confessions, Arab cultural values, and Jordanian sociopolitical circumstances are critical in formatting Jordanian Muslim women's identities. In regards to women's understanding of how they relate to Allah, both Muslim women and Christian women share the same understanding as being Allah's creations without discrimination from men. On the other hand, regarding women's understanding of their own identity, Christian women's identities are founded in a relationship with the trinitarian God

1. Bridges, "Analysis," 1.
2. Karokaran, "Cultural Alienation," 147–48.

Conclusion

as being created in the image of God. Muslim women understand their identity as based on both their relationship with Allah as well as other authorized males in family. They also understand that their marital life must be according to the Qur'an and that a woman needs to be in submission to her male authorities, including father, husband, brothers, and uncles in the family.

In many places in both holy books, women are considered socioculturally weak. Most verses for women in the Qur'an are considered as a reflection of the milieu of Arab women in the sixth century and the Prophet Muhammad's view of women from his experiences with his wives.[3] The Bible also reflects women according to Hebrew and Hellenistic perspectives. However, "the God of the Bible is not a continuation of the age-old deity of religious patriarchy," but he wants to "lead men and women in to the shared freedom of the messianic time."[4] Jesus shows through his examples that he understands women as of equal stature to men, responsible, and coworkers of his ministry. The attitude of Jesus towards women displays who a woman truly is and her original identity given by God.

Jordan is a strong Islamic country that follows the Sunni sect. As a traditional Islamic society, Jordanians value Islamic beliefs and traditions. Hence, there are prevalent conceptions among people in Jordan that "any Muslim that changes [his] religion is a traitor to Allah and a Christian brings great shame and dishonor to a person's family values and relationships."[5] Furthermore, many Muslims have negative conceptions against Christians due to their religious prejudices, historical experiences, such as Western colonialism, and experience with noticing immoral images from Western television programs.[6]

Jordanian Muslim women are dependent beings. Regardless of their education or social status, being a mother and a wife is still considered their primary identity. In order to keep their ideal identity, they are required to be modest and obedient, and in harmony with community and the traditional ideology of society. With communal cultural characteristics, it is natural for women to feel the necessity to get permission and obey the authority of their parents or husbands in regard to all kinds of their life matters. Jordanian women, however, have been recently facing the challenges

---

3. Beck, "The Religious Lives," 33.
4. Wood, *Theology*, 185.
5. Emetuche, "The Challenge," 5.
6. Ibid.

from globalization and secularization. Women nowadays are more able to have diverse perspectives of their contemporaries' lives. With a lot of opportunities for higher education and self-development, the social status of Jordanian Muslim women has improved. They have begun to build their identity under both the influences of conservative religious and sociocultural circumstances as well as secular-modernized civilizations.

Therefore, converts from a Muslim background have frequently experienced a radical dislocation of worldview and a crisis of identity.[7] On top of that, in the case of a woman, she faces a much bigger identity crisis than a man. James Huston describes that becoming a Christian is a process of "demolition of one's identity from the ruins of self-enclosure" and radical reconstitution "as a person-in-Christ."[8] Jordanian BMB women already stand in transitional states between old and new sociocultural ideologies. Conversion to a new faith exacerbates the dilemma they find themselves in by individual and independent choice in the decision-making process. It also causes experiences of new and unfamiliar understandings of their identities. In the process of conversion, they have gone through breaking the safe and familiar zone and created a new autonomous identity. All these processes cause them to have identity crises at the initial stage of new faith.

Missiological Theories in Research Findings

Bauman mentions fluid identity as a characteristic symbol of postmodernism. Along with secularism and globalization, postmodernism also influences young and intelligent Jordanian women. They have a fuller grasp of the intricacies of their circumstances and have built a more flexible self-understanding than the older generation of women. However, Jordanian society is still strongly bound to traditional norms for women, so even though young or intelligent women recognize changes of the times, they are still far from applying it to their daily lives, in particular at home. So sometimes, according to place and situation, their behavior is different from what they might say they believe in. In university, they enjoy freedom to mingle with male classmates and have no hesitancy to speak with strangers, but when returning to their home, they try to follow the family's or neighbors' traditions. With Bauman's description of our contemporary societies as a "'liquid' phase of modernity" in identity formation, BMB

7. Armangan, "Conversion," 508.
8. Huston, *The Mentored Life*, 12.

women in Jordan stand in a transitional state. They, however, are not only in a fluid state but often this liquid is viscous.[9] Regarding postmodern and transitional times, Castell also suggests three identities—Legitimizing, Projective, and Resistance identity.[10] In particular, Resistance identity is a useful concept to understand Jordanian sociocultural situations. He believes that people in contemporary society have a collective resistance to alienate from others and create boundaries.[11] However, Castell only deals with general phenomena caused by this Resistance identity in society and politics. He does not deal with more specific problems and issues in the formation of the identity, especially on an individual level. In case of Jordanian BMB women, Resistance identity is expressed as a hesitancy to make a decision to be a Christian because of distorted image of Christians.

Triandis and Gregg's cross-cultural sociopsychological model-collectivity is a good model to form general influences on Jordanian women's behaviors by its religious and sociocultural norms. These authors, however, only give a general feature that applies to males and does not give specific focus on women. It also does not give enough attention to the changing processes from traditionalism to individualism. Jordanian women are strongly affected by these processes and have built their identity to follow these norms. An ideal Muslim woman is the common feature that religion, culture, and society require women to be. However, at the same time with the rise of intellectualism, secularism, and nominalism of Islam, Jordanian society is changing rapidly and Jordanian women are beginning to benefit from these changes. In that sense, Josselson's categorization explains why Jordanian Muslim women have difficulty in making important decisions about their life by themselves. Because she deals, though, with general types of women's identity in North America, her models are not enough to discuss the influences by conversion and challenges from Islamic society. Under the unified requirements for women as good wives and daughters, most Jordanian BMB women grew up having no doubts about these factors until they are challenged by their conversion. It is because a Muslim woman's self-understanding of who she should be, the society's view of who she should be, and the Islamic view of who she should be are unified.

Regarding interim stages suggested by Rambo, Speelman, and Leone, most Jordanian BMB women went through emotional and mental confusion

9. Bauman, *Liquid Times*, 1.
10. Castells, *The Power*, 8–9.
11. Ibid., 9.

at the beginning stage of their new faith. They experienced discontinuity in regards to religious beliefs. They also perceived the possibility of relational barriers in regards to their family and friends, even though nobody was aware of their new beliefs. These scholars claim that the interim period occurs for two reasons in general: the change of their religious beliefs as well as the previous religions restrictions on them. These factors, however, do not acknowledge what is happening on the inside of the converts under the specific situations living in an Islamic society. Therefore, this research asserts that Jordanian BMB women in Islamic situations are challenged to create a new identity by conversion at the beginning stage. They already have a uniformed fixed and required identity from their previous religion which concurs with Islamic religious and cultural values and is dependent on male authorities. However, by conversion Jordanian BMB women are challenged to form a new identity which is to integrate all the situations they face and should be flexible, negotiated, and independent in a short period at the beginning stage of their new faith.

Missiological Implications and Suggestion for Further Study

Deciding how to help BMB women practically adapt well to their new faith at the beginning stage is the next step that needs to be researched and discussed. Evans also points out the growing need to help BMBs to find their identity.[12] It can be discussed in diverse ways, including theological, cultural-anthropological, and religious approaches. When a Muslim woman becomes a Christian, she needs to overcome many problems and challenges, such as discontinuities from her old beliefs, psychological conflicts, fear of new adventures, and finally to reconstruct her identities. Hence she faces a real life version of a "re-evaluation of all values" or a break from the "taken for granted *nomos*" which the person had been operating under.[13] Furthermore, she should be able to keep her Arab identity, while also being a part of the Christian community.

In order to reduce the negative impact of the identity crisis and help to create a new identity of BMB women, this section will focus on creating a sense of belonging to the new spiritual community in the identity formation stage of the nurturing process. I also suggest possible ways to

12. Evans, "Discipling," 159.
13. Armangan, "Conversion," 508.

help them in this process, based on the answers to the interview questions I asked BMB women and personal experiences.

To simplify, the concept of identity is recognition of who I am and where I belong. In general, conversion and identity issues are considered an individual decision in Western society, but the "I" concept needs to be readjusted to meet Jordanian circumstances. Jordanians have built their identities in communal circumstances. The Jordanian Muslim women I interviewed have answered self-understanding questions of themselves in a communal sense, and formatted their identities under the influence of Islam, traditional cultural values, and social circumstances. For BMB women in Jordan, conversion from Islam "parallels a break away from society."[14] Peter Berger strongly asserts this as follows: "The society is the guardian of order and meaning not only objectively, in its institutional structures, but subjectively as well, in its structuring of individual consciousness. It is for this reason that radical separation from the social world, or anomy, constitutes such a powerful threat to the individual."[15]

Therefore, Bridges states loneliness caused by seclusion from their Islamic society is one of the reasons why many BMBs turn back to Islam.

> The reason identified for this trend is loneliness. According to this report, Muslim converts to Christianity do not have fellowship with other believers. Most of them revert to Islam after a short time. Some say 90 percent of Muslim converts in the Middle East revert to Islam—if not to agnosticism—within the first year after they decided to follow Christ. In regard to the challenge of creating communities where none exist, the first step would be, when a true convert is identified, he could be extracted for a limited time.[16]

Therefore, Armangan suggests that in a societal-religious aspect, "providing Muslim converts an alternative community and a new meaning system may prevent them from early dropout."[17] Evans also points out that through the "experiences of many practitioners and researchers, as well as the testimony of ex-Muslim believers themselves," the personal relationship of BMBs with a mentor or other fellow believers is critical for their spiritual growth.[18] A Jordanian pastor, who disciples Marwaha in my inter-

14. Ibid.
15. Berger, *The Social Reality*, cited in Armagan, "Conversion," 31.
16. Bridges, "Analysis." 1.
17. Armangan, "Conversion," 508.
18. Evans, "Discipling," 160.

view, emphasizes the importance of a sense of community at the beginning stage of conversion.

> At first, she didn't understand anything about Christianity and many things needed to be explained to her. But taking care of her was the most important thing as her new Christian family. In this relationship, making her feel at peace was very important. We are the new people and the new society. Even though she goes through many things, she has to feel welcomed by the new community. She knows that we take care of her. Even before teaching the Bible, this welcome and feeling of belonging to the new community is very important for her. This will make her fear slowly decrease. She will feel that she has another family and can overcome the persecution. We have to accept BMBs and help them feel at home. We have to spend more time with them and let them be assured they have a close relationship with us. They need to understand we love them and are not just making them believe in Jesus or teaching the Bible.[19]

Furthermore, in the nurturing process, it is necessary to consider their whole situation rather than just follow a certain discipleship program from Western or other countries where they are legally permitted to convert to another faith. For Muslims, religion is "a community of communities."[20] Making them aware of their involvement in a new community through culturally considered fellowship and discipleship/mentoring is critical in helping them develop their new identity. Appropriate religious instruction that considers Arab culture and the Arab worldview can maximize continuity, minimize discontinuity, and lessen confusion in the process of conversion or nurturing.

- Jordanian BMB women should know deeply that they belong to God as a new creation in a new spiritual community given by God.

This is the primary consideration that BMBs need. In other words, they need to have inner assurance about their new identity built on Jesus Christ and new values from the Bible. Sondra Higgins Matthaei in *Making Disciples: Faith Formation in the Wesleyan Tradition* insists that:

> Christian identity means coming to know oneself as a Christian having assimilated the values, beliefs and lifestyle of one who professes to be a follower of Jesus Christ. John Wesley expressed this

---

19. Rev. A, interviewed with the author, Jordan, February 18, 2013.
20. Müller, *The Messenger*, 277.

"knowing" as receiving assurance of a new relationship with God through Jesus Christ and increasing in holiness—love of God and neighbor through the perfecting work of the Holy Spirit.[21]

BMB women have to know that their real value is from God, "who has created the world out of nothing and has made all human persons."[22] Our identity comes from God alone. Psalm 100:3 tells us "know that the Lord is God. It is he who made us, and we are his; we are his people, the sheep of his pasture." They have to know that they have new birth as an entity created in the image of God, redemption in Jesus Christ, and that the Spirit of God dwells inside of them. Spiritually and culturally they have rebirth as children of God and women of God. Their values are from God, not from male figures in their lives. In addition, giving them a solid biblical foundation about their new identity is a vital ingredient for them to release their "Islamic false beliefs" and face the truth. From the interviews, most of the BMB women have conflicts between getting rid of their old beliefs and integrating new beliefs at the beginning. Recognition of the different beliefs between Islam and Christianity, for example the love of God and the different views of the Prophet Muhammad, helps them to make a full transition to new faith.

- Culturally considered discipleship can maximize continuity and minimize discontinuity in BMBs' or seekers' conversion experiences.

Learning usually is easier when people can understand something new in light of what they already know. Middle Eastern cultures are in many ways similar to the Bible culture, for example in the way they understand hospitality.[23] The Hebrew paradigm is very similar to the Arab paradigm as well. Emetuche explains two different types of learning between Western and Eastern by quoting Larry Poston. Western learning employs Greco-philosophical inductive learning (Aristotelian methodology) in the teacher–student relationship. Most Jordanian BMBs have been oriented and learn "through modeling and motivation [which is] master–discipleship based,"[24] which is similar to many Eastern cultures.

In terms of Arab oral culture, "storytelling" is also a good way to disciple BMB women and to help them construct their new identities. The

21. Matthaei, *Making Disciples*, 22.
22. Harrison, *God*, 44.
23. Pietzsch, *Welcome Home*, 18.
24. Emetuche, "The Challenge," 6.

Identity Crisis

storytelling can be an alternative way to Q&A Bible study in the Arab culture. For their whole lives, BMBs have learned the Qur'an and Allah by recitation and memorization. Bailey presents that "... Oriental culture informs the text of the parables."[25] Since Jordanians are mainly oral communicators even though they are well-educated, "face-to-face" communication becomes more powerful through relationships as well. Since Arab society values relationship, oral contact is much closer to their heart.

Not only in regards to traditional Arab culture, but also in a universal contemporary context, storytelling emerges and applies to all generations. Today's people reject some central legitimizing myth, or overarching dogma, that claims to explain universal reality. They want to hear subjective experiences, or emotions in the way of story.[26] Bartholomew and Goheen introduce how narrative can help us find ourselves. They contend that the Bible narrative will answer the questions of "Where do we belong in this history? How does it shape our lives in the present?"[27] Carl E. Armerding also affirms that "story exegesis addresses the spiritual hunger of our day. Because story concerns not only admit the supernatural, but center on human experience, there is no separation between intellectual [or] cognitive and the affective."[28] The Bible story and individual storytelling can penetrate people's lives and hearts in depth, and result in holding them firmly in Jesus Christ. Stories can also be a means of raising those concerns that otherwise might be too painful to deal with in the cultural barriers that are still standing.[29] Sharing Christian lives through storytelling makes it less difficult for BMB women in Jordan to accept new lives and identities.

Disciplers also could develop alternative rituals to take the place of Islamic rituals. This will help them relate their new beliefs to their lives. Rambo states that rituals work as "integrative modes of identifying with and connecting to the new way of life."[30] Religion shares its own culture

---

25. Bailey, *Poet*, 29.

26. Drane, *The McDonaldization*, 157.

27. Bartholomew and Goheen, *The True Story*, 8.

28. Armerding, "Faith," 47.

29. One day, I shared a Bible story of a demon-possessed man in the Gerasa (Luke 8:32–36) with a Jordanian woman. After sharing, this woman with tears asked for advice concerning her possessed son, and wanted to meet Jesus to solve her problem. In the shame culture of Arab, they are used to keeping secrets like this, so such sick people are found within their household, but the Bible story touched this lady's heart, and she admitted her situation to a foreigner.

30. Rambo, *Understanding*, 108.

through symbols and emotions.[31] Religious activities such as prayer, rituals, miracles and other mystical experiences increase assurance of religious truth and strengthen emotional ties to the religious culture.[32]

- Knowing their belonging to their new community through personal fellowship with a Christian helper is helpful.

When Jordanian BMB women begin their spiritual journey, usually a spiritual mentor or helper who can be an evangelizer or Christian friend is involved. As aforementioned, BMB women need to belong to an alternative community in their lives, but it is hard for them to have general Christian communities, except for a personal relationship with the helper or a very few Christians or BMBs. In that sense, the primary concern the mentor or disciple has is to make them know who they belong to. Since Arab culture highly values personal relationships, the disciples should spend more time with new believers to build relationships and to build their identity in conversations. This is also the same principle as Jesus. Bill Hull states that before we try any kinds of programs following Christ's example is essential in discipleship (1 Pet 2:21; 1 Cor 4:16–17).[33] Jesus showed good models of nurturing by spending time and staying with his disciples, as well as demonstrating what kind of life his followers should live. Jesus taught his disciples by demonstration. He selected a few people and spent time with them. He brought his disciples wherever he went, and demonstrated obedience to God and what the life of believers should look like. Like Pastor A has shared, most interviewees mentioned that they had somebody who helped them grow in their faith and they emphasized the importance of building relationships and making them feel they belong to the new community.

> *Relationships are critical for BMB women. Family is also vital. If we give her a Christian family, it helps them. We have to speak about love a lot in our conversation and fellowship, and then later we can study the Bible. Before the Bible study, though, the relationship is important such as drinking tea and talking about the true love (Amani).*
>
> *Eat at the beginning. I think that reading the Bible every day is important, but fellowship and sharing my difficulties with a friend who prayed for me is the most important. I asked lots of questions at the*

---

31. Stark and Finke, *Acts of Faith*, 120.
32. Ibid., 120–21.
33. Hull, *The Complete Book*, 115.

> beginning. Later I learned how to act and what to do in certain situation as a Christian (Marwaha).

With teaching the correct Biblical theology of rebirth, spending time with BMBs lets them know they are truly joining a spiritual community. In addition, designing conversation which can create and maintain new identities for BMB women can be practiced naturally in fellowship. The modern tendency of defining identity is shaped in dialogue with, as well as sometimes in struggle against, the things our significant others want to see in us.[34] Berger and Lackmann in *The Social Construction of Reality* connect the importance of conversation to create and maintain one's identity as a way in which one understands/maintains their own reality.[35] They also showed how important continuous affirmation of one's new self-identity within community by using an example of Paul in the Bible. "Saul may become Paul in the aloneness of religious ecstasy, but he could remain Paul only in the context of the Christian community that recognized him as such and confirmed the 'new being' in which he now located this identity."[36]

Although a radical shift of conversion experience brings diverse problems for BMB women, a clear understanding of where they belong can lessen the chaos of changes in the process of new identity formation and transition effectively into their new Christian lives. A deeper level of further study and research is needed to understand the spiritual dimension of a new identity and role of BMB women in their family and the people in their communities.

This research focuses on difficulties related to issues of identities of BMB women from religious and sociocultural influences in Jordan. Through interviews, in the process and after conversion, BMB women have experienced change in the spiritual understanding of self. They have started to realize what the meaning of being in Christ is as a new creation in their inner beings. They could notice their spiritual freedom and power given by God and became agents of change in their understanding of self, life, and the societies to which they belonged.

In the process of forming the new identity of BMB women, therefore, they also need to recognize that their existing relationships with their family and people in their community should be transformed according to the word of God. It is true that their relationships with family and people in the

---

34. Taylor, "The Politics," 25.
35. Berger and Luckmann, *The Social Construction*, 152.
36. Ibid., 158.

community were big hindrances for them to come to Jesus. They, however, should be agents to transform these relationships. They have to shine the light of Jesus inside of them through their daily lives with those people rather than break the relationships and leave them. As a result, they need to develop another identity that includes their new role while transforming their existing milieu and relationships with people.

Appendix

A. Interview Questions with Jordanian BMB Women

Background Questions

1. Could you introduce yourself? (age, educational background, family, social status and class, marital status)
2. When and how did you believe in Jesus Christ?

Before Being a Christian

1. What was your life as a Muslim woman?
2. What was the image of Christian women to you?
3. Did you have any difficulty when you made a decision to become a Christian?
4. Which of the following are the most difficult hindrances to becoming a Christian?

    a. Fear of persecution for becoming a follower of Jesus

    b. Making such an important decision on my own

    c. Preconceptions, both negative and positive about Christianity

    d. Concern about your security or future

    e. Other reasons

Appendix

After Conversion

1. What are changes inside of you before and after being a Christian?
2. How long did it take for you to settle down to your new faith and why do you think takes time?
3. From your own experiences, what are the most difficult challenges BMB women face at the beginning phase of their new faith comparing to male BMB?
4. Do you understand the Bible when you study with Christians? What kind of way would be easier for you understand?
5. What are the difference between being Muslim and Christian as a woman?

B. Interview Questions with Jordanian Muslim Women

1. What is general life of a woman in Jordan?
2. What are the important virtues of Jordanian women?
3. What is ideal Muslim woman?
4. What is the image of Christian women to you as a Muslim?
5. What is the concept of honor and shame?

C. Interview Questions with Women Workers in Discipling Jordanian Female BMB

1. What is general life of a woman in Jordan?
2. What is Muslim women's identity or important thing in self-understanding?
3. What are the most difficult hindrances to becoming a Christian?
4. What are the most difficult challenges BMB women face at the beginning phase of their new faith comparing to male BMB?
5. What is image of Christian for Muslims?
6. Why do BMB women go back to Islam or step back from new faith?

Bibliography

Abu-Lughod, Lila. *Veiled Sentiments: Honor and Poetry in a Bedouin Society.* Berkeley: University of California, 1986.
"Adam—Creation of Eve." http://www.alim.org/library/biography/stories/content/SOP/14/1/Adam/Creation%20of%20Eve%20.
Adeney, Frances S. *Christian Women in Indonesia: A Narrative Study of Gender and Religion.* Syracuse: Syracuse University Press, 2003.
Adeney, Miriam. *Daughters of Islam: Building Bridges with Muslim Women.* Downers Grove, IL: InterVarsity, 2002.
Afkhami, Mahnaz. "Introduction." In *Faith and Freedom: Women's Human Rights in the Muslim World*, edited by Mahnaz Afkhami, 1–16. Syracuse: Syracuse University Press, 1995.
A. H. "Discipleship of Muslim Background Believers through Chronological Bible Storying." In *Ministry to Muslim Women: Longing to Call Them Sisters*, edited by Fran Love and Jeleta Eckheart, 146–73. Pasadena, CA: William Carey Library, 2000.
Al-Buti, Muhammad Said Ramadan. *Ela kul Fataten Tumin be-Allah* [To all people to believe Allah]. 8th ed. Beirut: Muasasat ar Risalah, 1987.
Al-Faruqi, Maysam J. "Women's Self-Identity in the Qur'an and Islamic Law." In *Windows of Faith: Muslim Women Scholar-Activists in North America*, edited by Gisela Webb, 72–101. Syracuse: Syracuse University Press, 2000.
'Ali, 'Abdullah Yusuf, trans. *The Meaning of The Holy Qur'an.* Beltsville, MD: Amana, 2008.
"Ali ibn Abi Talib: The Fourth Caliph of the Muslims." http://www.al-islam.org/restatement/59.htm.
Allen, John L., Jr. "Even in Jordan, Christian-Muslim Ties Not Always Easy." *National Catholic Reporter*, May 9, 2009. http://ncronline.org/ news/vatican/even-jordan-christian-muslim-ties-not-always-easy.
Al-Oudat, Mohammed. *Tribal Identity and State Power.* Berlin: Shaker, 2005.
Al Oudat, Muhammad, and Ayman Al Shboul. "Jordan First: Tribalism, Nationalism and Legitimacy of Power in Jordan." *Intellectual Discourse* 18/1 (2010) 65–96.
Al-Tall, Suhayr Salti. *Muqaddimah Hawla Qadiyat al-Mar'ah wa-al-Harakah al-Nisa'iyah fi al-Urdun* [Introduction of village women and women movement in Jordan]. Beirut: Al-Mu'assah al-'Arabiyah lil-Dirasat wa-al-Nashr, 1985.
Ammerman, Nancy, et al. *Studying Congregations: A New Handbook.* Nashville: Abingdon, 1997.
Anderson, Dana. *Identity's Strategy: Rhetorical Selves in Conversion.* Columbia: University of South Carolina, 2007.

Bibliography

Anwar, Etin. *Gender and Self in Islam*. New York: Routledge, 2006.

Armagan, Nur. "Conversion and Apostasy: A Sociological Perspective." In *Envisioning Effective Ministry: Evangelism in a Muslim Context*, edited by Laurie Fortunak Nichols and Gary R. Corwin, 56-61. Wheaton, IL: Evangelism and Missions Information Services, 2010.

Armerding, Carl. "Faith and Story in Old Testament Study: Story Exegesis." In *A Pathway into the Holy Scripture*, edited by Philip E. Satterthwaite and David F. Wright, 31-50. Grand Rapids: Eerdmans, 1994.

Arsu, Sebnem "Turks to Fight 'Honor Killing' of Women." *New York Times*, May 16, 2005.

Ask, Karin, and Marit Tjomsl. *Women and Islamization: Contemporary Dimensions of Discourse on Gender Relations*. New York: Berg, 1998.

"Asma Khader." http://ictj.org/about/asma-khader .

Azban, Ahmad Kamal. *Diwan Baladna: Arab Culture From an Arab's Perspective*. Amman: daira maktabe wataniye, 2010.

Badamasiuy, Juwayria Bint. *Status and Role of Women under the Shari'ah*. Abuja, Nigeria: Zkara, 1998.

Badr, Ḥabib, et al. *Christianity: A History in the Middle East*. Beirut: Middle East Council of Churches, 2005.

Bailey, Kenneth. *Poet and Peasant and Through Peasant Eyes: A Literary-Cultural Approach to the Parables in Luke*. Combined ed. Grand Rapids: Eerdmans, 1983.

Barazangi, Nimat Hafez. *Woman's Identity and the Qur'an: A New Reading*. Gainesville: University Press of Florida, 2006.

Bartholomew, Craig G., and Michael W. Goheen. *The True Story of the Whole World: Finding Your Place in the Biblical Drama*. Grand Rapids: Faith Alive, 2004.

Bartlotti, Debi. "Muslim Women in Crisis." In *Ministry to Muslim Women: Longing to Call Them Sisters*, edited by Fran Love and Jeleta Eckheart, 21-32. Pasadena, CA: William Carey Library, 2000.

Bauman, Zygmunt. "From Pilgrim to Tourist—or a Short History of Identity." In *Questions of Cultural Identity*, edited by Stuart Hall and Paul du Gay, 18-36. Thousand Oaks, CA: SAGE, 1996.

———. *Liquid Times: Living in an Age of Uncertainty*. Cambridge: Polity, 2007.

Beaumont, Peter. "Jordan Opens New Syrian refugee Camp." *The Guardian*, April 30, 2014. http://www.theguardian.com/world/2014/apr/30/jordan-new-syrian-refugee-camp-al-azraq.

Beck, Lois. "The Religious Lives of Muslim Women." In *Women in Contemporary Muslim Societies*, edited by Jane I. Smith, 27-60. London: Associated University Press, 1980.

Beek, Abraham van de. "Christian Identity Is Identity in Christ." In *Christian Identity*, edited by Ed. A. J. G. van der Borght, 17-32. Leiden: Brill, 2008.

Berger, Peter. *The Social Reality of Religion*. Harmondsworth, UK: Penguin, 1973.

Berger, Peter L., and Thomas Luckmann. *The Social Construction of Reality: A Treatise in the Sociology of Knowledge*. New York: Anchor, 1966.

Borght, E. A. J. G. van der. "Introduction." In *Christian Identity*, edited by E. A. J. G. van der Borght, 3-16. Leiden: Brill, 2008.

Brand, Laurie A. "Women and the State in Jordan." In *Islam, Gender, and Social Change*. edited by Yvonne Yazbeck Haddad, 100-123. New York: Oxford University Press, 1998.

Braswell, George W. *Islam: Its Prophet, Peoples, Politics and Power*. Nashville: Broadman & Holman, 1996.

Bibliography

Bridges, Erich. "Analysis: Many Converted Muslims Stand—or Fall—Alone." *BP News*, March 13, 1997. http://www.bpnews.net/4243.

"A Brief Illustrated Guide to Understanding Islam—Some Basic Islamic Beliefs." http://www.islam-guide.com/ch3-2.htm.

Brown, Colin, ed. *The New International Dictionary of The New Testament*. 3 Vols. Grand Rapids: Zondervan, 1975–78.

Brown, Daniel W. *A New Introduction to Islam*. Oxford: Wiley-Blackwell, 2009.

Bureau of Democracy, Human Rights, and Labor. "Jordan: Annual Report on International Religious Freedom, 2010." November 17, 2010. www.state.gov/j/drl/rls/irf/2010/148826.htm.

Bush, Richard C., et al. *The Religious World: Communities of Faith*. 2nd ed. New York: Macmillan, 1988.

Carrothers, Robert M. *Identity Consequences of Religious Conversion: Applying Identity Theory to Religious Changing*. Kent, OH: Kent State University, 2004.

Castells, Manuel. *The Power of Identity*. 2nd ed. Oxford: Blackwell, 2004.

Central Intelligence Agency. "Jordan." https://www.cia.gov/library/publications/the-world-factbook/geos/jo.html.

Chacko, James. *The Phenomenon of Christian Conversion with Particular Reference to Its Theology in the Indian Context*. Delhi: ISPCK, 2005.

Chapman, Colin. *Cross and Crescent: Responding to the Challenge of Islam*. 2nd ed. Downers Grove, IL: InterVarsity, 2007.

Choi, Youngkil, trans. *The Holy Quran*. Riyadh: Al-Munawara kingdom of Saudi Arabia, 2002.

"Christians in the Quran." http://www.muslimsforjesus.org/Christians%20in%20the%20Qur'an/Christians%20in%20the%20Qur'an.htm.

Clarke, L. "Women in Islam." In *Women and Religious Traditions*, edited by Leona M. Anderson and Pamela Dickey Young, 187–217. Toronto: Oxford University Press, 2004.

Coleman, Robert E. *The Heart of the Gospel: The Theology behind the* Master Plan of Evangelism. Grand Rapids: Baker, 2011.

Colby, Diana. "Islamic Reformation and Fundamentalism's Impact on Muslim Women." In *Ministry to Muslim Women: Longing to Call Them Sisters.* edited by Fran Love and Jeleta Eckheart, 64–78. Pasadena: William Carey, 2000.

Conn, Harvie M. "The Muslim Convert and His Culture." In *The Gospel and Islam*, edited by Don M. McCurry, 97–111. Monrovia, CA: Missions Advanced Research and Communication Center, 1979.

Cortez, Marc. *Theological Anthropology: A Guide for the Perplexed*. New York: T. & T. Clark, 2010.

Cragg, Kenneth. *The Call of the Minaret*. New York: Oxford University Press, 1956.

Creswell, John W. *Qualitative Inquiry and Research Design: Choosing Among Five Approaches.* 2nd ed. Thousand Oask, CA: SAGE, 2007.

Davary, Bahar. *Women and the Qur'an: A Study in Islamic Hermeneutics*. New York: Mellen, 2009.

Denzin, Norman K., and Yvonnan S. Lincoln, eds. *Handbook of Qualitative Research*. 2nd ed. Thousand Oaks, CA: SAGE, 2005.

Dickson, H. R. P. *The Arab of The Desert*. London: Unwin, 1949.

Doi, Abdur Rahman I. *Women in Shari'ah*. Kuala Lumpur: A. S. Noordeen, 1992.

Bibliography

Douglas, J. D., ed. *The New International Dictionary of the Christian Church*. Grand Rapids: Zondervan, 1974.

Drane, John. *The McDonaldization of the Church: Consumer Culture and the Church's Future*. Macon, GA: Smyth & Helwys, 2001.

El-Zahlaoui, Fr Joseph. "Witnessing in the Islamic context." In *Your Will Be Done: Orthodoxy in Mission*, edited by George Lemopoulous, 95–104. Geneva: WCC, 1989.

Emam, Dana Al. "Jordanian Women Remain Underrepresented in Politics." *Jordan Times*, March 26, 2013. http://jordantimes.com/jordanian-women-remain-underrepresented-in-politics.

Emetuche, Damian. "The Challenge of Discipling Muslim Background Believers." *Global Missiology English* 2/7 (January 2010) n.p. http://ojs.globalmissiology.org/index.php/english/article/view/5/13.

Erickson, Erick H. *Identity Youth and Crisis*. New York: Norton, 1968.

Esposito, John L. *The Future of Islam*. New York: Oxford University Press, 2010.

Evans, Edward. "Discipling and Training for 'Muslim Background Believers' Programme Design." in *Ministry of Reconciliation*, edited by John Stringer, 159–84. Amsterdam: Grassroots Mission, 2009.

———. "Discipleship Session 1: Understanding and Caring." Lecture, Amsterdam, December 31, 2012.

Evans, Mary J. *Woman in the Bible*. Cape Town: Oxford University Press, 1983.

Flanders, Christopher L. *About Face: Rethinking Face for 21st Century Mission*. Eugene, OR: *Wipf & Stock*, 2011.

Foh, Susan T. *Women and the Word of God*. Phillipsburg, NJ: Presbyterian & Reformed, 1979.

Gallagher, Nancy. "Women's Human Rights on Trial in Jordan: The Triumph of Toujan al-Faisal." In *Faith and Freedom: Women's Human Rights in the Muslim World*, edited by Mahnaz Afkhami, 209–31. Syracuse: Syracuse University Press, 1995.

Gaventa, Beverly R. *From Darkness to Light: Aspects of Conversion in the Testament*. Philadelphia: Fortress, 1986.

Geertz, Clifford. *The Interpretation of Cultures*. New York: Basic Books, 1973.

Gibbs, Eddie. "Conversion in Evangelistic Practice." In *Handbook of Religious Conversion*, edited by H. Newton Malony and Samule Southard, 123–36. Birmingham, AL: Religious Education, 1992.

Gilbert, Paul. "What Is Shame? Some Core Issues and Controversies." In *Shame: Interpersonal Behavior, Psychopathology, and Culture*, edited by Bernice Andrews, 3–38. New York: Oxford University Press, 1998.

Gillespie, V. Bailey. *The Dynamics of Religious Conversion: Identity and Transformation*. Birmingham, AL: Religious Education, 1991.

———. *Religious Conversion and Personal Identity*. Birmingham, AL: Religious Education, 1979.

Gilligan, Carol. "Different Voice in Moral decisions." In *From Christ to the World: Introductory Readings in Christian Ethics*, edited by Wayne G. Boulton, Thomas D. Kennedy, and Allen Verhey, 172–76. Grand Rapids: Eerdmans, 1994.

Goffman, Erving. *Relations in Public: Microstudies of the Public Order*. New York: Basic Books, 1971.

Goodwin, Jan. *Price of Honour*. London: Warner, 1994.

Green, Joel B. *Body, Soul, and Human Life: The Nature of Humanity in the Bible*. Grand Rapids: Baker, 2008.

Gregg, Gary S. *Culture and Identity in a Muslim Society*. New York: Oxford University Press, 2007.
Grenz, Stanley J. *The Social God and the Relational Self: A Trinitarian Theology of the Image Dei*. Louisville: Westminster John Knox, 2001.
Haddad, Yvonne Yazbeck. "Traditional Affirmations Concerning the Role of Women." In *Women in Contemporary Muslim Societies*, edited by Jane I. Smith, 61–86. London: Associated University Press, 1980.
Haider, Raana. *Gender and Development*. Cairo: American University in Cairo, 1995.
Hall, Edward T., and Mildred Reed Hall. *Understanding Cultural Differences: Germans, French and Americans*. Yarmouth, ME: Intercultural, 1990.
Halpern, Manfred. *The Politics of Social Change in the Middle East and North Africa*. Santa Monica, CA: Rand, 1963.
Hamada, Louis Bahjat. *Understanding the Arab World*. Nashville: Thomas Nelson, 1990.
Harrison, Nonna Verna. *God's Many-Splendored Image: Theological Anthropology for Christian Formation*. Grand Rapids: Baker, 2010.
Hassan, Riffat. "Islamic Hagar and Her Family." In *Hagar, Sarah, and Their Children: Jewish, Christian and Muslim Perspectives*, edited by Phyllis Trible and Letty M. Russell, 149–68. Louisville: Westminster John Knox, 2006.
Hiebert, Paul G. *Cultural Anthropology*. Grand Rapids: Baker, 1983.
———. "Worldview Transformation." In *From the Straight Path to the Narrow Way: Journeys of Faith*, edited by David H. Greenlee, 23–34. Waynesboro, GA: Authentic Media, 2006.
Hijab, Nadia. "Islam, Social Change, and the Reality of Arab Women's Lives." In *Islam, Gender and Social Change*, edited by Yvonne Yazbeck Haddad and John L. Esposito, 45–55. New York: Oxford University Press, 1998.
Horner, Norman A. *A Guide to Christian Churches in the Middle East: Present-Day Christianity in the Middle East and North Africa*. Elkhart, IN: Mission Focus, 1989.
Hourani, Albert. *A History of the Arab Peoples*. Cambridge, MA: Belknap, 1991.
Huda. "What Does the Quran Say About Christians?" http://islam.about.com/cs/jesus/f/christians.htm.
Hudson, Michael C. *Arab Politics: The Search for Legitimacy*. New Haven, CT: Yale University Press, 1997.
Huston, James M. *The Mentored Life: From Individualism to Personhood*. Colorado Springs: NavPress, 2002.
Hull, Bill. *The Complete Book of Discipleship*. Colorado Springs: NavPress, 2006.
Ipgrave, Michael. "Affinity, Inclusion, and Mission Christian Resources for Living with Difference." In *Humanity: Texts and Contexts: Christian and Muslim Perspectives*, edited by Michael Ipgrave and David Marshall, 21–31. Washington, DC: Georgetown University Press, 2011.
James, Carolyn Custis. *Lost Women of the Bible: Finding Strength and Significance through Their Stories*. Grand Rapids: Zondervan, 2005.
Jansen, Wilhelmina. "Contested Identities: Women and Religion in Algeria and Jordan." In *Women and Islamization: Contemporary Dimensions of Discourse on Gender Relations*, edited by Karin Ask and Marit Tjomsland, 73–102. New York: Berg, 1998.
Jawad, Haifaa A. *The Rights of Women in Islam: An Authentic Approach*. New York: St. Martin's, 1998.
"Jordan Population 2014." http://worldpopulationreview.com/countries/jordan-population/.

Bibliography

"Jordanian Kills Sister to 'Cleanse Family Honor.'" *Al Arabiya News*, April 30, 2013. http://english.alarabiya.net/en/News/middle-east/2013/04/30/Jordanian-kills-sister-to-cleanse-family-honor-.html.

Jørgensen, Jonas Adelin. *Jesus Imandars and Christ Bhaktas: Two Case Studies of Interreligious Hermeneutics and Identity in Global Christianity*. Frankfurt: Peter Lang, 2008.

Joseph, Suad. "Introduction: Theories and Dynamics of Gender, Self, and Identity in Arab Families." In *Intimate Selving in Arab Families*, edited by Suad Joseph, 1–20. Syracuse: Syracuse University Press, 1999.

Josselson, Ruthellen. *Finding Herself: Pathways to Identity Development in Women*. San Francisco: Jossey-Bass, 1987.

———. *Revising Herself: The Story of Women's Identity from College to Middle*. New York: Oxford University Press, 1996.

Kahn, M. Muhsin, trans. "Translation of Sahih Al Bukhari." http://www.muslimaccess.com/sunnah/hadeeth/bukhari/index.htm.

Karokaran, Anto. "Cultural Alienation of Converts and Radical Inculturation of Faith." In *Mission and Conversion: A Reappraisal*, edited by Joseph Mattam and Sebastian Kim, 147–81. Delhi: Fellowship of Indian Missiologists, 1996.

Katiğçibaşi, Çiğdem. *Family, Self, and Human Development across Cultures*. Mahwah, NJ: Lawrence Erlbaum, 2007.

Keller, Catherine. *From a Broken Web: Separation, Sexism, and Self*. Boston: Beacon, 1986.

Keohane, Alan. *Bedouin*. London: Kyle Cathie, 1994.

Keskin, Tigrul. "The Sociology of Islam." In *The Sociology of Islam: Secularism, Economy and Politics*, edited by Tugrul Keskin, 1–20. Reading, UK: Ithaca, 2011.

Khan, Maulana Wahiduddin. *Woman in Islamic Shari'ah*. Delhi: Islamic Centre, 1995.

Khawalde, Silman, and Dan Rabinowitz. "Race from the Bottom of the Tribe that Never Was: Segmentary Narratives amongst the Ghawarna of Galilee." *Journal of Anthropological Research* 58/2 (Summer 2002) 225–43.

Kim, Jungwi, ed. *The Encyclopedia of Islam*. Seoul: Hamunsa, 2002.

Kim, Sebastian. "Differing Concepts of Community Identity: Debates over the 'Racial and Religious Hatred Bill.'" In *Community Identity: Dynamics of Religion in Context*, edited by Sebastian C. H. Kim and Pauline Kollontai, 107–21. Edinburgh: T. & T. Clark. 2007.

Kim, Seyoon. *Women God Made*. Seoul: Tyrannus, 2004.

King, Diane E. "Middle Eastern Belongings: Impositions, Ironies, Bodies, Lands." *Identities: Global Studies in Culture and Power* 15 (2008) 261–70.

Kong, Ilju. *Revival of the Arab Churches*. Seoul: Jerusalem Public, 2000.

———. *Understanding the Arab Culture*. Seoul: Miraen, 1999.

Kraft, Kathryn Ann. *Searching for Heaven in the Real World: A Sociological Discussion of Conversion in the Arab World*. Oxford: Regnu, 2012.

Lee, Dongjoo. *The Gospel and Religions*. Seoul: Asia Center for Theological Studies and Mission, 2006.

Lee, Wonsam. "Jinn and Folk Religion in Islam." *Korean Islamic association* 13/2 (2003) 2–19.

Leone, Massimo. *Religious Conversion and Identity: The Semiotic Analysis of Texts*. Oxford: Routledge, 2004.

Lewellen, Ted C. *The Anthropology of Globalization: Cultural Anthropology Enters the 21st Century*. Westport, CT: Bergin & Garvey, 2002.

Lewis, Michael. *Shame: The Exposed Self.* New York: Free Press, 1992.
Library of Congress. "A Country Study: Jordan." December, 1989. http://lcweb2.loc.gov/frd/cs/jotoc.html.
Lindholm, Charles. *The Islamic Middle East: An Historical Anthropology.* Malden, MA: Blackwell, 1996.
Lofland, John, and Norman Skonovd. "Conversion Motifs." *Journal for the Scientific Study of Religion* 20/4 (1981) 373–85.
Lyons, Nona Plessner. "Two Perspectives: On Self, Relationships, and Morality." In *Mapping the Moral Domain: A Contribution of Women's Thinking to Psychological Theory and Education*, edited by Gilligan Caro et al., 21–48. Cambridge, MA: Harvard University Press, 1988.
Maalouf, Tony. *Arabs in the Shadow of Israel: The Unfolding of God's Prophetic Plan for Ishmael's Line.* Grand Rapids: Kregel, 2003.
Mahameed, Shweish. *The Justice of the Witness: Two Perspectives in Islamic Sharia and Sociology.* Amman: The National Library, 1997.
Mandryk, Jason, ed. *Operation World: The Definitive Prayer Guide to Every Nation.* 7th ed. Colorado Springs: Biblica, 2010.
Marranci, Gabriele. *The Anthropology of Islam.* Oxford: Berg, 2008.
Marshall, Paul A., ed. *Religious Freedom in the World.* Lanham, MD: Rowman & Littlefield, 2008.
Mathews, Alice. *A Woman: God Can Lead.* Grand Rapids: Discovery House, 1998.
Matthaei, Sondra Higgins. *Making Disciples: Faith Formation in the Wesleyan Tradition.* Nashville: Abingdon, 2000.
McFadyen, Alistair I. *The Call to Personhood: A Christian Theory of the Individual in Social Relationship.* New York: Cambridge University Press, 1990.
McGuire, Meredith B. *Religion: The Social Context.* 5th ed. Belmont, CA: Wadsworth Thomson Learning, 2002.
McKeown, James. *Genesis.* Two Horizons. Grand Rapids: Eerdmans, 2008.
McKim, Donald K. "The Mainline Protestant Understanding of Conversion." In *Handbook of Religious Conversion*, edited by H. Newton Malony and Samule Southard, 123–36. Birmingham, AL: Religious Education, 1992.
McNeal, Melani. "Contextualization or the Affirmation of Patriarchal Norms? The Case for Breaking Cultural Norms to Reach Muslim Women." In *Doing Mission in the Arab World*, edited by John Stringer, 141–52. Amsterdam: Grassroots Mission, 2008.
———. "Do Muslim Women Really Need Saving? Mission, Reconciliation and Gender in the Arab World." In *Ministry of Reconciliation*, edited by John Stringer, 71–89. Amsterdam: Grassroots Mission, 2009.
McQuilkin, Robertson. *Understanding and Applying the Bible.* Chicago: Moody, 1992.
Mernissi, Fatima. *Beyond the Veil: Male-Female Dynamics in a Modern Muslim Society.* Rev. ed. Indianapolis: Indiana University Press, 1987.
Meyer, Bright, and Peter Geschiere, eds. *Globalization and Identity: Dialectics of Flow and Closure.* Malden, MA: Blackwell, 1999.
Minces, Juliette. *The House of Obedience: Women in Arab Society.* Translated by Michael Pallis. London: Zed, 1982.
Moaddel, Mansoor. "Religion and the State: The Singularity of the Jordanian Religious Experience." *International Journal of Politics, Culture and Society* 15/4 (Summer 2002) 527–68.

Bibliography

Moghissi, Haideh. *Feminism and Islamic Fundamentalism: The Limits of Postmodern Analysis*. 2nd ed. New York: Zed, 2002.

Moran, Lee. "Honor Killing Victim Stabbed to Death by Her Brother in Jordan: Cops." *New York Daily News*, May 2, 2013. http://www.nydailynews.com/news/world/honor-killing-victim-killed-brother-cops-article-1.1332901.

Mostert, Christiaan. "Christian Identity as Baptismal Identity." In *Christian Identity*, edited by E. A. J. G. van der Borght, 51–65. Leiden: Brill, 2008.

"Mughal Empire." Victoria and Albert Museum. http://www.vam.ac.uk/page/m/mughal-empire/.

Muhammad, Ghazi bin. *The Tribes of Jordan: At the Beginning of the Twenty-First Century*. Amman: Hashemite Kingdom of Jordan, 1999.

Müller, Roland. *The Messenger, the Message, the Community: Three Critical Issues for the Cross-Cultural Church-Planter*. Istanbul: CanBooks, 2006.

Musk, Bill. *The Unseen Face of Islam: Sharing the Gospel with Ordinary Muslims at Street Level*. Grand Rapids: Monarch, 1989.

"Muslims Befriending Non-Muslims." http://www.thereligionofpeace.com/Quran/009-friends-with-christians-jews.htm.

Nida, Eugene A. *Message and Mission: The Communication of the Christian Faith*. Rev. ed. Pasadena, CA: William Carey Library, 1990.

Nikaido, S. "Hagar and Ishmael as Literary Figures: An Intertextual Study." *Vetus Testamentum* 51 (2001) 219–42.

Noort, Ed. "Abraham and the Nations." In *Abraham, the Nations, and the Hagarites: Jewish, Christian, and Islamic Perspectives on Kinship with Abraham*, edited by Martin Goodman et al., 3–31. Leiden: Brill, 2010.

Norris, Rebecca Sachs. "Converting to What? Embodied Culture and the Adoption of New Beliefs." In *The Anthropology of Religious Conversion*, edited by Andrew Bucker and Stephan D. Glazier, 171–82. Oxford: Rowman & Littlefield, 2003.

Okoye, James Chukwuma. "Sarah and Hagar: Genesis 16 and 21." *Journal for the Study of the Old Testament* 32/2 (2007) 163–75.

Oyserman, D., H. M. Coon, and M. Kemmelmeier. "Rethinking Individualism and Collectivism: Evaluation of Theoretical Assumptions and Meta-Analyses." *Psychological Bulletin* 128/1 (2002) 3–75.

Patai, Raphel. *The Arab Mind*. New York: Macmillan, 1983.

Peace, Richard V. *Conversion in the New Testament: Paul and the Twelve*. Grand Rapids: Eerdmans, 1999.

Philips, Abu 'Ameenah Bilal. *The Jinn*. Riyadh: International Islamic, 2000.

Pietzsch, Horst B. *Welcome Home: Caring for Converts from Islam*. Cape Town: Life Challenge Africa, 2004.

Pitt-Riverse, Julian. "Honour and Social Status." In *Honour and Shame: The Values of Mediterranean Society*, edited by J. G. Peristiany, 19–78. Chicago: University of Chicago, 1966.

The Pooya/Ali Commentary. http://quran.al-islam.org/.

"Qualitative Measures." October 20, 2006. http://www.socialresearchmethods.net/kb/qual.php.

Ramadan, Tariq T. "The Way (Al- *Sharia*) of Islam." In *The New Voices of Islam: Rethinking Politics and Modernity*, edited by Mehran Kamrava, 65–98. Berkley: University of California, 2006.

Rambo, Lewis. *Understanding Religious Conversion*. New Haven, CT: Yale University Press, 1993.
Rambo, Lewis, and C. E. Farhadian. "Converting: Stages of Religious Change." In *Religious Conversion: Contemporary Practices and Controversies*, edited by C. Lamb and M. D. Bryant, 23-34. London: Cassel, 1999.
Reissacher, Evelyne. "North African Women and Conversion." In *From the Straight Path to the Narrow Way: Journeys of Faith*, edited by David H. Greenlee, 109-24. Waynesboro, GA: Authentic Media, 2006.
Roald, Anne Sofie. *Women in Islam: The Western Experience*. New York: Routledge, 2001.
Robbins, Richard H. *Cultural Anthropology: A Problem-Based Approach*. 4th ed. Belmont CA: Thomson Wadsworth, 2006
Robins, Philip. *A History of Jordan*. Cambridge: Cambridge University Press, 2004.
Rynkiewich, Michael. *Soul, Self, and Society: A Postmodern Anthropology for Mission in a Postcolonial World*. Eugene, OR: Cascade, 2011.
Saeed, Abdullah. "Trends in Contemporary Islam: A Preliminary Attempt at a Classification." *The Muslim World* 97 (2007) 395-404.
Saliba, John A. *Understanding New Religious Movements*. Grand Rapids: Eerdmans, 1996.
Schleifer, Aliah. *Motherhood in Islam*. London: The Islamic Academy, 1986.
Schlorff, Sam. "Muslim Ideology and Christian Apologetics." *Missiology: An International Review* 21/2 (April 1993): 173-85.
Schrieter, Robert J. *Constructing Local Theologies*. Maryknoll, NY: Orbis, 1985.
Shafaat, Ahmad. "The Punishment of Apostasy in Islam, Part 1: The Quranic Perspective." February 2006. http://www.islamicperspectives.com/Apostasy1.htm.
Sharify-Funk, Meena. *Encountering the Transnational: Women, Islam and the Politics of Interpretation*. Burlington, VT: Ashgate, 2008.
Sharkey, Heather J. "Empire and Muslim Conversion: Historical Reflections on Christian Missions in Egypt." *Islam and Christian-Muslim Relations* 16/1 (January 2005) 43-60.
Shoup, John A. *Culture and Customs of Jordan*. Westport, CT: Greenwood, 2007.
Siddiqui, Mona. "Being Human in Islam." In *Humanity: Tests and Contexts*, edited by Michael Ipgrave and David Marshall, 15-21. Washington, DC: Georgetown University Press, 2011.
Smith, Wilfred Cantwell. *Belief and History*. Charlottesville: University of Virginia Press, 1977.
———. *The Meaning and End of Religion*. Minneapolis: Fortress, 1991.
Spectorsky, Susan. "'A'ishah bint Abi Bakr." In *Middle Eastern Muslim Women Speak*, edited by Elizabeth Warnock Fernea and Basima Qattan Bezirgan, 27-36. Austin: University of Texas, 1977.
Speelman, Gé M. *Keeping Faith: Muslim-Christian Couples and Interreligious Dialogue*. Zoetermeer: Uitgeverij Meinema, 2001.
Stark, Rodney, and Roger Finke. *Acts of Faith: Explaining the Human Side of Religion*. Berkley: University of California, 2000.
Storti, Craig. *Figuring Foreigners Out: A Practical Guide*. Yarmouth, ME: Intercultural, 1999.
Stowasser, Barbara Freyer. "Gender Issues and Contemporary Quran Interpretation." In *Islam, Gender and Social Change*, edited by Yvonne Yazbeck Haddad and John L. Esposito, 30-44. New York: Oxford University Press, 1998.

Bibliography

———. *Women in the Qur'an, Traditions, and Interpretation*. New York: Oxford University Press, 1994.
Strauss, Anselm L. *Mirrors and Masks: The Search for Identity*. Glencoe, IL: The Free Press, 1959.
Tangney, June Price, and Ronda L. Dearing. *Shame and Guilt*. New York: Guilford, 2002.
Tangney, June Price, and Jessica L. Tracy. "Self-Conscious Emotions." In *Handbook of Self and Identity*, edited by Mark R. Leary and June Price Tangney, 446–78. 2nd ed. New York: Guilford, 2012.
Taraki, Lisa. "Islam Is the Solution: Jordanian Islamists and the Dilemma of the 'Modern Woman.'" *The British Journal of Sociology* 46/4 (December 1995) 643–61.
Taylor, Gabriele. *Pride, Shame and Guilt: Emotions of Self-Assessment*. New York: Oxford University Press, 1985.
Travis, John. "The C1 to C6 Spectrum." *Evangelical Missions Quarterly* 32/2 (1996) 304–10.
Theron, Phillipe. "Devastating Grace: *Justificatio Impii* and I-dentity." In *Christian Identity*, edited by E. A. J. G. van der Borght, 33–50. Leiden: Brill, 2008
Triandis, Harry C. *Individualism and Collectivism*. Boulder, CO: Westview, 1995.
Wadud, Amina. "Alternative Qur'anic interpretation and the Status of Muslim Women." In *Windows of Faith: Muslim Women Scholar-Activists in North America*, edited by Gisela Webb, 3–21. Syracuse: Syracuse University Press, 2000.
Wallis, Jim. *The Call to Conversion: Why Faith Is Always Personal but Never Private*. San Francisco: HarperSan Francisco, 2005.
Walls, Andrew. "Converts or Proselytes? The Crisis over Conversion in the Early Church." *International Bulletin of Missionary Research* 28/1 (January 2004) 2–6.
———. *The Cross-Cultural Process in Christian History*. Maryknoll, NY: Orbis, 2002.
———. *The Missionary Movement In Christian History*. Maryknoll, NY: Orbis, 1996.
Walther, Webke. *Women in Islam: From Medieval to Modern Times*. Translated by C. S. V. Salt. Princeton, NJ: Markus Wiener, 1993.
Ward, Keith. *Religion and Community*. London: Oxford University Press, 2000.
Wehr, Hans, and J. Milton Cowan, eds. *Arabic-English Dictionary: The Hans Wehr Dictionary of Modern Written Arabic*. Beirut: Librairie du Liban, 2000.
Weiss, Phlip. "A Jordanian Complains About His King and the Zionist." *Mondoweiss: The War of Ideas in the Middle East*, September 13, 2010. http://mondoweiss.net/2010/09/a-jordanian-complains-about-his-king-and-the-zionists.html.
Weng, Ng Kam. "The Image of God, Human Dignity, and Vocation." In *Humanity: Texts and Contexts*, edited by Michael Ipgrave and David Marshall, 3–14. Washington, DC: Georgetown University Press, 2011.
Wessels, Antonie. *Arab and Christian? Christians in the Middle East*. Volklingen, Ger.: Pharos, 1995.
Wilken, Robert Louis. "Christianity Face to Face with Islam." *First Things*, January 2009. http://www.firstthings.com/article/2008/12/001-christianity-face-to-face-with-islam-12 htm.
Willemse, Karin. *One Foot in Heaven: Narratives on Gender and Islam in Darfur, West-Sudan*. New York: Brill, 2007.
Wood, Laurence W. *Theology as History and Hermeneutics: A Post-Critical Conversation with Contemporary Theology*. Lexington, KY: Emeth, 2005.

Woodlock, Rachel. "Many Hijabs: Interpretative Approaches to the Questions of Islamic Female Dress." In *The Sociology of Islam: Secularism, Economy and Politics*, edited by Tugrul Keskin, 395–418. Reading, UK: Ithaca, 2011.

"World's Most Powerful Women." http://www.queenrania.jo/media/news/worlds-most-powerful-women.The Qur'an. http://quran.al-islam.org.

Wright, Christopher J. H. "Implications of Conversion in the Old Testament and the New Testament." *International Bulletin of Missionary Research* 28/1 (January 2004) 14–19.

———. *The Mission of God; Unlocking the Bible's Grand Narrative*. Downers Grove, IL: InterVarsity, 2006.

Yalman, Suzan. "The Art of the Safavids before 1600." October 2002. http://www.metmuseum.org/ toah/ hd/safa/hd_safa.htm.

Zwemer, Saumel M. *Arabia: The Cradle of Islam*. Caldwell, ID: Caxton, 1900.

———. *The Law of Apostasy in Islam: Answering the Question Why There Are so Few Moslem Converts, and Giving Examples of Their Moral Courage and Martyrdom*. London: Marshall Brothers, 1924.

———. *Moslem Women*. West Medford, MA: The Central Committee on the United Study of Foreign Missions, 1926.

Subject Index

Allat, 67
Al-Uzza, 67
Arab; 'assabiyya, 90; culture, 175; fatalism, 90; hospitality, 90, 91, 173; oral tradition, 53, 173; traditionalism, 1, 76, 81, 85, 87, 88, 145, 149, 155, 169; people, 1, 10, 75, 76, 83, 86, 87, 88, 95, 161; Arab spring, 149; women, 167
Assumption, 4, 22

Bauman, Zigmunt, 10, 18, 24, 144, 149, 168
Bedouin, 6, 57, 64, 77, 83, 84, 90, 91, 94; raiding, 90
Behavior, 10, 11, 19, 20, 30, 32, 33, 38, 40, 53, 60, 91, 95, 98, 113, 116, 121, 123, 137, 137, 144, 149, 152, 155, 156, 160, 163, 168, 169
Belonging, 13, 26, 47, 50, 57, 58, 90, 93, 95, 159, 161, 162, 164, 170, 175
Bible, 2, 26, 29, 39, 53, 116, 126, 142, 143, 151, 167, 172, 174, 176; Old Testament, 12, 43, 48, 53, 56, 126; New Testament, 7, 12, 49, 52, 59, 126
BMB, 1, 3, 6, 9, 22, 26, 53, 58, 59, 60, 96, 97, 116, 122, 124–32, 143–46, 151–80; confusion, 16, 21, 121, 134, 143, 151, 159, 163, 164, 169, 172; difficulty, 97, 116, 133, 139–42, 154, 162, 169; threat, 3, 36, 96, 149, 155, 171; decision, 3, 4, 15, 25, 59, 65, 84, 87, 97, 122, 153, 155, 169, 179; loneliness, 130, 171; emotion, 14, 16, 20, 86, 133, 140, 155, 158, 162, 164, 169, 174, 175
Boundary, 19, 57, 83, 103, 112, 136, 153, 160
Buddha, 1
Buddhist, 1, 23
Bureaucratic, 62, 63

Castells, Manuel., 10, 18, 19, 57, 145
Church; ancient, 68, 70, 172; orthodox, 68; protestant, 13, 64, 68, 70, 74
Collectivism, 8, 25, 75, 90, 161; collectivist, 8, 10, 20, 86
Communalism, 88, 90, 93
Christianity, 1, 3, 4, 15, 19, 26, 42, 68, 74, 75, 83, 119, 124, 127, 128, 140, 150, 151, 156, 160, 164, 173
Christian; assurance, 142, 149, 172, 173, 175, 120, 121, 123; belief, 143; believer, 7; body of Christ, 51; commentators, 56; community, 170, 175, 176;

Subject Index

Christian, *cont.*; faith, 47, 157, 162; helper, 175; hermeneutics, 13; identity, 4, 49, 50, 69, 172; image, 114, 169; inner man 51; in the Qur'an 70–74; judeo, 29; message, 17; theology, 13; tradition, 48; understanding, 12; women, 11, 95, 96, 99, 100–113, 115, 120, 166; workers, 6
Conservatism, 63, 75
Contemporary, 5, 10, 18, 24, 37, 75, 76, 86, 89, 147, 155, 168, 169, 174
Conversation, 52, 60, 175, 176
Conversion, 4, 6, 7, 9, 11, 12–17, 23, 24, 97, 122, 133, 141, 150, 153, 157, 163, 168, 172, 176; converts, 3, 6, 15, 16, 17, 24, 79, 134, 143, 153, 156, 166, 168, 170, 171; revert, 171

Delimitations, 5
Divorce, 29, 33, 34, 35, 38, 52, 79, 122, 125, 128, 142, 154
Discipleship, 24, 172, 175; discipler, 174; nurturing, 170, 172, 175
Dreams, 43, 67, 118, 126, 142, 150

Equality, 5, 30, 78, 136; inequality, 31
Emic, 23
Etic, 23

Fear, 34, 40, 67, 94, 118, 119, 121, 126, 128, 130, 139, 140, 159, 170, 172
Fellowship, 42, 45, 51, 118, 127, 162, 172, 175, 176
Feminism, 74, 81, 148; feminist, 5, 36, 38, 81, 148
Freedom, 13, 15, 23, 29, 44, 45, 57, 78, 115, 120, 121, 131, 136, 140, 141, 156, 160, 167, 176
Folk Islam, 66; jinn, 65, 67

Fundamentalism, 148, 149

Globalization, 10, 81, 149, 155, 168
God; assembly, 69; bible, 167; creation, 44–46, 172; epiphany, 58; grace, 121; image, 42–47, 49, 167; lord, 173; love, 173; relationship, 53, 173; sovereignty, 59; Trinitarian, 166; true, 1; voice, 125, 142; worship, 28
Guilty, 94, 139

Hadith, 10, 12, 27, 29, 30, 36, 39, 41, 42, 53, 65, 66, 67, 87, 98
Hagar, 53- 58; Ishmael, 53- 58, 61
Harmony, 86, 135, 167
High contextualization, 143
History, 5, 18, 34, 36, 40, 56, 58, 62, 90, 148, 156, 174
Holy Spirit, 13, 47, 48, 51, 120, 173
Honor, 29, 75, 80, 83, 84, 88, 90, 91, 92, 96–99, 115, 128, 130, 137, 155, 159, 160
Honor killing, 33, 80, 81, 128

Identity; communal, 51; dependent, 146, 160; fixed and required, 134, 146, 158–60, 170; integrated, 146, 162, 164; independent, 22, 94, 146; legitimizing, 18, 169, 174; negotiated and flexible identity, 146, 158; projective, 18, 169; religious, 3, 9, 15, 79, 134, 159; resistance identity, 16, 18, 144, 155, 169; uniformed identity, 146, 162
Identity crisis, 3, 4, 8, 9, 11, 15, 16, 17, 21, 24, 133, 153, 163, 168, 170
Individualism, 8, 25, 88, 161, 169
Insider movement (C5 and C6), 5, 143

Subject Index

Intellectualism, 147, 169
Interim stage, 9, 11, 15, 16, 169, 170
Interview, 23, 95, 96, 140, 142, 143, 146, 158, 164, 171, 173, 179; Crossing, 116; interviewee, 98, 113, 114, 141, 150; muslim, 97; semi-structured, 23; women workers, 127, 180
Islam; activities, 118; apostasy, 78–79, 128, 153-4; conservatism, 63; customs, 80; doctrine, 27, 65, 78, 143; education, 33; ethics, 41; fundamentalism, 149, 155; history, 40, 156; ka'ba, 54, 55, 67; Khalifa, 30; pillars, 65, 99 : revivalism, 76, 80, 127; rituals, 66, 151, 174; shahada, 65, 78, 99, 114; sharia, 5, 6, 37, 78, 79, 80, 152, 133, 190; shia, 65; society, 36, 76; 87, 88, 122, 147, 148, 150 169,; state, 70; tradition, 27, 29, 30, 33, 40, 148, 150; scholar, 81; symbols, 160; ummah, 32, 33, 66, 75, 88–90, 92, 145, 152, 162; understanding, 32, 35; value, 32, 76, 78, 156

Jesus, 1, 2, 3, 7, 31, 39, 42, 46, 47, 49, 50, 51, 52, 55, 58, 59, 60, 71, 73, 118, 119, 120, 122, 123, 124, 125, 139, 141–47, 151, 158, 162, 166, 167, 172, 173, 174, 175, 177
Jordan, 67–71, 75–91, 96, 116; history, 62, 74, 89; middle class, 81, 82, 147; tribalism, 63, 64, 86; women, 11, 23, 61, 77, 80–85, 91, 93–95, 98, 127–31, 137, 146–49, 152, 157, 159, 167, 169
Josselson, Ruthellen., 8, 10, 11, 21, 22, 25, 82, 93, 157, 169
Judgment day, 71

Liberation, 5

Manat, 67
Mernissi, Fatima., 5, 80, 87, 88, 89, 152
Middle East, 25, 68, 74, 82, 115, 129, 153, 171; culture, 57, 173; history, 58; society, 148, 161; view, 5
Modesty, 29, 32, 39, 75, 77, 83, 88, 91, 98, 116, 128, 159
Modernism, 63, 75, 145
Morality, 38, 42, 78, 88, 100–112, 152, 158
Muslim, 2, 3, 4, 7, 9, 10, 24, 27, 29, 31, 35, 53, 64, 66, 69–82, 88, 92, 115, 125, 151, 152, 155, 159, 161, 164; behavior, 156; Brotherhood, 63; calendar, 31; community, 36; culture, 20; family, 59, 92, 118, 119; identity, 20; law, 92; order, 33; society, 20, 33; women, 5, 6, 11, 23, 26, 34, 38, 40, 50, 87, 93, 94, 95, 96, 97, 98, 99, 114, 122, 127, 154, 156, 160, 161, 163, 166–172; world, 61
Mughals, 61

Nafs, 27, 28
New creation, 58, 157
Nominalism, 169

Obedience, 34, 37, 39, 65, 88, 92, 135, 137, 159
Otherness, 94, 161
Ottoman, 61, 62, 70, 74

Patriarchalism, 81, 87
Persecution, 3, 55, 121, 163, 172, 179
Politics, 5, 18, 24, 61, 62, 63, 64, 74, 75, 76, 77, 81, 84, 89, 127, 147, 169
Polygamy, 31, 34, 154

195

Subject Index

Postmodernism, 10, 11, 17, 146, 148, 168
Prophet Muhammad, 65, 66, 67, 71, 73, 123, 126, 139, 143, 152, 167, 173

Qualitative research, 22, 23
Qur'an, 65, 66, 88

Rambo, Lewis R., 9, 11, 14, 16, 145, 153, 162, 169, 174
Relatedness, 94, 161
Religion, 89, 90, 91, 92, 98, 99–110, 114, 115, 116, 122, 128, 133, 137, 151, 152, 156, 158, 160, 164, 166, 167, 170, 172; activity 121, 125; allegiance, 88; beliefs, 145, 155, 159, 170; community, 152; duty, 99–111, 114, 118; education, 151; interpretation, 86; morality, 152; norm, 169; practice, 115; ritual, 151; worldview, 147
Repentance, 12, 13; returning, 12, 168

Safavids, 61
Secularism, 146, 147, 168, 169
Seekers, 2, 3, 4, 5, 7, 151, 173
Self, 7, 8, 9, 10, 11, 13, 14, 16, 17, 20, 21, 22, 27, 28, 32, 36, 45, 47, 48, 50, 51, 52, 67, 76, 88, 92, 95, 97 128, 129, 134, 136, 141, 149, 155, 158, 161, 162, 163, 166, 168, 169, 171, 176; identity, 38, 134
Shame, 20, 32, 59, 60, 87, 96–100, 115, 116, 135, 137–39, 155, 167

Status, 8, 18, 19, 35, 74, 83; Allah, 29; Bedouin, 6; legal, 155; Muslim, 79; parent, 87; women, 5, 26, 27, 29, 48, 51, 53, 54, 77, 81, 83, 97, 136, 140, 142, 160, 167, 168, 179
Submission, 53, 92, 94, 159, 160, 167
Sunni, 5, 10, 64, 65, 167

Tafsir, 36, 37
Transition, 10, 11, 17, 19, 20, 25, 146, 149, 168, 169, 173, 176

Western, 44, 56, 74, 76, 81, 97, 151, 172; colonization, 127, 167; concept, 11, 148; culture, 19, 75, 76, 85; influence, 76, 147; learning, 173; modernity, 20, 63; power, 62, 74; society, 171; value, 144; world, 161
Women's identity; drifters, 10, 21, 22, 93, 94; guardians, 10, 21, 28, 93, 157, 171; pathmakers, 10, 21, 93, 94; searchers, 10, 21, 22, 93, 94, 157, 171
Women's right, 5, 30, 32, 34, 37, 52, 84, 85, 147
Worldview, 4, 9, 10, 22, 26, 28, 86, 147, 157, 159, 168, 172

Young generation, 20, 114, 136, 137, 138, 149, 150; girl, 95; people, 13, 15, 81; women, 114, 116, 149, 168

Zam Zam, 54